THE USES OF SPORT

Sport plays an important part in cultural life around the world, but until recently it has remained on the sidelines of academic Cultural Studies. Putting sport at the centre of cultural enquiry, *The Uses of Sport* investigates the implications for sport in the pre-Cultural Studies tradition of cultural commentary, before moving on to a critical engagement with a number of themes pertinent to contemporary Cultural Studies, including: community and social capital; cultural populism; cultural materialism; ethnographic enquiry; sport and the city; and the link between sport and cultural policy.

Overall, *The Uses of Sport* provides a resource for the theoretical location of sport within culture and popular culture. It takes a provocative stance, challenging theoretical trends that have emerged within Cultural Studies since the 1980s, arguing that sport and other cultural phenomena are usefully examined by more traditional modes of cultural analysis.

John Hughson is Senior Lecturer in the School of Physical Education, University of Otago, Dunedin, New Zealand. He is co-author with David Inglis of *Confronting Culture: Sociological Vistas* (Polity, 2003). **David Inglis** is a lecturer in sociology at the University of Aberdeen. He is a founding editor of the journal *Cultural Sociology*. **Marcus Free** is a lecturer in Media and Communication Studies at Mary Immaculate College, University of Limerick. He has published various articles on football fandom and national identity, sport and media representation, and television drama.

THE USES OF SPORT

A critical study

*John Hughson, David Inglis
and Marcus Free*

Routledge
Taylor & Francis Group

LONDON AND NEW YORK

First published 2005
by Routledge
2 Park Square, Milton Park, Abingdon, Oxon, OX14 4RN

Simultaneously published in the USA and Canada
by Routledge
270 Madison Avenue, New York, NY 10016

Routledge is an imprint of the Taylor & Francis Group

© 2005 John Hughson, David Inglis and Marcus Free

Typeset in Bembo by Taylor & Francis Books Ltd
Printed and bound in Great Britain by TJ International Ltd, Padstow, Cornwall

British Library Cataloguing in Publication Data
A catalogue record for this book is available from the British Library

Library of Congress Cataloging in Publication Data
A catalog record for this book has been requested

ISBN 0–415–26047–7 (hbk)
ISBN 0–415–26048–5 (pbk)

CONTENTS

INTRODUCTION

In one of the stories in his book *The Grim Smile of the Five Towns* (1907), Arnold Bennett tells of the death of the fictional painter Simon Fugue. Fugue, a son of the Potteries in North Staffordshire, was a rare representative of that region within the high arts. However, the narrator in Bennett's story is flabbergasted to find a poster for a local evening newspaper announcing the signing of a new centre-forward to the local soccer team, while making no mention of Fugue's passing. Upon complaint to a local professional man, the narrator is bluntly told that the death of a painter is unimportant when compared to the arrival of a talented footballer and the attendant hope of the team's survival within the First Division. Should the team go down, 'ten thousand homes would go into mourning' (Bennett 1907: 276).

This fictional anecdote gives a glimpse of the real cultural importance that sport has acquired within countries like England, over the last century at least.[1] It also foreshadows debate about the cultural basis of sport, how sport is considered in relation to high culture and how it has been constituted as a form of popular culture. These debates are central matters of discussion in this book. The title of the book is borrowed from Richard Hoggart's *The Uses of Literacy* (1958 [1957]), and it shares Hoggart's broader interest in the social uses of culture. Hoggart's book became a foundational text to a new academic discipline formally constituted with the opening of the Centre for Contemporary Cultural Studies (CCCS) at the University of Birmingham – with Hoggart as Director – in 1964. The intention of this book is to locate the cultural phenomena of sport within the intellectual framework of Cultural Studies. The debt to Hoggart within our endeavour is significant. As we go on to show in Chapter Two, Hoggart wrote little about sport, but the implication of his approach to the study of culture and popular culture for sport is of utmost importance. This is recognised, if only in passing, by most academics who have written books in relation to sport and Cultural Studies. What our book seeks to do is to provide a detailed discussion of commentary and analysis by a number of key cultural critics, such as Hoggart and others associated with Cultural Studies (in terms of the academic discipline and cultural studies more generally), to see how respective positions on culture

1

allow us to understand more fully the cultural significance of sport. However, rather than just using Cultural Studies to understand sport we modestly attempt to invert the intellectual process, to some extent, to integrate sport into Cultural Studies and related cultural analysis. We do this based on our assumption that Cultural Studies needs sport as much as sport needs Cultural Studies. In Chapter Four we look at the indictment of Cultural Studies by some academics; their claim that Cultural Studies has largely ignored sport. We believe that to overcome this oversight sport needs to be written into cultural analysis as much as cultural analysis needs to address sport as an external object of enquiry. Our chapters proceed with this ambition in mind.

The acknowledged debt to Hoggart betrays a particular orientation to Cultural Studies. Along with contemporaries Raymond Williams and E.P. Thompson, Hoggart is generally regarded as one of the foundational figures of intellectual inspiration for Cultural Studies. The particular strand of Cultural Studies associated with these figures has subsequently been referred to as *culturalism* (Milner 1994). Culturalism was eventually surpassed as the key mode of enquiry within Cultural Studies by structuralism. Whereas culturalism is derived from the observation and reporting of human experience, structuralism is derived from the study of language and the related belief that cultural meaning is set within the structure of grammar. As Cultural Studies became increasingly concerned with the texts of popular culture, the attraction of structuralism strengthened as scholars turned to the related area of semiotics (the study of signs as a system of language) to unlock the meanings of cultural texts. We can appreciate the relevance of structuralism and semiotics to the cultural study of sport with regard to the analysis of the symbolism and textual representation of sport, primarily in sporting texts coming through the mass media and advertising. However, it is our belief that the retreat from culturalism has not always been to the benefit of the study of cultural forms and this misgiving applies especially to sport. By its very nature, sport is about physical activity and human movement, and textual studies of culture do not adequately come to terms with the intrinsic dynamism of sport. Much contemporary textual based Cultural Studies is about the body as a site of meaning, but this form of cultural studies tends to either reduce the body to a text or to study stationary bodies. Sport is about moving bodies and requires a mode of analysis that attempts to capture the flow of movement without stationing the human body within a textual frame. We believe culturalism to be a most appropriate mode of analysis for studying the dynamism of sporting culture. We are aware of long standing claims that the culturalist and structuralist 'paradigms' can be reconciled (Hall 1981), but remain unconvinced that such reconciliation has been achieved within Cultural Studies.

Culturalism has a specifically British pedigree, with traces of German intellectual ancestry. If we are to name the guiding principle of culturalist thought then it is *lived experience*. An emphasis on lived experience arises within British writing on culture from at least the late eighteenth century. It derives from a blend of traditions, principally romanticism and humanism. We examine the romantic and humanistic roots of culturalism in Chapter One of the book before moving on to discuss the emergence of distinctively culturalist thought via a consideration of Hoggart and Williams in Chapter Two. It is the emphasis on lived experience that draws us to culturalism in our attempt to understand sport as a cultural phenomenon. The concern of culturalism is in the feelings and emotions that generate and emerge from the lived experience of people. The focus is on collective experience and, therefore, shared feelings and emotions held and lived out at some societal level. Culturalist writers such as Hoggart and Williams value individual experience, but their intellectual projects are primarily concerned with culture in a collective context, thus they speak of people rather than of individuals. Our interest in sport as a cultural form is similarly motivated. We recognise that sport offers individuals an important means of emotional expression but our interest is in the collective experience of sport, indeed, in how sport fits into what Williams (1961) referred to as the 'structure of feeling' of particular historical periods. We are interested in how sport fits into wider cultural contexts that exist in particular societies at given times.

Intrinsic to the view of sport as lived experience is an interest in how people make collective use of sport and draw cultural meaning from their engagements with sport both as participants in and as spectators of sport. Accordingly, we have entitled the book, *The Uses of Sport*. The subtitle of the book *A Critical Study* requires further explanation. A critical study suggests a book that is at the cutting edge of its intellectual field, one that takes on existing debates and positions, exposes them to scrutiny and offers alternative if not necessarily superior arguments. To some readers our book will appear as a step back into an earlier age of Cultural Studies, and the above discussion admits to as much. However, we would argue that this does not render our subtitle a misnomer. As we have indicated, Cultural Studies is currently dominated, and has been for a number of years, by positions that display little allegiance with culturalism and in some cases decry it. What we attempt to do in much of the book is to provide a return to culturalism, not in a regressive way, but in a way that shows the continuing relevance of a culturalist disposition to aspects of cultural life, sport in the case of our book. In so doing we take issue with a number of analytical positions on sport that are drawn from themes within contemporary Cultural Studies. This is particularly the case in Chapter Five where we expose what we believe to be the deficiencies in analysing sport as a form of postmodern culture. Our own position will no doubt draw criticism in reply and, we would hope, lead to further constructive debate. For now, we make claim to provision of a critical study on the basis of our departure from and critique of current theoretical trends in the cultural study of sport. We also hope that our contribution will be read as an endorsement of the importance of culturalism to Cultural Studies more generally, and if it is accepted in this way, that sport will be taken more seriously within the mainstream of Cultural Studies scholarship.

Cultural Studies has itself been regarded as a critical discipline. From its inception it proposed that forms of culture previously occluded from the academic agenda be put onto the table for serious discussion. Initially, this was inspired by the championing of working-class culture in the writings of Hoggart, Williams and Thompson. This was a radical departure from the elitist cultural tradition in which culture was taken to mean established areas within the arts and humanities. Academic study of culture was thus concerned with classical music, art history, classical literature and, with the emergence of English studies, English literature. Hoggart was of the first generation of working-class scholarship students to be educated within this tradition. He has always held the tradition dear while wanting to expand the parameters of what is studied as culture. Hoggart's account of pre-war English working-class culture provided in *The Uses of Literacy* (1958 [1957]) showed the richness of this cultural life and its importance in both aesthetic and social terms. Williams's *Culture and Society* (1958), published around the same time, at the end of the 1950s, made a more direct claim for the location of working class culture within an ongoing tradition of cultural commentary and analysis. Williams raised an explicit class based challenge to the study of culture, contending that cultural evaluation was traditionally the preserve of the bourgeoisie. Once we move beyond this bias, we can genuinely study culture as a 'whole way of life' and broaden cultural analysis to the working class and the forms and practices that make up their cultural life.

Williams, and to a greater extent, Hoggart, did not shed the mode of cultural criticism into which they had been educated and they did not recommend a cultural anything goes. They accepted that distinction and discernment will reside within working-class culture and the uses made of culture by working-class people. They therefore inspired but did not give license to the emergent equation within Cultural Studies of working-class culture with popular culture. We believe that the ascendancy of popular culture as the primary concern of Cultural Studies is problematic for the social study of culture as initially promised by Hoggart and Williams. In some contemporary manifestations within Cultural Studies, popular culture becomes declassed as individuals are seen to create their own identities through cultural consumption, irrespective of the class backgrounds they bring to the point of cultural consumption and cultural usage. Sport is one area of culture where the inadequacy of such an orientation is all too obvious. At a number of points in the book we will indicate the importance of retaining an emphasis on the classed nature of sports with regard to the cultural history of particular sports and the ways in which people engage with sports as participants and spectators. We also recognise the importance of accounting for the relationship between sport and other key sources of social identity such as gender and race. We agree that, where appropriate, sport should be studied as a form of popular culture, but always in cognisance of the social factors that have bearing on the ways that cultural items are made sense of and put to use.

Cultural Studies emerged formally within the academy as a disciplinary amalgam of English literary studies and sociology. Culturalism, as inspired by Hoggart and Williams, and developed in the work of some subsequent scholars such as Paul Willis, is a product of that union (Inglis and Hughson 2003: 88–111). It is our belief that much of the work within contemporary Cultural Studies has strayed almost entirely from the foundations of both literary studies and sociology, and hence from culturalism. The shift towards an interest in the structures of language and signs promotes a shift away from sociology's interest in 'social structures' and literary studies' humanistic interest in culture. So-called poststructuralist analysis deconstructs the structures of language and signs but offers no return to the primary concerns of sociology and literary studies. As an intellectual project culturalism proposes the possibility of exploring the sensuousness of culture as experienced by people within collective, community contexts. The proposition comes mainly out of literary studies and its deliberate evocation of human spirit. However, this is a decidedly non-theoretical understanding of culture. The theoretical starch for culturalism comes from sociology and its principal concerns with social structures and processes. Without sociology, notions such as community tend to exist purely at a romantic level. Hoggart, as the least sociological of culturalist writers, is often accused of romanticising his working-class community. On the other hand, Williams, who comprehensively developed his own account of the sociology of culture, provides a theoretically informed version of culturalism – cultural materialism – as discussed in Chapter Six of this book. Our major intellectual influences in *The Uses of Sport* can thus be attributed to the cultural humanism of Hoggart and the cultural materialism of Williams.

The book is organised into chapters developed thematically from our starting point in culturalist Cultural Studies. Chapter One charts the prehistory of Cultural Studies by examining the conservative and mildly liberal traditions of English cultural commentary, which gave rise to the romantic and humanistic temperaments that underpin the later leftist culturalism of Hoggart and Williams. We look at the implications for sport within this tradition, particularly with regard to the precarious position of sport within debates that distinguish between civilisation on the one hand and culture on the other.

Chapter Two concentrates on the key culturalist writers Hoggart and Williams, particularly on the way that each of these writers makes the notion of community central to their understanding of a genuinely democratic and sustainable collective cultural life. Although neither of these writers has much to say about sport we can deduce from what they do say that sport has an important role to play within their envisaged 'common cultures'. The cultural analysis of both Hoggart and Williams is helpful to understanding the communal significance and everday meanings of sport.

Chapter Three continues with the theme of community but turns from a British focus to an American one. This takes us away from Cultural Studies as such, into more general considerations about culture, democracy and public life that are keenly debated within American intellectualism. We are particularly interested in the chapter to look at the 'fall of public man' thesis as proffered by Richard Sennett and to look at the implications for sport as a form of public culture.

Chapter Four takes us directly into the territory of Cultural Studies by looking at sport as a form of popular culture. We move from debates about mass culture, to those concerned with developing distinctions within popular culture, to those over the alleged trend towards the uncritical celebration of popular culture. We locate sport within these debates as well as discussing the claim that sport has largely been excluded from research and publishing within the academic mainstream of Cultural Studies.

Chapter Five takes a particularly critical stance on the theoretical trend within Cultural Studies towards postmodernism. We accept that rather immense cultural changes have occurred from the time of the Second World War, but we contend that these changes are not usefully characterised within a new era known as postmodernity, nor is a new theoretical means known as postmodernism required to explain what has happened. The chapter presents a case for locating sport within late modernity rather than postmodernity and for returning to more conventional modes of theoretical analysis for its explication.

Chapter Six takes us further into the theoretical territory of the sociology of culture. We look at the social factors that underpin the material relations of culture, specifically addressing the key sociological dimensions of class, gender and ethnicity. We consider the structural and ideological bases of power relations and how domination within the realm of culture is challenged through cultural practice; sport in our case. Raymond Williams's notion of 'cultural materialism' is particularly important to our considerations about how power is contested within culture.

Chapter Seven examines the experience of sport in relation to the body. We draw insight from phenomenological philosophy, principally the ideas of Maurice Merleau-Ponty, to develop an understanding of the instinctive bodily movements involved in sporting practice. We look especially at examples of 'star' performers in professional sport. Although the body movements in sport are often described as natural, in a manner attributed entirely to individual peculiarity, we contend that the embodied experience of sport is shaped within cultural contexts. To explain the co-existence of nature and culture within human movement we refer to Pierre Bourdieu and the concept of 'habitus'.

Chapter Eight discusses means of research, specifically looking at how sport might be studied, in both participant and spectator modes, as forms of 'lived experience'. We consider the claim of ethnography to provide a first hand experiential understanding of the meanings that people invest into and take from their engagement with sport and sport related activities. We initially consider a particularly humanistic form of ethnographic reportage that we refer to as 'panoramic ethnography', and look at examples of this writing pertinent to sport. We then consider the participant observation ethnography, more familiar to sociology and Cultural Studies, and discuss the difficulties and advantages of this type of research for studying sporting cultures and subcultures.

Each chapter is followed by a Connections section. These sections make pertinent links to concepts and issues extending from the central themes of the substantive chapters. The Connections sections discuss related examples from sport and point to further readings within the sport academic literature. The exception is the Connections section to Chapter Six, which concentrates on explicating important theoretical themes stemming from the discussion in that chapter.

The substantive chapters are followed by a concluding commentary focussed on the policy implications for sport from a culturalist position. We consider the place of sport within cultural policy – and in relation to social policy – and reflect critically upon the rhetorical and symbolic incorporation of sport into the recent 'City of Culture' campaigns in Britain. Following the concluding commentary is a brief section containing discussion questions, each pertaining to the substantive chapters and the themes they address.

Note

1   The importance of sport to English working–class life is sensuously evoked by Priestley (1980 [1929]: 5–6) in a well known early passage of the novel *The Good Companions*, where he describes the deep cultural significance of an afternoon at the football.

1

SPORT, CULTURE AND CIVILISATION

We commence the book with a chapter seeking to locate sport within what might be referred to as the prehistory of Cultural Studies. By this particular use of the term prehistory, we mean the intellectual tradition from which Cultural Studies, as an area of study within the academy, was spawned. Given our recognition of Britain as the birthplace of institutional Cultural Studies, we are particularly interested in the tradition of cultural commentary that informed the pioneering work of Richard Hoggart and his contemporary Raymond Williams, and with how sport might be viewed in relation to this tradition. Williams's classic 1958 text *Culture and Society* traces a lineage of British writers from 1780–1950, which elevates culture onto an intellectual and aesthetic plane above the more practical realm of society. Williams accounts for a history of ideas dating from the period of the Industrial Revolution and represents culture in terms antithetical to an increasingly mechanised society − often described as civilisation. Before coming to Williams and Hoggart (in the next chapter), and looking at how these two writers invert the critique of − yet maintain attachment to − the preceding tradition of British cultural commentary, we want to consider the implications for sport of this particular tradition. Are we to consider sport as existing within the realm of culture or civilisation? How does sport connect with thoughts about the reconciliation of culture with civilisation?

Kulturkritik and romanticism

The roots of the aforementioned British tradition reside in a borrowed tradition of German cultural commentary. This tradition, known as the *Kulturkritik*, is associated with a number of German philosophical writers on culture, principally Johann Gottfried von Herder (1744–1803) who explicated a rupture between culture and civilisation in the late eighteenth century (Mulhern 2000: xvi). Herder believed that culture is in harmony with nature whereas civilisation is distinctly man-made and developed from the artifice of human affairs, particularly politics and economy. From this perspective, civilisation must not be allowed to inhibit the lived experience of culture in its various forms. Mulhern (2000: xv) notes that when interpreted in English, *Kulturkritik* means 'cultural criticism'. Passing into usage in England this 'cultural criticism' takes on national specificity and bears relevance to what becomes the cultural dimension of an ongoing 'condition of England' debate. We thus agree with Mulhern that in the English context it is more appropriate to speak of a de-italicised Kulturkritik, and we continue to do this where relevant in the chapter. We look briefly at how a Kulturkritik emerged in England in the commentary of Samuel Taylor Coleridge (1772–1834) in the early 1800s, how it was developed in the Victorian period by Matthew Arnold (1822–83), and worked into – what might be described as a proto cultural studies – the cultural criticism of F.R. Leavis (1895–1978) and T.S. Eliot (1888–1965) in the first half of the twentieth century. Our discussion of these key writers within the English Kulturkritik is related to the respective intellectual positions of romanticism, humanism and culturalism. It is our intention to indicate – and further evidence will arise in subsequent chapters – that these positions have lingering importance to the lived cultural experience of sport in contemporary times. Let us set out the position before reflecting on the implications for sport.

The seeds for an English Kulturkritik can be found in the early writing of Edmund Burke (1729–97) on the philosophy of aesthetics, dating back to the early period of the Industrial Revolution. According to Burke, art is the ultimate source of social cohesion and harmony; 'it is the mediatress between man and the natural world' (Ackroyd 1976: 42). This view creates not a reverence for the objects of art – as is often mistakenly ascribed to one of Burke's intellectual inheritors, Matthew Arnold – but an essential respect for the 'humane purpose' of art. Culture – interpreted as art – thus acquires a moral significance as the living repository of human values. Burke thus elevates culture onto a plane above other aspects of life, although he does not specify a categorical rift between culture and society. Coleridge is perhaps the first prominent English intellectual to do so during a series of public lectures in the first decade of the 1800s. It is possible that much of Coleridge's excursus was original, although the influence of post-Kantian German thought was so apparent that Coleridge was accused by critics of plagiarism, a claim he emphatically denied (Holmes 1998: 276). Coleridge's later lectures in the series gave acknowledgment to German theorists, including von Herder, thus establishing an explicit connection between English and German cultural criticism. Cultural criticism in both of these national contexts was decidedly anti-capitalist in tone. However, rather than being indicative of a pre-Marxist form of socialism, this criticism was aimed primarily at the deleterious social and environmental impact of capitalist industries following the Industrial Revolution. Politically radical in the early part of his life, Coleridge turned to conservatism in his later years, this position culminating in the publication of *On the Constitution of the Church and State* in 1830. Although depicted as capricious by critics, Coleridge's views on humanity remained largely consistent and were indicative of the common ground shared by the conservative and radical mindset.

Coleridge initiated an English Kulturkritik with his differentiation between 'cultivation' and 'civilisation'. For Coleridge, civilisation constitutes the 'ordinary progress of society' (Williams 1958: 63), a mixture of necessary affairs with the possibility of corruption. Cultivation is tantamount to culture, it is the embodiment of human value offering the means by which individuals might glimpse, if not attain, perfection. From this perspective, cultivation is anything but ordinary, a point later inverted by Williams and taken up as the chief bone of contention by academic Cultural Studies. For Coleridge, cultivation is independent of civilisation but stands in judgement of it (Williams 1958: 63). In practical terms this is to be performed by a cultural elite referred to by Coleridge as the clerisy. His religiosity is apparent enough here as he presupposes an inextricable linkage between the Church, the state and the nation. He calls for the clerisy to propagate a 'moral science' as the means of guidance for the 'numerous classes'. His cultural conservatism is further evinced in his view of the clerisy as the guardians of the national culture; 'treasures of the past' must be preserved as a guide to the present and future. As elitist as Coleridge's position sounds, and indeed is, he wants elements of cultivation to be diffused through 'the whole community'. This is the hallmark of the conservative position on culture. Culture – understood in terms of the fine arts – is the preserve of a cultivated elite, but its essential goodness is to the benefit of the community at large.

John Stuart Mill (1806–73) referred approvingly to Coleridge in seemingly oxymoronic terms as a radical Tory (cited in Walsh 1967: 193), an element of conservatism that has never been prominent in party politics and is almost non-existent in parliamentary forums today. Mill's comment arose in his comparative discussion of Coleridge with the unlikely bedfellow of Jeremy Bentham (1748–1832), the philosopher who outlined the principles of utilitarianism in the late 1780s. Mill's attempt to reconcile the ideas of Coleridge and Bentham – judged by Williams in *Culture and Society* (1958) as ultimately unsuccessful – appears as an attempt to soften his own utilitarian position. Utilitarianism intends a rather practical approach to philosophy. Utility, taken to mean 'the greatest happiness of the greatest number', is its cornerstone and is seen as the most sensible steering principle for social life and associated political and economic policy making. Utilitarianism recognises the primacy of the individual and the pursuit of self-interest as a perfectly understandable and legitimate aim for human beings. The role of government should be to provide the most conducive social conditions for individuals to pursue their interests in an unhindered manner. From the perspective of utilitarianism, society itself is seen as 'no more than the aggregation of individuals brought together in the realisation of their individual goals' (Jary and Jary 1999: 713). Utilitarianism provided the philosophical underpinning of the modern liberal state and the various policy manifestations that have arisen since, including economic rationalism (Milner 1994: 9).

Andrew Milner (1994) argues that British Cultural Studies and the preceding tradition of cultural commentary developed as a critique of the position on culture implicit in utilitarianism. While Milner commences with Arnold, we are proposing here a similar spirit of critique commencing with Coleridge. Coleridge offers a collectivist position that remains essentially at odds with utilitarianism despite the conciliatory aspects identified by Mill (and later by the literary theorist I.A. Richards). Coleridge's social philosophy is primarily aimed, as indicated above, at the 'advancement of knowledge' throughout society. This is at once the social value of cultivation, and the clerisy and the National Church assume their institutional purpose towards this end (Walsh 1967: 194). Coleridge's position is concerned with the maximisation of social good, rather than the maximisation of self-interest. His social outlook – society viewed in holistic terms – is the converse of Bentham's image of society as an aggregation of individuals pursuing their own interests. Coleridge could never accept the reduction of culture to a matter of preference with each individual entitled to cultural pleasures of their choice. This is not to say that Coleridge was opposed to self-expression, indeed self-expression is fundamental to the romantic movement of which Coleridge was a key figure. Ernst Fischer (1963: 52) described romanticism as a 'contradictory protest' because it at once opposed capitalism and promoted aesthetic individualism. However, self-expression for Coleridge was of the imagination, that most important human faculty he described as 'the living power and the prime agent of all human perception' (James 1961: 38–9). Coleridge's discussion of imagination pertained to the art of poetry but connects with his social thought in regard to his dissatisfaction with the state of the world in the way that it impedes artistic sensibility.

Although a cultural elitist in his emphasis on cultivation, Coleridge shared the respect of the romantic movement for 'folk art'. Romanticism sought an attachment with folk traditions to re-establish a sense of cultural unity across an increasingly fragmented society. The individualist and collectivist tendencies within romanticism were thus linked by a quest for what Fischer (1963: 62) refers to as 'a synthesis of the personality and the collective'. Romanticism thus evoked *the people* as the embodiment of an endangered, if not lost, organic community. This concept of the people as an organic community appears in subsequent cultural commentary, prominently in the work of Leavis and Eliot where class differences in cultural location are explained in terms of a natural cultural hierarchy within society. However, the appeal extended to cultural commentary on the non-Marxist left. Hoggart, for example, although distinguishing between 'them' and 'us', assumed an organic community in which cultural barriers need not be rigid because culture is ultimately shared. Both the right and left of what becomes retrospectively known as the culturalist paradigm within Cultural Studies thus take inspiration from the organic view of culture developed by Coleridge, particularly as a riposte to the atomistic cultural developments in their own time. Aspects of

11

Coleridge's romanticism were challenged within subsequent English commentary – Leavis and Eliot were both critics – but he was undeniably a formative figure in what develops into an English Kulturkritik.

Kulturkritik and humanism

As stated earlier our interest here is to consider how sport, as a form or aspect of culture, is implicated within the emergent Kulturkritik tradition. It is our view that if we are to explain the cultural phenomena of sport via Cultural Studies, then we need to have some understanding of how sport might be placed within the preceding intellectual tradition. Let us take stock at this point and then move on to consider the implications of other writers within the tradition. Coleridge, it will be apparent, did not write about sport and it is not our intention to impute a position on sport to him.[1] The same point applies to other writers in the chapter, although we find some passing references to sport, particularly in the work of Eliot. We will see that although sport is not readily associated with the Kulturkritik aesthetic interpretation of culture, it necessarily has a place within that tradition's parallel understanding of culture as 'a whole way of life'. This understanding of culture as organic and natural, and lived out in various forms of folk culture – crafts, arts, leisure activities, including sport – is concomitant with the conservative and elitist desire to protect and nurture the artistic canon. Culture is natural and all forms of culture have their place within the cultural hierarchy. From this perspective sporting traditions are to be respected as they are seen as a valuable and possibly intrinsic dimension to community relations. The Kulturkritik repulsion for the utilitarian position on culture would certainly extend to sport. The threat to – in some cases the complete shattering of – traditional affiliations between sport and local communities that has occurred over the last many years is one indicator of the extent to which the utilitarian ethos has invaded sport through the insidious twin manifestations of commercialisation and professionalism. Campaigns against such developments as the forced amalgamation of football teams are inclined to be interpreted as socialistic as they are pitted against business interests, however certain elements within the protest are no doubt motivated by conservative cultural concerns perhaps in keeping with a Kulturkritik temperament.

The romanticist mood of the post-Enlightenment cultural tradition in Britain was matched by a humanistic temperament that developed in the latter part of the nineteenth century, which is most famously associated with the work of Matthew Arnold. While romanticism is inclined to be antirational and often underpinned by religious conviction, humanism favours rational thought and tends to prioritise the secular. From the position of religious romanticism, such as that found in Coleridge, humans are incapable of seeking out perfection as perfection resides solely with God. This results in an inherently conservative understanding of culture. From a humanist position, the ultimate importance of secular life is in the individual pursuit of human perfection. Humanists may or may not be religious believers, but those who are recognise a potential for human perfection that exists in relation to, but categorically apart from, the perfection of God. For some humanists, such as Arnold, culture provides the major means through which individuals can seek perfection. The emphasis placed on individual potential and development through culture has resulted in humanism being interpreted as politically liberal and thus Arnold has been described as a liberal humanist. Arnold is often the first cultural writer addressed in Cultural Studies textbooks and is usually depicted (sometimes rather facilely) as a cultural elitist who has been completely superseded by the more 'radical' writers within contemporary Cultural Studies.

Arnold is best known for the book *Culture and Anarchy*, originally published in 1869 and thoroughly revised by Arnold in 1875. From this book comes Arnold's famous association of culture with 'the best which has been thought and said in the world' (Arnold 1932 [1869]: 6). This phrase is often taken as the key indicator of Arnold's cultural elitism, but it is often misinterpreted. As Lesley Johnson (1979: 29) importantly notes, 'Arnold did not equate culture with "the best which has been thought and said" ', but believed culture to be in a constant state of development and that it could develop most beneficially out of a critical engagement with the best thoughts and ideas. Like the romantics Arnold accepted the balance of conceptual tension of culture in relation to aesthetics and society. However, *Culture and Anarchy* is principally a book about politics, in which Arnold placates his own fears about the growth in mass democracy by pronouncing his faith in the socially corrective possibilities of culture. Arnold was not entirely opposed to democratic reform and, from his position as Inspector of Schools, he argued for reforms within the education system based on the principle of meritocracy. However, while believing the education system to be ripe for change, he also believed it to be the most appropriate institutional forum for maintaining social standards and cohesion. This would occur as schools transmitted culture via a curriculum concentrated on 'the best which has been thought and said'. The necessity of culture for Arnold was as a protection against the deleterious impact of mass culture, which, he believed, would accompany the democratic extension of electoral franchise. Democracy by political decree was not truly democratic for Arnold, as it did not result in making people equal. The true hope of democracy lay in culture because culture exposes all men (*sic*) to 'an atmosphere of sweetness and light'. Culture 'seeks to do away with classes' and to elevate the masses above their 'raw and uncultivated state' (Arnold 1932: 70, 76).

In seeing culture as the pursuit of human perfection, Arnold's understanding of culture goes beyond the intellectual emphasis implied by his preoccupation with 'the best which has been thought and said'. Indeed, for Arnold, culture involves 'the development of all sides of human nature' (Johnson 1979: 28). As the son of Thomas Arnold, the famous headmaster of

Rugby School and the figurehead associated with the introduction of 'muscular Christianity' to the English public school system, Matthew Arnold no doubt thought about the relationship of sport to culture and cultural advancement. Holt (1989: 95) suggests that Arnold (quoted in Briggs 1965 [1954]: 153) has sport in mind when he lauds the egalitarian merits of the public school, where the bringing up 'side by side' of 'the bottle-merchant's son and the Plantagenet' are indicative of the 'beneficial salutary inter-mixture of classes'. From this interpretation sport takes on a supplementary role within Arnold's social view of culture, as a means of overcoming class barriers as the sons of aristocrats play alongside the sons of factory-owners in rugby and other sports. Arnold's social view of culture has obvious similarities to the romantics in that he is interested in the whole way of life of a society. However, his view is dynamic rather than static, and his humanistic temperament refuses to see individuals confined to preordained stations in life. This provides for a different view of culture to that of conservatively minded romantics such as Coleridge who work with a rather fixed hierarchical view of lived culture in association with an organic image of the people. From this latter view the social importance of culture is that everyone respects their station and keeps to their place. In contrast, Arnold's humanistic view of culture provides the important social possibility of people being brought together. He thus denies the existence of immutable social barriers based on assumed natural hierarchies.

Another key difference between Arnold and the romantics is his promotion of Hellenism. Arnold believed the English cultural mood – developed under the influence of Christianity – to be characterised by Hebraism, evincing a tendency of scepticism towards human perfection. For Arnold (1932 [1869]: 132), an overemphasis on Hebraism results in a preoccupation with obedience and an effective stifling of human expression. He appealed to Hellenism as an equally worthy spiritual discipline alongside that of Hebraism; Hebraism is important, but its *strictness of conscience* needs to be balanced with the *spontaneity of consciousness* offered by Hellenism. Arnold's interest in Hellenism represents a particularly important development in cultural commentary for our considerations, because it is a step out of the realm of imagination, characteristic of Coleridge, into a more total understanding of the human spirit comprised of mind and body. After all, the ancient Greek quest for human perfection involved both intellect and physique. Physical training for the Greeks was necessarily associated with preparation for combat and was therefore part of a stringent disciplinary regime, but 'the athletic male body was unquestionably a cultural ideal' (Guttmann 1996: 17), as attested by representations in artwork surviving from the age. This prompts consideration of athleticism, and therefore sport, in relation to culture understood in aesthetic as well as – and in conjunction with – social terms: a theme discussed in previously published work by two of the present authors (Inglis and Hughson 2000).

Arnold's emphasis on the individual and human perfection should not be taken to mean that he was opposed to the collectivist spirit that had emerged from English conservative cultural commentary. He stands in relation to the romantics, being particularly sympathetic to an organic view of society if not one forever marked by rigid class hierarchies. Most importantly, Arnold rejects the instrumental form of individualism associated with utilitarianism, clearly opposing the self-interest trend of his day when an 'Englishman's right to do what he likes' had become taken for granted (Arnold 1932 [1869]: 76). This is indicative of the tendency to anarchy that so concerned Arnold. While much critical attention within Cultural Studies is focused on Arnold's fear of the mass as a social entity, he was perhaps more concerned with the mob mentality that contradictorily finds expression in the aggressive assertion of individual rights. Rather than disliking the masses themselves, Arnold disliked the essentially middle-class utilitarian mood which had pervaded the lower social echelons. He believed the problem would be exacerbated by the increasing Americanisation of English culture. The problem with American culture for Arnold was that it had been exposed to the crudest interpretation of democracy, whereby individuals are free to choose whatever they like according to their preferences, no matter how ill-informed or unrefined these preferences might be. Such a situation results in moral decline as society loses the cultural standards necessary for the practical guidance of a moral life (cf. Johnson 1979: 21). Arnold's fears of the impact of Americanisation became embedded within the English intellectual psyche and amplifications of his critique appear on both the right and left of subsequent cultural criticism – interestingly, the hatred of Americanisation provides a unifying theme for the twentieth-century culturalist writers to the time of Hoggart. In a moment we discuss this theme as it emerged in the work of F.R. Leavis; at this point we consider the related implications of this particular line of anti-Americanisation argument for sport.

Arnold believed that the drift to Americanisation and into cultural 'anarchy' could be rectified in England by the diffusion of culture through state institutions, through schools in particular. However, his liberal spirit was tempered by conservatism and in the absence of recommendation for significant structural change in society, his hopes for cultural regeneration across social classes appear fanciful (cf. Milner 1994: 23). Had social reform proceeded only in the manner proposed by Arnold, the class barriers he wanted to see overcome would still be far closer to those of the Victorian period than they are today. Cultural activities and the possibility of cultural advancement (in Arnold's own vision) would be much more tightly constrained by class background than they presently are. Sport as a social leveller would have gone little further than the realm of the public school discussed above with reference to Arnold. Arnold's hopes rested on culture having a natural transforming capacity. He believed culture to be super-ordinate to society and that culture itself promised the breakdown of social class barriers. Arnold could therefore argue that democracy need not be imposed by radical political reform, as it would come through the dissemination of culture via the education system. His elitist view of culture thus coincides with a top-down understanding of democracy – to favour radical democratic change was, for Arnold, to advance *anarchy* over *culture*.

Leavis: sport and the 'organic community'

Arnold's conservative–liberal version of a Kulturkritik position became very influential upon subsequent writing, and found particular resonance in the cultural commentary of the Cambridge literary intellectual F.R. Leavis. However, the optimism of Arnold is less evident in Leavis. The inverted ordering of terms in Leavis's own Kulturkritik title, *Mass Civilisation and Minority Culture* (1930), is meant to indicate that Arnold's worst fears – culture being swamped by anarchy – had been realised by the 1930s. Leavis was a supreme cultural elitist and took the Arnoldian epithet of 'the best which has been thought and said' as an end as much as a means to culture. His book *The Great Tradition* (1993 [1948]) sets out, in purely subjective terms, a literary canon of the few truly great English writers. In so doing he explicitly defines culture in association with aesthetic objects, in contrast to Arnold's definition of culture in terms of a process (Johnson 1979: 102). Furthermore, Leavis rejects Arnold's primarily social definition of culture by moving closer to a romantic understanding of culture existing not only above but also apart from society. He sounded more like Coleridge than Arnold in professing the need for an established cultural elite (albeit one 'not to be identified with any social class') to guard over culture, which he redefined as 'the picked experiences of ages' (Leavis and Thompson 1933: 82). A minority culture needed defending by a cultured minority, against the impending ravage of mass culture.

As with Arnold, the biggest threat to English culture came for Leavis through the perceived contagion of Americanisation. Leavis followed the line of Arnoldian critique by arguing that a culture opened to the democracy of mass sentiment resulted in 'standardisation' and 'levelling down' (Leavis and Thompson 1933). This critique was set out in another Kulturkritik inspired title, *Culture and Environment* (1933), written by Leavis with the assistance of Denys Thompson. This book might now be seen as the first Cultural Studies textbook, offering a series of questions to students by which they could apply the analysis of literary criticism to the emergent popular culture forms of the day. The interpretation of popular culture presented by Leavis is hardly neutral and the student/reader is clearly being invited into an appraisal resulting in condemnation. Leavis is particularly critical of the commercialism of American popular culture, which he tacitly associates with the vilest of utilitarian intention. He is especially repulsed by the parasitic industry of advertising – 'the genial bloodthirstiness of the "ad. men" of the U.S.A.' – which he clearly sees as antithetical to his desired understanding of culture as

16

a repository of moral value (Leavis and Thompson 1933: 31). Leavis goes on to invert the language of utilitarian economics to parody the American sense of self-achievement. For Leavis, the American boast of enjoying 'the highest "standard of living" in the world' is entirely indicative of a concomitant failure to recognise the cultural malaise into which that nation had drifted (Leavis and Thompson 1933: 64).

Leavis appeared to relish using American based studies to sharpen and validate his criticisms. For example, he quotes at length from the study *Middletown* (1929), by the sociologists R.M. and H.S. Lynd to show the atomising effect on social life when local networks of interpersonal communication are superseded by mass mediated forms of communication. The account of individuals experiencing estrangement in an increasingly depersonalised culture portends criticisms by more contemporary American cultural critics to be discussed in Chapter Three. For Leavis, the *Middletown* study betrayed the 'decay of social life and the arts'; it evinced a non-community where 'individuals came together to escape from their loneliness and the emptiness of their lives and to nourish their sense of herd solidarity' (Leavis and Thompson 1933: 65). Leavis (Leavis and Thompson 1933: 68) contrasted this image of American cultural life with England's 'rich tradition of recreation' that resided in the pre-industrial 'organic community'. His vision was unapologetically backward looking and repeated the romantic equation of community with social life prior to the Industrial Revolution. It also indicates that despite refusing to define culture in social terms, Leavis – in keeping with the Kulturkritik – recognises an alternative understanding of culture as lived experience within a common tradition. He opens *Culture and Environment* with the classic quote:

> What we have lost is the organic community with the living culture it embodied. Folk-songs, folk-dances, Cotswold cottages and handicraft products are signs of expressions of something more: an art of life, a way of living, ordered and patterned, involving social arts, codes of intercourse and a responsive adjustment, growing out of immemorial experience, to the natural environment and the rhythm of the year.
>
> (Leavis and Thompson 1933: 1–2)

His reference to 'social art' is particularly interesting. Although uncompromising in his adherence to the idea of culture – perhaps best put with a capital C – existing within a 'great tradition', Leavis allowed that artistry could be seen within the normal course of social life of the common people as they engage in their pastimes and leisure pursuits. Leavis, perhaps unwittingly, suggests a distinction between leisure and culture, the former a social terminology, the latter an aesthetic terminology. His explicit reference to the social activity of leisure – *Culture and Environment* features a chapter titled 'The use of leisure' – stakes an unexpected claim for Leavis within the then-incipient sub-field of the sociology of leisure. His discussion proceeds in unacknowledged class terms, accounting for the decline in standards of working class – both white and blue collar – leisure activities. Modern leisure is seen by Leavis in direct relation to the world of work. As work becomes increasingly meaningless to individuals, this is reflected in the mindless escapism of their pastimes. Leavis traces the decline by drawing on the writing of the nineteenth century author George Sturt, who noted that the tiresome and laborious nature of industrial work permeated the worker's life beyond work hours. Sturt (quoted in Leavis and Thompson 1933: 71) asks, 'after a day like the coal-carter's, where is the man that could refresh himself with the arts, or even the games, of civilisation?' This is, in itself, an insightful quote, as the Kulturkritik-inspired Leavis would clearly want to differentiate between the arts and games of civilisation and the arts he associates with culture. The main purpose for Leavis in drawing upon Sturt, however, is to lend historical weight to his claim about the deleterious impact of industrialisation upon the common culture.

For Leavis, this decline can only be worsened once American culture takes hold in Britain. Like work, he believed leisure lost dignity under industrialisation and this was a circumstance ripe for exploitation by crass commercialised forms of popular culture that were superficially attractive and addictive to the non-discerning consumer. With the arrival of a mass produced popular culture the division between work and labour is widened in the most artificial manner. Leavis believed people are drawn into consuming popular culture as a release from the tedium and senselessness of work, the pure escapism of Hollywood films being the most obvious example. The problem with films for Leavis is that they nullify a meaningful critical engagement, reducing the viewer to a passive recipient of formulaic storylines. They appeal to the most tawdry of human emotions and can completely destroy the capacity within the individual to be receptive towards true culture – the arts and literature. Here Leavis reveals his humanist temperament. Like Arnold he believed that all humans have an innate capacity for the appreciation of culture – culture is classless – and he hated mass popular culture for denying this possibility to the majority of people. However, the reality he accepted was that in modern society culture would continue to be appreciated by only a limited few, hence his reference to the 'minority culture'. His underlying disposition is to liberal humanism, but his dogged defence of the 'minority culture' against 'mass civilisation' promoted a cultural conservatism that would serve to strengthen class boundaries rather than overcome them.

Although not addressing sport, Leavis provides further insight for us into how sport might be related to the British Kulturkritik tradition of cultural commentary. Of particular importance is his reference to leisure as a distinct form of cultural activity removed from culture understood in relation to the high arts. Once this distinction is stated, sport can be thought of as clearly located within the category of leisure. Leavis would be disinclined to bother about thinking of sport in relation to aesthetics, a logical outcome of the Kulturkritik distinction between culture and civilisation. For Leavis, leisure (and hence sport) takes place within the latter realm. Again though, as for earlier Kulturkritik thinkers such as Coleridge, the cultural life of the people within the civilisation at large remains important and worthy of respect. Much has been made within academic Cultural Studies of Leavis's fear that mass produced popular culture would damage the 'minority culture'. This is certainly part of his concern but we do well not to overstate it. Leavis was surely aware that the high arts would be sustained for a minority elite audience and readership in one way or another, no matter how much the masses became engrossed by a vacuous Americanised popular culture. His cultural criticism, as evinced by the quotation from *Culture and Environment* above, was very much concerned with a decline in standards of the common culture. For Leavis there should be a natural relationship between work and leisure. Work should be rewarding and fulfilling, and if this is the case people will pursue pastimes which fill their leisure hours with an equivalent degree of satisfaction. He was gravely concerned that as work became increasingly trivial and degrading for people in industrialised Britain they would become inclined to seek out pastimes of equally dubious value.

Leavis would no doubt be horrified – if not surprised – by the current state of spectator sport in Britain. As a mediated form of popular culture sport has all the traits of flashy excess that Leavis associated with popular culture subject to the influence of Americanisation. It would be almost impossible to register his level of disdain for the popularity of pseudo-sports such as professional wrestling, but he would perhaps be equally alarmed by the uprooting of tradition in sports such as association football brought by hyper-commercialisation and so-called progress. Sport may be placed within the context of Leavis's quotation on the relationship between a common culture and the 'organic community', being a form of lived culture, indicative of shared social experience, and a natural expression of social intercourse. Leavis – sounding like a functionalist sociologist – would acknowledge the role of sport as a means of creating and maintaining social order and patterning. Conversely, it is reasonable to believe that he would be resentful of the breakdown of traditions that increasingly severs any meaningful link between sports teams and local communities. There would be a more agreeable place for amateur and junior sport if we apply Leavis's perspective to a view of contemporary leisure life, but a note of caution would be sounded with regard to the extent of competitiveness that might be observed at this level. Leavis the humanist would no doubt want sport to involve a natural expression of individual and team skills, and would reject the tendencies towards rationalisation and instrumentality that encroach upon amateur sport once it is placed within highly organised contexts such as regional competitions, where winning becomes the paramount goal. From this perspective, sport might not be about the pursuit of human perfection in the way that culture is, but it should certainly be about natural self-expression and not the pursuit of contrived self-interest in the manner of utilitarianism.

Eliot: sport in the 'common culture'

A similar position on culture to Leavis's was advanced by his contemporary, T.S. Eliot. Best known for his poetry, Eliot also wrote cultural commentary and criticism, the most prominent of these works being *Notes Towards the Definition of Culture*, published in 1948. Eliot also believed culture to occupy a separate realm from civilisation and that culture, understood as the high arts, was the preserve of a privileged elite. However, he also accepted an interpretation of culture in association with the everyday leisure activities of the populace at large and came close to a sociological definition of culture as constituting 'the whole way of life'. He clearly believed that culture, so understood, is based in tradition and grows out of an organic community. His best known quote from *Notes Towards the Definition of Culture* sounds very similar to Leavis, if even more quaintly English in the examples of common culture he cites:

> Derby Day, Henley Regatta, Cowes, the twelfth of August, a cup final, the dog races, the pin table, the dart board, Wensleydale cheese, boiled cabbage cut into sections, beetroot in vinegar, nineteenth-century Gothic churches, and the music of Elgar.
>
> (Eliot 1964 [1948]: 30)

Although sport does not feature in Eliot's discussion we see it clearly identified in his vision of the cultural life of the English people. It takes its place alongside other leisure activities within a natural state of affairs that has been established over time. Like Leavis, Eliot opposed the upsetting of cultural traditions and believed English society to be in a state of cultural decline. He feared the impact of an emergent mass culture and would be completely hostile to trends within contemporary leisure, including sport, which reflect commercial prerogatives rather than the communal interests of the people. The range of sporting activities included within Eliot's definition gives recognition to both amateur and professional sport and to the classed bases of sport. For Eliot there is no antagonism implied by these differences. Amateur sport sits comfortably alongside professional sport within the panoply of cultural life in England, and sports find their place naturally within the social hierarchy, the social elite having developed their own sporting traditions – often extending out of the public school system – and the working classes having their own sporting traditions. Like Leavis, Eliot was anti-utilitarian in his view of culture, and this would apply to sport. We can see from Eliot's quotation above that sport is intrinsically tied to his idea of the organic community and this would be anathema to sport serving crude self-interests. Eliot's position, like that of Leavis, prompts a possible critique of the tendency for sport to be organised according to utilitarian principles. Such a critique, as indicated in the discussion of Leavis, could apply to both amateur and professional sport and, more broadly, to the way sport is used as a form of ideology within public discourse to promote a general utilitarian ethos within Western societies.

Together, Leavis and Eliot ushered in a form of cultural commentary that, however unwittingly or with reservation, prompted the academic study of popular culture (cf. Dworkin 1997: 82). Their position might be described as right culturalism, standing in converse relationship to the left culturalism of the early Cultural Studies figures Richard Hoggart and Raymond Williams. We must be careful not to conflate the figures of Leavis and Eliot within Cultural Studies, they had differences particularly along political lines. Unlike Leavis, Eliot was an ardent conservative and was disinterested in liberal notions of high culture being potentially accessible to all individuals. Eliot argued that culture is inextricably linked to family background and upbringing and that this is a natural situation, one that cannot be altered by well intentioned social engineering. He, therefore, explicitly locates culture within a hierarchy of social class. For both Leavis and Eliot the main interest is in culture understood as the high arts, the minority culture as they referred to it. By the time both of them were writing, sociology and anthropology had developed as academic disciplines and they were drawn into accounting for culture from the perspectives of these disciplines. This is to say that they were unable to do anything other than consider culture as 'a whole way of life'. In the case of Eliot, Johnson (1979: 128) suggests that the surrender to sociology was made rather reluctantly and that the brief catalogue of common leisure activities in his famous quotation was given with some cynicism. Raymond Williams (1958: 234) claims that Eliot slides between definitions of culture, ultimately imposing his high culture definition onto his popular culture definition. Williams does not explain how Eliot does this, but we can presume he means that moral value pertains to popular culture as it does to high culture. The relationship can never be identical as high culture is intrinsically moral, whereas popular culture can only be moral by example, in message and conduct. For both Eliot and Leavis, traditions of leisure will be developed within and through the organic community, forming a common culture. Sport will be a significant part of this cultural life and should therefore provide a means of conduct through which people can at once enjoy themselves and behave morally.

Sport, manners, morals and civilisation

A less prescriptive, more sociologically descriptive, account of the link between sport and moral conduct is to be found in the work of the German scholar Norbert Elias. Having left Germany in the 1930s, Elias became a prominent professor of sociology in Britain and (along with Pierre Bourdieu) is the best known of twentieth-century sociologists to systematically address sport in his published writing. Elias (1996) rejected the distinction within the German *Kulturkritik* tradition between 'culture' and 'civilisation', believing that such a distinction disenabled the sociological analysis of culture. A major concept within Elias's sociological analysis was the 'civilising process', a historical process embedded in class relations through which observable patterns of social conduct could be interpreted and explained. Elias was interested in the most routine and taken for granted forms of human behaviour. This is exemplified by his discussion of the conventions and customs associated with spitting and nose blowing. Elias believed that even these most elementary bodily practices were set within class relations, and that the ways in which these practices were conducted in public altered over the years as members of the working class conformed to their perceptions of middle class behaviour. This is the 'civilising process' in a nutshell: a general trend that occurred in Western nations between the Middle Ages and the twentieth century whereby the 'civilised' standards of behaviour of the upper classes extended increasingly across society. For Elias, this is indicative of how the power of class relations works in the historical context of modernity. Coercive forms of power give way to consensual means as the lower classes come to see themselves in the image of those above them in the hierarchy of the social structure.

Elias recognises sport as being highly illustrative of the civilising process at work. In collaboration with his former student Eric Dunning (Elias and Dunning 1986), Elias discussed how the emergent behavioural practices in a number of sports can be explained with reference to the civilising process. *Inter alia*, Elias and Dunning examined the historical development of different types of football from a sprawling and completely unruly battle between undefined groups of opponents, occurring over an indefinite period of time and often across one village to the next, to the highly regulated, time bound and spatially circumscribed sports that we know today as association football (soccer) and rugby. Dunning (1999: 62) notes how English public schools used football to regulate the disorderly behaviour of their male pupils. Football was used as a form of institutional catharsis whereby boys were able to expend energy in a controlled and regulated manner. Unlike the football of working class tradition, the public school variant was played on a confined area and according to rules, largely determined by senior prefects of the school. This circumstance, of working class tradition being brought to the progeny of the social elite, was effectively inverted as the regulated version of football found its way back to the working class, coinciding with other 'civilising' developments in England in the Victorian period.

Football thus provides an example of how sport, as a type of working class cultural tradition, was co-opted by the upper classes and then, largely unintentionally, given back to the working class in a refined form. As the upper echelons of the working class were becoming increasingly embourgeoisified (enjoying better incomes and taking on the customs and mannerisms of the middle class), they welcomed a regulated and codified form of football, which penalised violent play. Elias and Dunning (1986: 21) provide a similar historical example in boxing. Fist fighting had long been used by men within the lower classes to settle neighbourhood disputes, but once taken up by the social elite for a similar purpose and as a less drastic alternative to pistol duelling, boxing was made 'civilised' by the introduction of gloves and various rules to limit the violence of pugilistic engagement. With the codification of the Marquis of Queensbury rules in 1857 boxing was formalised as a sport, bearing the characteristic bourgeois imprimatur of amateurism. Amateurism thus emerges from these class relations and, with its bourgeois ethos, became a distinctive trait of English sport. Contemporary concerns about the decline of tradition within professional sport appeal to this ethos, often unwittingly. The high and popular cultural sensibilities of sport are thus historically intertwined in a way that illustrates Elias's misgivings about maintaining distinctions between culture and civilisation.

Elias also used sport to show that the civilising process is not completely unidirectional in class terms. Once a general social consensus has been reached on a 'threshold of repugnance' with regard to acceptable human behaviour, it has the potential to reach upwards socially as well as downwards. The residual barbarism of the upper classes is most apparent within their distinctive sporting practices, none more so than the sport of foxhunting. However, according to Elias, the barbarism of foxhunting has been tempered over time as the bourgeoisie gives ground, even if not totally conforming, to acceptable social standards on violent conduct. Elias (in Elias and Dunning 1986: 163) thus claims that foxhunting 'shows very clearly the general direction of a civilising spurt'; whereas earlier forms of foxhunting reflected a desire for killing animals, the *raison d'être* of the modern codified version of foxhunting is the chase. The sanctioned limitations of the modern hunt are scrupulously followed including the protection of other animals, such as hares, from the hounds in chase of the fox. Protection also extends to all foxes other than the one sought at the outset of the hunt.

From a conservative or right culturalist position these conventions may vary over time, but they stem ultimately from the essence of the hunt as a cultural activity rather than from sociological circumstance, as suggested by Elias. Right culturalists can take inspiration from the view on hunting advanced by the philosopher Ortega in his 1942 publication *Meditations on Hunting*. For Ortega, hunting is an activity devoid of any 'utilitarian element' (Inglis 2004). The true purpose of hunting resides within the very nature of the activity, 'seeking to capture the prey'. That foxhunting has ended up as a rather exclusive leisure domain for the upper classes is, from this perspective, a reflection of the fact that these classes are able to hunt without utilitarian intent in that they hunt for neither food nor profit but just for the sake of the hunt itself. Social factors thus intervene in how hunting is actually experienced but, for Ortega, the human significance of hunting rests primarily in a cultural rather than a social understanding.

Scruton and the hunt: sport in contemporary Kulturkritik

It is perhaps somewhat surprising that the most eloquent defence of foxhunting by a contemporary conservative writer – and a philosopher at that – does not make reference to Ortega. We refer here to the short book *On Hunting* by Roger Scruton. For Scruton (1998a: 68) foxhunting is of 'ancient and venerable' character and, although arcane, steeped in ceremony and hierarchically ordered, is not as elitist as is commonly believed. The hunt is open to and actively enjoyed by individuals across the social classes according to Scruton. For Scruton, foxhunting is genuinely tribal and free of artificially contrived democratic arrangements. That it is a sport mainly associated with the upper classes is more a question of civilisation than one of democracy. According to Scruton (1998a: 68), 'those with the highest civilisation are most in need of forgiveness for it'. In Kulturkritik mode, Scruton argues that civilisation 'denaturalises' man and, therefore, that the most civilised of men, namely the aristocracy and their class associates, seek out activities that return them to nature. Foxhunting offers such a return through forgiveness from the affairs of civilisation. It provides a step back into genuine – pre-civilisation – tradition, a relief from 'human artifice' and a return to the 'fold of nature' (Scruton 1998a: 69). Scruton thus speaks of the hunt as 'those centaur hours' when the hunter unites with his/her steed, 'the blood of another species flows through your veins, stirring the old deposits of collective life' – a return to 'real life'. Thus, for Scruton, foxhunting stands above and provides relief from civilisation. Perhaps this is why hunters are prepared to endure what is undoubtedly a rather arduous leisure activity. The Victorian novelist Anthony Trollope (1865: 16–17) pondered how any man (*sic*) could actually like hunting. Scruton's point is that some men need it.

Scruton thus presents his defence of foxhunting in terms familiar to right culturalism. But, as such, and for a confessedly Arnoldian thinker, Scruton (1998b: 2) must maintain a distinction between sport and 'high culture' in terms of the 'best which has been thought and said'. Scruton achieves this distinction by suggesting that although different from the arts, sport may exist on a moral plain close to high culture as long as it stays true to nature – hence his exuberance for foxhunting. From this position, as sports move away from a relationship with nature they decline in cultural value. Even sports arguably bearing an apparent closeness to nature – angling and shooting are the given examples – do not, for Scruton (1998a: 138), have the moral worth of foxhunting because machinery (hooks and bullets) is involved at the point of capture or felling of the prey. It is reasonable to surmise that Scruton would see most popular sport as also removed from nature and therefore lacking in moral worth. His rejection of rock music is based on such an interpretation. Scruton (1998b: 90) argues that the melody, rhythm, harmony and tone of rock are 'externalised' from the music, which is artificially and mechanically constructed, resulting in 'a barrage of amplified noise'. However, rock music does offer a means of collective engagement that might interest Scruton under different circumstances – i.e. if rock music had artistic merit. Scruton (1998a: 86) sees sport as more promising in this regard as it promotes a collective enthusiasm indicative of human instinct. He argues that the 'essence of sport' is the arousal of acute interest and that the 'highest form of animal interest [including our own species] is the collective interest of the pack'. On this basis Scruton contends that team sports excite more passion in followers than individual sports; 'the quiet absorption of the Wimbledon stalls bears no comparison to the riotous exultation of a Wembley football match'.

While Eliot offered a glimpse of sport within 'the whole way of life', Scruton presents an account of sport *as* a way of life – the lived and felt experience of sport. Trollope had warned against sport being taken too seriously (Dunning, in Elias and Dunning 1986: 215). While Scruton would agree with Trollope's attendant claim that sport 'should be a pleasure and not a business' he would argue that sport is both a necessary and very serious pleasure because of its intrinsic relationship to human nature. However, Scruton's understanding of the cultural basis of sport steeped in nature is so rigid that few sports could gain acknowledgment as being culturally worthy. There is almost an inevitability about the celebration of foxhunting when viewed in context with Eliot and Leavis's account of the organic community and the implications for sport. By shifting towards a sociological and/or anthropological understanding of culture Eliot and Leavis – explicitly in the case of Eliot – put sport onto the agenda of conservative cultural commentary. However, this involves sport within the common culture but not the lofty heights of culture perceived in terms of the high arts. Scruton takes sport closer to this exalted level of culture by claiming for foxhunting an almost pure relationship with nature. Scruton depicts foxhunting as at once natural and extraordinary, offering a release from the mundane existence of civilisation. From this depiction, sport – in the form of foxhunting – performs a cultural role understood in Kulturkritik terms. Scruton's choice of a sport that is clearly class bound reflects the same naivety or blinkeredness that we get with other Kulturkritik writers when writing about high culture, particularly in the conservative liberal variant of Arnold and Leavis where culture itself is perceived as class neutral but the means of attainment, in reality, are class bound.

The Kulturkritik position offers a means of considering sport in relation to cultural traditions and of defending such traditions against the utilitarian impulse of commercialisation. However, in its attempt to elevate culture above civilisation the Kulturkritik eradicates class relations from the realm of culture. This is effectively what Scruton does in his celebration of foxhunting. Even within Leavis and Eliot's common culture class relations are something of an irrelevance, as the common culture reflects the organic community of pre-industrial society. Accordingly, the class relations of sport – as an aspect of the common culture – are not a consideration from this Kulturkritik perspective. It took the emergence of what might be described as a left strain of Kulturkritik, in the writing of Richard Hoggart and Raymond Williams, to open English cultural commentary to meaningful considerations of class. It is to these writers that we turn next as we look at sport from a view of culture as 'ordinary'.

Note

1   Of Coleridge's literary contemporaries, the Scot, John Wilson, is notable for 'dividing his attention' between sport and literature. For Wilson, 'poetry, sport and revelry were three fountains of inexhaustible inspiration; and it was from an intimate blending of … all three that his … work proceeded' (Herford 1899: 73).

CONNECTIONS

The right culturalist position, particularly in its conservative guise, suggests an affiliation between culture and nature. We saw Scruton's justification for the sport of foxhunting presented on the grounds that it promotes a natural relationship between man, beast and environment (although our discussion of Scruton did not focus on this latter dimension). Without revisiting Scruton's example we want to explore the relationship between culture, nature and sport in this Connections section, concentrating on the natural environment. We consider a culturalist temperament towards the sport/nature nexus and ask whether this temperament has currency within contemporary sporting cultures based on thrill seeking.

While writers like Scruton emphasise the necessary link between culture and nature it is important to distinguish between the two terms. Culture, in one of its derivations, is associated with cultivation, and this can be taken to mean the human cultivation of what exists in an untouched natural form. Culture alters nature as humanity impacts upon the environment and animal species. Culture also embraces the notion of humanity moving beyond its own natural state of being; to become 'cultivated' in this sense is to move beyond primitivism. Eagleton (2000: 3) notes that within the Western intellectual tradition, culture and nature exist in dialectical relation: nature produces culture which (in turn) changes nature. According to Eagleton (2000: 5), 'the very word "culture" contains a tension between making and being made', and we can see this tension lived out in a host of cultural practices including those associated with sport. Within the culturalist tradition culture has an essential ethical link

---

with and commitment to nature. Culturalists believe that as creatures of nature humans should maintain an affinity with nature and that culture should reflect this affinity. How might this be the case with sporting culture?

Eagleton (2000: 6) comments, 'it is part of the point of the word "nature" to remind us of the continuum between ourselves and our surroundings'. This has been a point of constant concern to the cultural geographer John Bale, in his fascinating writings on sport, culture and place. In the book *Landscapes of Modern Sport*, Bale (1994: 39) looks provocatively at the particular cultural status of sport contending that as 'a cultural and not a natural phenomenon, sport imposes itself on the natural landscape and therefore, at root, is anti-nature'. However, this does not mean that sport is unable to reconcile itself with nature. Sport can exist in harmony with nature in certain circumstances depending on how sporting cultures and their relationships with nature and environment are developed. Bale (1994: 41) notes that the 'sport being anti-nature' position is most emphatically put by Johann Galtung (1994), who claims that sport carries a Western notion of 'deep culture', holding that 'nature is there to be controlled'. Put into practice this means sport as culture is given primary importance and nature is used as seen fit to serve the interests of sporting culture. A likely result is environmental degradation (on varying scales) as landscapes are altered to accommodate sporting practices. Bale (1994: 44) notes that the emergence of 'serious sports' in the modern period has resulted in rather drastic alterations aimed at reducing natural interference and encumbrance of sport performance. Sports administrators have in many cases sought to have sport played in 'environmentless' conditions (Bale 1994: 45). As contemporary sport becomes increasingly concerned with the measurement and quantification of performance and sports action and scoring processes are subject to greater technological scrutiny, nature, more than ever, is regarded as a nuisance to be overcome. Be it the wind and rain blowing across a tennis court or the fallibility of the naked eye of the cricket umpire, nature is neither to be left to its own devices nor to be trusted within the precision-conscious world of contemporary sport.

However, by this stage we are talking quite clearly about scientific intrusion into sport and any reference to culture must be understood in this context. The greater intrusion of science into sport occurs in tandem with utilitarian intentions of the mainly commercial – but also public (in the form of the state) – powers that administer and control sport as a cultural institution. Culture within this context is quite removed from an understanding of culture developed within the British intellectual tradition, as discussed within the current chapter. The romantic roots of culturalism, as found in Coleridge and Wordsworth – and in keeping with the Kulturkritik – are completely concerned with distancing culture from civilisation. From this perspective, and within the historical context, culture is seen in symbiosis with nature, whereas civilisation in the form of the industrialisation of the English countryside is blamed for the defilement of nature. Culture takes on the responsibility of the artistic preservation of nature, and art movements such as the Pre-Raphaelite Brotherhood promoted the faithful representation of nature within art. However, within this tradition culture and nature are not necessarily seen in static relationship. Some of the key figures we would associate with the culturalist tradition were aware of the aesthetic rewards of a physical engagement with nature. For example, the Victorian art critic John Ruskin waxed lyrical about the beauty of the Alps, not only in admiration from a distance but also from the sensual arousal gained from episodes of rambling in their foothills (Hilton 2002: 69). Going further, and in defiance of Ruskin's criticism of mountain climbers, the Cambridge literary theorist I.A. Richards became a committed mountaineer and his writings include essays on mountaineering along with his prolific literary criticism. Importantly, Richards (1976 [1927]: 244) notes the intensity and preoccupation of the mountaineer with the activity of climbing itself, but he goes on to declare the susceptibility of the mountaineer to the 'ordinary beauty of the mountains' as experienced by those who view from below, and to claim a 'privileged enjoyment of their extraordinary beauty' for those who dare to venture 'upon their ridges'.

Mountaineering could be considered as an inchoate form of what are today referred to as 'extreme' sports. As noted in a recent academic book on extreme sport – *To the Extreme: Alternative Sports, Inside Out* – the term extreme is today associated with consumption items, fashion, celebrity and even sexual technique (Rinehart and Sydnor 2003: 3). This association sits uncomfortably with the desired image of alternativeness customarily sought by those engaged in so-called extreme sporting activities, but it betrays the curious relationships, namely sponsorships and endorsements, that some of these sports and proponents thereof have struck with commercial interests. This trend has been accompanied by the introduction of familiar forms of sporting contests to sports that otherwise choose to dissociate themselves from conventional sporting organisation. Nevertheless, extreme sports maintain an alternative status in that they are generally not recognised as legitimate sports on the same footing as 'mainstream' sports and, in some cases, their claim to be legitimately known as sport would be challenged by those favouring a limited extension of the definition of sport. Extreme sports often differ from established sports in that they are not conducted within dedicated sport sites such as sport stadiums. They occur in a variety of landscapes, some urban, some rural, some not on landscapes at all but in water or the sky. There are indications that extreme sport devotees are mindful of the ecological implications of the activities in which they engage. Rinehart and Sydnor (2003: 10) note that 'extreme sports are sometimes connected to a new world order, a transnational village, the peaceful brotherhood of our planet'. In such circumstances we might be hopeful about the respect given to the environment within these sporting cultures. However, there is reason to remain cautious. By their very name, extreme sports are concerned with pushing participants to the limit of performance, and under such circumstances the environment once again is at risk of becoming subject to the prerogatives of sport. Only when sporting cultures are attuned to the environments within which they are conducted can sport be at one with nature.

SPORT, COMMUNITY AND THE COMMON CULTURE

In the previous chapter we discussed a position associated with what we called the prehistory of Cultural Studies. In the current chapter we move on to consider sport in relation to what are generally regarded as the foundational texts of Cultural Studies and the related work of their authors, Richard Hoggart and Raymond Williams. As we have identified in our introduction, *The Uses of Literacy* (1958 [1957]) by Hoggart and *Culture and Society* (1958) and *The Long Revolution* (1961) by Williams inspired the emergence of Cultural Studies within the academy. In this chapter we examine the writings of these authors with a view to looking at how sport might be accounted for culturally, once culture has been dislodged from the elitist moorings of the foregoing tradition of commentary and criticism. As indicated in the previous chapter, Hoggart and Williams present a left culturalist position that remains sympathetic to the Kulturkritik sensitivity to culture being aloof from civilisation but explicitly locates culture within the context of class. At this early point it is important to note that we are not proposing a conflation of the ideas of Hoggart and Williams.[1] Although sharing the view that culture needs to be understood through its expression within class relations, Hoggart and Williams differed in their political orientations to the working class and in their attitudes to working class engagement with popular culture. Our task is to discern how sport might be accounted for within the respective visions of these key figures within the left culturalist strand of Cultural Studies.

Sport and the 'older' order

From the opening chapter of *The Uses of Literacy* (first published in 1957) Hoggart makes it clear that he is interested in discussing culture in relation to the way of life of the people who constitute the English working class. Hoggart offers more of an account than a definition of the working class, and it is distinctly and evocatively the account of an insider. Hoggart draws on his own background as an orphan growing up in the Hunslet area of Leeds to provide an auto-ethnographic picture of working class life that might be applicable to a range of towns in the north of England in the 1930s. *The Uses of Literacy*, subtitled *Aspects of Working-class Life with Special Reference to Publications and Entertainments*, is a book of two halves, but need not be defined as a 'schizophrenic' book (as some criticism would have it). Schizophrenic implies the contradiction of a confused mind, an imputation unmerited by Hoggart. The first half of *The Uses of Literacy* outlines 'an "older" order' of working class life drawing on Hoggart's personal reflections as mentioned above. The second half of the book discusses a process referred to by Hoggart as 'yielding place to the new'. Hoggart's overall theme is consistent. In the older order of the working class prior to the Second World War Hoggart recognises authentic community life revolving around valued folk traditions and associated pastimes. With the increasing popularity of 'mass entertainment' and particularly the onset of Americanised youth culture in the 1950s, Hoggart believed the traditions of working class culture, and the spirit of community that such culture fostered, to be imperilled. Hoggart wrote little about sport, but it can be deduced that sport has a significant place within his older order and that sporting traditions are under threat from the cultural upheaval that disrupted working class life from the 1950s.

Hoggart's enduring contribution to Cultural Studies is, perhaps, his genuine fascination with the everyday life of working class people. In his chapter 'The "real" world of people', Hoggart discusses the way in which members of the working class engage with popular culture and incorporate its texts into their routine conversation. Hoggart (1958 [1957]: 108) provides a glimpse of the importance of sport to working class people when he declares that it 'vies with sex as the staple of conversation' at work. Hoggart does not elaborate but we are given the impression that workers would spend their minimal breaks from work discussing football and boxing as well as other types of sport. The newspapers of the 1930s, particularly the tabloids, featured columns on a variety of sports, and it is likely that these would have fuelled discussions of sport around the shop floor. Many such discussions may have focussed on sports of local interest, as reports on darts, pigeon racing and bowls were included in the sports pages alongside sports of national prominence such as football, cricket and horse racing (Holt 1989: 193). Workplace discussion might also have involved activities on the seamier side of sporting life that remained popular in the 1930s, activities such as bare-knuckle fist fighting and dog fighting (Brailsford 1992: 108). Hoggart does not discuss such activities, news of which would have been delivered by word of mouth rather than the sports columns in newspapers.

Hoggart also remarks on another theme of interest to contemporary Cultural Studies (see Chapter Five), the sports hero. Hoggart (1958 [1957]: 109) claims that 'the great boxers and footballers and speedway riders naturally become heroes'. Naturally, because they possess the characteristics admired by 'working-class sports-lovers' of the 'hunter and fighter and daredevil' exhibited by display of 'strength and muscle, speed and daring, skill and cunning'. For Hoggart these are natural traits and the sports arena provides a modern forum for a modern hero blessed with such traits and commensurate abilities. Hoggart's sports hero is, thus, likened to 'the hero of saga' and enjoys an intimate connection to the people. His representation of the sports hero takes no account of the contrived celebrity, which we might associate with the contemporary sports hero and the obsession with a marketable image rather than any genuine relationship with sports fans. The trend towards the celebrity sports hero was recognised in early post-war football by the short-story writer Brian Glanville. In 'The footballers' (cited in Walsh 1964) Glanville notes the enormous financial rewards and attendant star status available to players in Italian football in the late 1950s and registers the portents of the emergence of such possibilities for footballers in Britain. Glanville's consummate knowledge of football culture made him more prescient than Hoggart of the arrival some forty years later of the David Beckham generation of sports heroes. Interestingly, Glanville detected that professional footballers were not only interested in financial rewards and material items but also craved a form of moral validation in their celebrity status. As William Walsh (1964: 186) notes in his summary of Glanville's writing, footballers accepted (and expected) 'worship in an almost objective, non-involved way as something merely right and proper'. This is the antithesis of Hoggart's classical image of the sports hero who earns his status through a relationship of mutual adoration – projected into the sporting performance – not through narcissism and hubris. Hoggart (2004: 83) makes passing criticism of the 'celebrity status' within contemporary football in his recent book *Mass Media in a Mass Society*.

Hoggart's interest in the class bound nature of cultural life is well exemplified by his discussion of a further sporting relationship – that between the referee and spectators. While Hoggart sees sport as essentially connected to community life, it is important to note that his view of community is different to the organic notion of community found in the right culturalism of Leavis and Eliot. With particular reference to the sport of rugby league football (a sport that has enjoyed regional popularity in the north of England since the late 1800s), Hoggart (1958 [1957]: 109) notes a 'common distrust' held for the referee by spectators. He is careful to point out that the level of distrust goes beyond the type of barracking that arises as spectators blame the referee for taking decisions that contribute to their team's loss of a match. Rather, Hoggart is speaking of what he believes to be a 'deeply ingrained feeling' of hostility towards the referee as an authority figure. Although the collective dislike usually results in little more than a chorus of well rehearsed imprecations, the dislike is significant or, as Hoggart puts it, 'pervasive'. Hoggart is tacitly locating this dislike of the referee into the dichotomous expression of class relations that he refers to in *The Uses of Literacy* as 'Them' and 'Us'.

From the perspective of working class people, Hoggart (1958 [1957]: 72) claims that 'the world' is divided into 'Them' and 'Us'. The world of 'Them', the cultural life of 'the bosses', is perceived to be a world removed from the world of 'Us', the working class. The terminology itself is an expression of resentment and indicative of a perception that the world of 'Them' is deliberately closed off from 'Us'. Hoggart maintains that particular resentment is held towards those in positions of boundary maintenance, those who take on the role of keeping 'Us' in place. This might refer to the policeman, the civil servant in various departments or the schoolteacher, as well the rugby league referee whom Hoggart actually compares to a headmaster. We come to further understand Hoggart's point about the dislike of the referee being 'deeply ingrained' and 'pervasive'. The referee's actual authority may apply to the football match but his authority is symbolic of the class relations of the workplace. In some ways the referee might be more resented than the foreman or manager because his exertion of authority transpires within the leisure domain of the worker and could therefore serve as a reminder – perhaps subliminally – of the relations of the workplace. It would follow from this – and it would seem Hoggart had this in mind – that vitriol directed at the referee reflects something more than annoyance with decisions taken against the favoured team. Indeed, the referee may well be a fall guy who takes the pent-up abuse that is felt towards other authority figures, but not expressed publicly. This leads into thoughts about the cathartic role of sport, in this case spectator sport. The football stadium has provided a public forum for the expression of the collective frustration arising from class relations. This occurrence has been subjected to various interpretations within the sociology of soccer literature (for a review see Giulianotti 1994a).

One of the criticisms made of *The Uses of Literacy* is that while it provides an account of the leisure life of the working class, it does not say much about working class life in the workplace. While this may be regarded as a limitation in Hoggart's study of the working class, it should serve to focus our attention on the importance of his writing to the analysis of leisure within both Cultural Studies and sociology. The title of Hoggart's famous book is something of a misnomer, a reflection of both Hoggart's academic background within English literary studies and his emergence as an unsuspecting sociologist. A key concern in Hoggart's book is the examination of public reading habits, a theme explored by Q.D. Leavis in her proto-Cultural Studies classic *Fiction and the Reading Public*, first published in 1932. However, despite F.R. Leavis's claim that Hoggart was merely repeating work that his wife had done twenty-five years before, Hoggart's book, as apparent from our discussion, extended to leisure themes beyond reading and popular literature – both *publications and entertainments*, as Hoggart's subtitle indicates. Indeed, Hoggart might well have named the book *The Uses of Leisure* to account for the range of working class leisure practices covered in his discussion. Hoggart's writing provided a Cultural Studies companion to the incipient sub-field in the sociology of leisure, which emerged from a growing interest within the sociology of work towards the social relations of consumption. Relations of consumption began to rival the traditional concern with relations of production as

33

sociologists examined the range of social practices applicable to the 'affluent worker' of the economically revived post-war period.

The Uses of Literacy is, then, a seminal book about the lived cultural contexts of working class leisure. It concentrates on leisure practices in both the private and public domains of working class life, indeed Hoggart professed to being interested in the interconnections between these two domains. Hoggart's detailed accounts of domestic life gave a glimpse of the activities of women in a manner that previously was found only within British fictional writing. However, Hoggart's account of working class life in pre-war Britain has been criticised for the limitation of its masculinist perspective. Notably, in *Landscape for a Good Woman* (1986), Carolyn Steedman sketches an alternative account of life for working class women in 1930s Britain, based on her own mother's life. A problem with Hoggart – who, to be fair, reflects the social reality of his time – is that his account of public leisure is mainly, although not exclusively, focussed on the leisure activities of men. This can tend to read as an uncritical celebration of male social behaviour, a tendency that has been amplified within some of the contemporary Cultural Studies writing on sports fandom. The privileging of men within public leisure domains can result in important concepts such as community being exemplified through fundamentally masculine endeavours. For example, when discussing the 'older order', Hoggart highlights the proud association between working class communities and their football teams, which are made up predominantly of 'our lads'. Hoggart's narrative alludes specifically to his local rugby league team Hunslet. He writes of the heady celebration following Hunslet's victory in the national rugby league competition: the parading of the trophy followed by an evening of conviviality with 'crowds of lads prepared to risk staying out hours after their bedtime for the excitement of seeing their local champions' (Hoggart 1958 [1957]: 108). This sporting celebration is a very masculine affair and indicative of the gendered social relations that pervade Hoggart's account of the public experience of working class leisure. Again, this is not to say that Hoggart excludes women from his account, he does talk about the involvement of women in community life at various points throughout the book. What it indicates is that gendered barriers circumscribed leisure activities, sport marking off a particularly masculine domain.[2]

The reason for Hoggart's concentration on leisure as a separate domain from work is to be found in his own orientation to the English tradition of cultural commentary examined in the previous chapter. Hoggart is a progeny of the English Kulturkritik and he maintains – albeit in a modified way – the idea of a dichotomy between culture and civilisation. Indeed, it is this intellectual disposition that underlies his fascination with the leisure activities of the working class. Hence, he is more interested in the forms of cultural life that stem from the social relations of work – class relations – than he is in the relations of the workplace itself. Hoggart would be inclined to see investigations of the latter as an appropriate brief for sociologists of work. The novelty of Hoggart is that, unlike the writers of the tradition from which he emerges, he believes the working class lead a distinctive form of cultural life which warrants examination in its own right. He approaches his task as both a moral and an analytical imperative; working class culture has nobility and it demands scholarly attention. Hoggart's break with the Kulturkritik tradition comes with his recognition and championing of working class culture, hence his designation as a left culturalist. The conservatism – right culturalism – of Kulturkritik writers disposed them to regard society as naturally hierarchical. Whilst they feared the destruction of minority culture by the masses they were disinclined to recognise the existence of classes, as this is to recognise the existence of an unnaturally imposed social hierarchy. In optimistic mood they write of 'the people' and of the different social echelons being bound together within an organic community, culture providing the moral wellspring for an ongoing communal existence.

Hoggart is not opposed to the notion of an organic community. Indeed, throughout his writing career he has maintained a humanistic belief in the existence of essential common values that pre-exist artificial social divisions such as class. In recent writing, Hoggart (1995: 328) claims that despite the decline of many valuable customs in British society, we can still witness the existence of a spirit of neighbourliness – the manifestation of common values – across class barriers. He speaks of the importance of community, but warns against multifarious usages of the term to represent the diversity of contemporary social collectivities, from 'the gay community' to 'the skinhead community' (Hoggart 1995: 164–5). Hoggart prefers an essentialist and holistic understanding of community, pertaining to the national citizenry. Hoggart trusts that this underlying belief in community is carried over into deed, being lived out in local and neighbourhood contexts. In relation to this understanding of community, Hoggart refers to a 'common culture', premised again on the belief that humanistic values precede the divisive interests that accrue from class relations. Thus, while Hoggart recognises the existence of class to the extent that it gives rise to cultural forms, he still works with the humanistic idea of the Kulturkritik that culture, and the possibility of community that culture fosters, take precedence over man-made civilisation. This creates a problem with Hoggart's representation of working class culture. We might be able to speak of working class culture and both respect and study it, as Hoggart proposes, but from a humanistic stand-point working class culture – arising from the artificial division within social relations – cannot be culture in essence, pure and holistic.

Hoggart is, thus, caught in a Kulturkritik bind. While wanting to move beyond the elitist implications of the Kulturkritik for the lived experience of culture, Hoggart remains shackled to the logic of its intellectual position on culture. He is faced with the difficulty of promoting the cultural life of the working class while working within an intellectual framework contending that there is a level of culture that transcends socially constructed working class culture in its various forms and contexts. As a result Hoggart imbues working class culture with essentialist qualities and values that are socially pre-existent. From here, despite references to the 'Them' and 'Us' mentality of the working class, Hoggart tends to discuss aspects of working class culture in relation to a general notion of community rather than a particularistic understanding of working class community. Hoggart's discussion of amateur sport in *The Uses of Literacy* is illustrative. In his concluding chapter Hoggart (1958 [1957]: 329) discusses how semi-formal sport clubs and activities provide a means through which young working class people can 'react positively to both the challenge of their environment and the useful possibilities of cheap mass-production'. Concentrating on cycling, Hoggart notes that working class youth extract from this sport particular benefits of 'companionship, hard exercise, and fresh air'. Underlying Hoggart's remarks is the idea of a cultural distinction between the natural and the artificial; similar to the distinction stated explicitly by Scruton. Sport can be healthy for people, not only physically but also culturally. Importantly for Hoggart, it holds the potential of maintaining significant, if limited, communal bonds in spite of the wider rupturing of community affiliations in contemporary society. It is also clear enough that Hoggart foresaw the possibility of participation in sport benefiting from the mass production of commercial goods. In the remark quoted above, Hoggart is specifically referring to the affordability of bicycles that allows working class people to engage in weekend cycling trips and friendly competitions. Hoggart quite decidedly refers to the purchase of sports equipment, such as bicycles, as one of the 'useful possibilities of cheap mass-production' as opposed to what he characterises in the second part of *The Uses of Literacy* as the less useful, indeed harmful, possibilities of mass consumption and the associated youth culture that emerged in post-war Britain.

Sport and the yielding of place to the new

In the second half of *The Uses of Literacy* Hoggart speaks of the older order 'yielding to the new'. Here he criticises the emerging forms of 'consumer culture' that, from his point of view, were having a harmful impact on working class youth in post-war Britain. Hoggart does not see the problem of mass marketed and culturally debased youth leisure styles and habits emanating from the working class, but blames the intrusion of American popular culture into British working class leisure traditions. Hoggart focuses his criticism on particular leisure sites. He is especially troubled by the milk bar as a location where young people gather to get their fill of American popular culture. Hoggart (1958 [1957]: 246) laments the transformation of young British men into 'juke box boys' who affect a Humphrey Bogart-like slouch and wear clothing in the style of American youth. He speaks of a 'spiritual dry rot' associated with related activities such as hanging around listening to rock and roll music on 'nickelodeons'. This new form of leisure and related conspicuous consumption plunges young people into a 'hollow cosmos', a void of 'puff pastry' culture 'with nothing inside the pastry'. Hoggart believed youth in post-war Britain to be buying into a cultural mythology based on imaginings of America. With reference to the young milk-bar crowd he declares (1958 [1957]: 248): 'their clothes, their hair-styles, their facial expressions all indicate ... [that they] are living to a large extent in a myth-world compounded of a few simple elements which they take to be those of American life'.

Hoggart's criticisms of the Americanisation of British cultural life echo those of Leavis before him. The main difference is that while Leavis articulated his concerns in relation to the deleterious impact on standards of excellence within the arts acknowledged as a minority culture, Hoggart lamented a decline in the standards of cultural life and the leisure traditions of the working class. However, despite these differences both feared that the emerging forms of mass produced items of popular culture and the artificial forms of cultural consumption and engagement that they gave life to threatened to undermine the natural flow of cultural life, whether perceived in relation to 'the people' or the working class. The notion of an organic community lurks within the ideas – and hopes – of both writers, and both, in their different ways, looked for community in the past. Leavis's vision of the organic community came from the rural idyll of pre-industrial England, whereas Hoggart's organic community developed from the customs and traditions that were formed in the working class neighbourhoods of industrial cities and towns up to the years prior to the Second World War. Again, Hoggart does not actually say much about sport, but from what he does say it is clear that both amateur and professional sport, for him, is part of the urban working class cultural tradition, and important to the prospects of community in the future. However, in passing comment he makes it clear enough that the continuing importance of 'sports clubs' as a cultural institution for youth is threatened by Americanised youth culture (Hoggart 1958 [1957]: 249).

In the previous chapter, it was noted that current campaigns against the closure and amalgamation of football clubs are, perhaps, closer to conservative sentiments of community than to socialist inspired protest. Hoggart would give qualified support to this form of community campaign. Hoggart was not politically conservative, but he was passionate about the preservation of traditions of community that he believed to be beneficial to the working class. Francis Mulhern (2000: 60) contends that in Hoggart, 'the post-war British labour movement found its own Matthew Arnold'. This is something of a misrepresentation of Hoggart. The working class may have found its own Matthew Arnold, but not so the labour movement. Although a Labour Party member throughout his career, Hoggart has always been a moderate amongst left-leaning intellectuals. His indebtedness to Kulturkritik thought – including an ongoing acknowledgment to Matthew Arnold – no doubt influenced his political orientation. While Hoggart's account of working class life is rich and highly evocative – indicative of the Romantic influence within the British Kulturkritik tradition – he is not particularly informative about the connections between working class culture and leisure and politics. Had Hoggart been more aware of, or interested in, such connections he may well have had more to say about sport in *The Uses of Literacy*.

Formal organisational links were established between sport and the British labour movement in the interwar years, principally with the formation of the National Workers' Sports Association in 1930 (Jones 1988: 107). Sport, and its place within working class culture, became a contested terrain for labour intellectuals and activists during this period. Those who thought positively of sport recognised its popularity with working class people, and believed it could be used as a means for recruitment to union membership. There was also a humanistic socialist view held by some within the labour movement that sport, conducted within a sociable and co-operative environment, can provide a counter to the destructively competitive and utilitarian spirit of industrial capitalism (Jones 1988: 116). However, some figures within the labour movement were less sanguine about the positive benefits of sport. At the purely organisational level, some trade union leaders were concerned that the formation of sports bodies within the movement would lead to a situation of the tail wagging the dog, with sport becoming the predominant interest over labour and industrial matters, for many members. A related intellectual concern was the belief held by some trade unionists that sport is both barbaric – in some of its forms – and trivial, in the latter sense serving to distract working class people from the crucial business of politics and labour militancy (Jones 1988: 117).

Richard Hoggart left his position as Director of the Centre for Contemporary Cultural Studies at the University of Birmingham to take up a senior diplomatic appointment with UNESCO at the end of the 1960s (Hoggart 1992: 147). Interestingly, his departure from academe coincided with the most volatile outbreak of student radicalism of the period. Hoggart's left culturalist orientation to Cultural Studies appeared out of step with the student body that had risen below him, and he was criticised by CCCS postgraduate students who wanted the Cultural Studies programme to move completely away from its origins in English cultural humanism to continental radical philosophy and social theory, principally, neo-Marxism (Hoggart 2001: 310). Hoggart was no Marxist and he was particularly unmoved by the fashionable turn towards the Italian theorist Antonio Gramsci and his concept of hegemony (see Chapter Six for a discussion of Gramsci and hegemony). Even in more recent writing Hoggart suggests that other writers – such as the American essayist Henry Adams – had laid out similar ideas, if by different name, some years before Gramsci (Hoggart 1995: 69, 185). However, although swimming against the changing intellectual tide, Hoggart was by no means an irrelevance, and he remained influential on aspects of the work done by young scholars at the CCCS. Although making no claim to be an ethnographer, the impressionistic, retrospective and panoramic ethnographic account of working class cultural life provided by Hoggart in the first part of *The Uses of Literacy* paved the way for the dedicated ethnographic studies of working class youth culture in the late 1960s and the 1970s, even though these studies focused on the types of youth gatherings decried by Hoggart in the second section of his book (see Chapter Eight).

One such contribution was John Clarke's (1973; 1976; 1978) ethnographic study of skinhead subculture. Although embracing Gramscian theory, Clarke's discussion of community bears similarity to Hoggart. Clarke's sensitive account of how the young men attempt to 'magically recover' a feeling of lost working class community through their subcultural activities romanticises – albeit not uncritically – both the subcultural life of the young men and the working class past to which they seek to return. Clarke recognises soccer support as a key dimension of the skinhead cultural life and argues that the breakdown of traditional working class communities explains the formation of skinhead groupings and their engagement in soccer hooliganism. Clarke (1976: 99) recognises working class communities as being in a state of 'real decline' and the skinheads' involvement in soccer related violence as a misguided means of recreating a lost working class masculinity in which lads from one town or neighbourhood defend their patch against those from another. While Hoggart would not share Clarke's explanation for soccer hooliganism in Marxist terms, he would concede that such activities are a result of a decline in the cultural life of the working class and the communal relations that such life fosters. Being intertwined within the culture of working class community, the traditions and customs of sport must be unsettled as patterns of working class community break down.

Clarke was one of the earliest academic commentators on English soccer to note how the administrative changes being sought to modernise the professional game impacted upon supporter cultures. In particular, Clarke (1978: 37–60) noted how the traditional rowdiness and revelry of soccer crowds – indicative of weekend working class masculinity – was challenged by a trend towards 'disinfected commitment' and 'contained partisanship'. Clarke's observation was prescient and despite corporate lip service to the importance of tradition, the various changes to the football watching experience, including all-seated stadiums and the prohibitive costs of season tickets, have certainly promoted a sanitised form of supporter culture, one often associated conveniently with the most evocative of conservative icons, the family. A number of recent ethnographic studies have examined how some male youth supporter groups – usually characterised as hooligans – rebel against such changes not only by engaging in boisterous behaviour but also by criticising soccer administration initiatives through alternative media forums such as fanzines (see, for example, Giulianotti 1997). These studies usually discuss the social practices of football supporter subcultures as being indicative of social resistance, resembling similar claims made for male youth subcultures in the ethnographic studies published by the CCCS, the volume *Resistance Through Rituals* (Hall and Jefferson 1976) being particularly prominent in this regard.

The cultural study of working class youth in the context of sport spectatorship extends Hoggart's observation of the 'Them' and 'Us' mentality on the terrace – between supporters and sport authorities – to an examination of the micro-politics of sports fandom and how the cultural activities of socially marginalised young men might be used as a means of reclaiming a sense of collective social importance. Hoggart's Kulturkritik disposition would prevent him going down such an avowedly political path, and whereas studies, from those of the CCCS subcultural ethnographers to the recent football subculture ethnographers, tend to focus on the spectacular aspects of youth cultural life, Hoggart remains relentlessly interested in the ordinary. As indicated above, Hoggart soon became unfashionable within Cultural Studies and, although a continuing respect is shown to him, his culturalism remains largely unfashionable today.

Hoggart's legacy to the cultural study of sport is most apparent in the work of social historians. Richard Holt's exemplary historical account in *Sport and the British* (1989) provides an overview of how sport is intricately entangled within the everyday cultural life of the British people. Of cultural histories on particular sports, Dave Russell's *Football and the English* (1997) is noteworthy as is Wray Vamplew's study of horse racing in *The Turf* (1976). Vamplew has been particularly adept at exploring the historical nexus between sport and other aspects of working class leisure, principally gambling and drinking (Vamplew 1988; Collins and Vamplew 2002). Within early Cultural Studies work Brian Jackson's ethnographically informed study of cultural activities in Huddersfield, in *Working Class Community* (1968), is most closely reminiscent of Hoggart's left culturalist account of the routines of working class leisure. Jackson surveys a number of recreational and leisure activities and pieces them together to provide a mosaic of working class cultural life within his native Yorkshire town – one not far from Hoggart's own Leeds. Jackson devotes a chapter to the sport of bowls, examining how working class customs are embedded within the culture of bowls and how this results in organisational similarities with other working class sports such as rugby league. Jackson also discusses the similarities in custom between these sports and other organised working class recreations, specifically brass band competitions.

Although there is continual reference within contemporary Cultural Studies to a concern with the study of 'everyday life', the near obsession exhibited by many scholars for celebrity, fashion and glamour suggests a fetish for the spectacular rather than an interest in the ordinary. The characteristic English belief in culture being 'about tranquillity rather than excitement' (Cannadine 2002: 161) is absent from this scholarship. A scholarly fascination for the spectacular in sport will perhaps result in more studies on various high profile professional sports, sports on the border of show business and burlesque – such as professional wrestling – and 'extreme' sports involving risk to life and limb. Studies of spectacular forms of sports fandom associated with more conventional sports as well as newer forms of sport and sport entertainments are likely to proliferate. These are, reasonably enough, legitimate areas of interest within the cultural study of sport and have been interestingly explored by a number of academics, for example, Mazer's (1998) fascinating study of professional wrestling. However, we would warn against an overemphasis on spectacular forms of sport and sports fandom within Cultural Studies. This tendency risks neglecting the ordinariness of sport participation, viewing and following. It is important that the cultural study of sport also produces work focused on the ordinary everyday practices of sport if we are to gain an understanding of how sport fits into contemporary patterns of community life and of the cultural meanings arising from the sport-supporting experience of the 'ordinary' sports fan.

Sport and the 'common culture'

The acceptance of the ordinariness of culture within Cultural Studies is most often attributed to the pioneering cultural commentary and analysis of Raymond Williams. In this regard his 1958 essay 'Culture is ordinary' is most often cited (Williams 1989a [1958]: 3–18). It is easy to interpret Williams's phrase as a riposte to the tradition of English cultural criticism that he recounts in *Culture and Society*, and Williams does have objections to the elitist characterisation of culture implied by his forbears. However, to claim that culture is ordinary is as much an extension of the ideas of Leavis and Eliot as it is a response to their cultural snobbery. As discussed in Chapter One, both Leavis and Eliot accepted social interpretations of culture involving a whole way of life and when they came to consider these inter- pretations they broadened the realm of cultural activity to include the pastimes and recreational interests of ordinary people. Williams preferred this social definition of culture to the conventional idealised definition of culture pertaining to a state of human perfection. However, to truly understand the social nature of culture, Williams argued for the need to move beyond the sociologically neutral category of the people as discussed by Leavis and Eliot. Williams accepted a Marxist analysis of society being made up of conflicting classes and that culture transpired within the context of class relations and locations. In moving towards a particular class based view of culture Williams sought the 'conjunction' of the ideal and social definitions of culture. People would seek out standards of excellence through literature and their engage- ment with other art forms, but their uses of culture always occur within a classed social context.

41

Williams had considerable faith in the members of the working class and he objected to the intellectual disdain directed towards them by cultural critics on both the right and the left. In particular Williams rejected the tendency of both Leavis and Eliot and Marxist cultural scholars to characterise the working class as a mass (Dworkin 1997: 91). For Leavis and Eliot the democratisation of culture leads to a dull majority or mass culture that will undermine standards of cultural excellence. For pessimistic Marxist critics the spread of commercialised popular culture serves to nullify political resistance and risks reducing the working class to a stupefied mass. Williams believed that the term mass should be confined to describing demographic shifts of people into cities. When used in relation to culture it takes on particular ideological functions. Williams (1958: 300) famously contended, 'There are in fact no masses; there are only ways of seeing people as masses.' Williams believed that the term masses is an objectification of working class people and a metonymical reduction of the working class to the media – namely the mass media – of popular culture. Unlike right culturalist critics Williams refused to accept that the people (the working class) would become mindless captives of film and television. He believed that traditional cultural activities would remain in one form or another and hoped that individuals would discriminate in their consumption of mass mediated popular culture. Unlike both Leavis and Eliot and also Hoggart, Williams did not lament the Americanisation of popular culture in Britain. Williams recognised and resisted the tendency of each of these critics, but particularly Hoggart, to sound like fuddy-duddies, associating American popular culture with undesirable trends in youth culture and lifestyles. This is not to suggest that Williams embraced cultural relativism. In *The Long Revolution* he clearly makes the case for retaining cultural distinctions within popular culture.

> Can we agree ... that football is indeed a wonderful game, that jazz is a real musical form and that gardening and homemaking are indeed important? Can we also agree, though, that the horror-film, the rape-novel, the Sunday strip-paper and the latest Tin-Pan drool are not exactly in the same world, and that the nice magazine romance, the manly adventure story and the pretty, clever television advertisement are not in it either?
>
> (Williams 1961: 336)

Williams's use of the term 'not exactly in the same world' is interesting. The latter cultural world alluded to by Williams is that of the commercial marketplace which produces cultural items purely as sellable commodities. The cultural items listed by Williams in relation to this world are tawdry and designed to titillate; they appeal to the basest of human sentiments. The other cultural world to which Williams refers contains cultural items that are 'real'; we can assume that these items are the products of authentic cultural expressions that have possibly been developed over time. Interestingly, for our purposes, Williams includes football in this cultural world and there is no doubt that he had a healthy respect for sport spectatorship as an enriching form of entertainment. Williams (1961: 337) claimed that the need for sport is 'as real as the need for art'; both are integral to 'a good living culture'. Williams was also something of a sports fan himself, claiming in a newspaper column that 'Sport, is of course one of the very best things about television; I would keep my set for it alone' (cited in Boyle and Haynes 2000: vii). How Williams would assess some of the current developments within television sport and the ways in which sporting traditions have been disturbed to satisfy the commercial imperatives as deemed by television executives is something to be investigated. First, however, we need to consider further Williams's social thinking about culture to get an appreciation of how cultural distinctions can be made within a social context. Williams's assignation of cultural forms into different worlds may seem arbitrary or subjective if viewed purely in an aesthetic sense, but his reasons for drawing cultural distinctions, and the particular distinctions drawn, are made on social grounds.

The key term here for Williams is 'common culture'. In *Culture and Society* Williams (1958: 317) claims that 'we need a common culture, not for the sake of an abstraction, but because we shall not survive without it'. Williams, thus, clearly indicates his belief in the practical importance of cultural discussion and in the need of cultural commentary to go beyond ivory tower debates between intellectuals. In this early usage of the term, Williams intends that common culture provides a means of grasping the connection between the apparently different understandings of culture, i.e. culture as lived experience and culture as selective tradition. Leavis and Eliot had, as we have seen, suggested similar possibilities but their commitment to the notion of common culture was quite different to that of Williams. While they associate culture with lived experience they never really provide a sense of culture being lived by common people. In contrast, Williams argued for a dynamic rather than a passive approach to culture. For him, the 'distinction of a common culture' is the collective making by its members, through ongoing common decision making the common culture is constantly 'made and remade' (Williams 1958: 337). Here Williams emphasises the practical engagement of the people in the making of a common culture, in a similar fashion to the later claim by the historian E.P. Thompson (1963) that the working class 'makes' its own history. Thompson criticised Williams for not being Marxist in his interpretation of the class relations of common culture. He believed Williams was too accommodating to the right culturalists in referring to culture as a 'whole way of life' (Dworkin 1997: 102). For Thompson culture was a 'whole way of struggle'. Nevertheless, Williams's understanding of common culture was located in class and reflected the inspiration of Marx. Williams (1958: 327) believed that the possibility of a common culture resides within the working class because of its collective character (to be contrasted with the individualistic character of the bourgeoisie). The common culture, like the working class itself, comprises 'the idea of solidarity'; it is 'the real basis of society'. This is comparable to Marx's broader point that a genuine social interest (albeit a largely unconscious one) resides within the working class. At the core of both Williams's and Marx's positions is a belief in the idea of the working class as the true bearers of democratic life. Thus we find Williams preoccupied in *The Long Revolution* and other essays from the late 1950s and early 1960s with argument for the establishment of public cultural arrangements based on commonality and equality of membership.

Williams's recommendations are concentrated on artistic and literary activities and, for the most part, emphasise the importance of increasing public funding of the arts at local and regional levels. His focus on the arts at the local level is indicative of Williams's belief that common culture is most meaningfully constituted within the context of community. Williams drew from his own youthful memories of working class village life in Wales to argue that organisational decision making at the community level allows for democratic self-management (Williams 1989b [1977]). He contended that community decision making was not just a matter of tradition but an important guiding principle for future organisational operation. Williams welds together sociological understandings of social relations (class) and social location (place) into a proto-Cultural Studies understanding of community that is tinged with romanticism. Hoggart offered a similar, albeit less sophisticated, interpretation of community. However, Hoggart's declared non-Marxist position on class resulted in a social democratic view of community whereas Williams's sympathy to Marxist class theory results in a position closer to democratic socialism. Indeed, Williams's position on community is similar to British guild socialism of the early twentieth century. In *Culture and Society* Williams (1958: 189) notes that the emphasis in guild socialist thinking on community rather than the state provides an important direction for the basis of class action; i.e. concentrated on the local rather than the national level. Whereas the guild socialists argued for the democratic intrusion of workers into the control of industries, Williams believed that a similar argument could be made in relation to culture. He saw this as entirely in keeping with a socialist tradition that owed intellectual debts to the great British cultural democrats Ruskin and Morris. Williams's own recommendations for the democratisation of the arts thus offer a practical extension of guild socialism into the realm of culture.

Only connect: sport, new technologies, new associations

In the concluding section of the chapter it is pertinent for us to further extend these considerations to sport. Although Williams did not take a programmatic interest in sport in the way that he did in the arts, his brief discussion of sport in his 1974 book, *Television: Technology and Cultural Form*, is insightful. Williams (1974: 67) tacitly discusses 'spectator sport' in inverted relationship to the arts; sports have traditionally been enjoyed by the many, the arts by a privileged minority. Whereas the arts will be democratised as they are extended into a common culture at the local level, Williams suggests that the democratic and communal traditions of sport are potentially upset once sports are popularised through the media and exposed to the processes of commercialism and sponsorship. Williams does not propose a course of action to defend sporting traditions and, indeed, is somewhat sanguine about the possibilities offered to sports viewing by technological developments in television broadcasting. Marshall McLuhan has taken these thoughts further, by considering the 'match' between technologies and certain sports (McLuhan and Fiore 2001 [1968]: 171). However, in declaring baseball and cricket unsuited to television, McLuhan failed to anticipate the prerogative of sports impresarios to alter the game to suit the medium. Sporting traditions have undoubtedly been disturbed by media intrusion, whether harmfully is a matter open to debate.

It is also unquestionable that community based traditions in sport have been affected by the economic rationalisation that occurs in the name of the professionalisation of sport. The sport in Britain most usually discussed in relation to the rupturing of community relations is association football. Within early academic writing on football hooliganism the severance of football teams from their local communities was cited as a primary cause of young working class men's disaffection as they lamented the passing of a tradition familiar to their father's generation. Ian Taylor (1971: 142–3) referred to a 'sub-culture of soccer' existing within working class communities. The sub-culture comprises the men (*sic*) 'involved in the building and sustaining' of local football teams. The football team forms part of the locally generated common culture, it is for Taylor a 'common concern'. By the 1960s the 'soccer sub-culture' was threatened by various forces associated with what Taylor refers to as football's 'embourgeoisification'. Combined with very real changes to the sport's material organisation is a perception that supporters are being denied any representation in the running of their beloved football clubs. Disgruntled fans associate the almost total intrusion of business into the administration of football with the disappearance of a tradition of 'participatory democracy'.

However, as Jeffrey Hill notes (2002: 27), proclamations of association football in Britain as the 'people's game' should be approached with caution. The actual involvement of 'the people' in football, once it was established into a commercial enterprise and organised into a national league, was limited. At the time of the Football League's formation in the late 1880s, working class supporters could hold shares in their local clubs, but even at this early stage of professional development their dividend holdings were minimal. Businessmen who also dominated club boards held the great proportion of shares. Football teams typically enjoyed local working class support while club management remained in the hands of the local bourgeoisie. The control of clubs followed a cynical pattern whereby directors would turn to local communities in times of hardship but restrict outside involvement when times were good. This was especially the case when match attendances soared in the immediate post-war boom period (McKibbin 1998: 349). Awareness of such arrangements does not detract entirely from the view of football clubs being community based, but calls for sober reflection. We can perhaps see Hoggart's 'Them' and 'Us' distinction in this light, having particular validity at the community level. The team belongs to 'Us' but is owned by 'Them'. Local middle class involvement in football club affairs will be tolerated to the extent necessary for financial viability, but nevertheless resented because it extends workplace relations into the domain of leisure. In the contemporary post-industrial context, where relations between the bourgeoisie and the working class have lessened as a source of social tension, local business financial involvement might be more appreciated than it once was. Where wealthy local businessmen basically bankroll football teams – for example Sir Jack Hayward and Wolverhampton Wanderers (Inglis 1996: 409–11) – they tend to be revered by working class supporters, since ownership provides supporters with the semblance of the club remaining local.

However, such an arrangement for keeping the football club within the community is far from participatory democracy and the inclusion of football in the 'common culture' in the manner desired by Williams. Given the highly developed commercial corporate ownership of contemporary football – and the intrusion into club ownership by 'foreign' tycoons, such as Roman Abramovich at Chelsea – the 'people's game' would seem further from the grasp of the people than ever. However, this is not to say that all hope should be lost in the attempt to incorporate football into a common culture. Working class action against the commercial corporatisation of football might take various forms. Taylor described the working class hooligans of the late 1960s and early 1970s as a 'resistance movement'. This seems at best fanciful, as, even if they were venting their protest at football's so-called 'embourgeoisification', hooliganism offers nothing positive towards reclaiming the football team for the local community. In contrast to such nihilistic protest, there are current campaigns actually aimed at establishing a collective voice in running football clubs.

An example is Supporters Direct. Supporters Direct is a British government funded scheme that assists supporter group initiatives in establishing co-operative and mutual ownership of football clubs. Specifically, it assists community based groups to establish trusts that are registered as industrial and provident societies. The trust is owned corporately (in a public, non-commercial sense) and run on a non-profit basis. The main stated aim of the trusts is democratic representation within the football club and the building and consolidation of a genuine link between clubs and local communities. Mutual supporters' trusts, not surprisingly, have become particularly popular with supporters of the English Football League's lower divisions, but are also present in some elite Premiership clubs.

Supporters Direct originated in a campaign by two supporters' organisa-tions (Independent Manchester United Supporters Association (IMUSA) and Shareholders United Against Murdoch (SUAM)) to stop the proposed merger of English football club Manchester United and Rupert Murdoch's satellite broadcaster BSkyB. Under pressure from supporters' groups, in October 1998, the British government Trade and Industry Secretary referred the deal to the Monopolies and Mergers Commission (MMC), to consider whether it would adversely affect broadcasting competition. If so, this might have been contrary to the 'public interest'. An anti-competitive situation in the sale of broad-casting rights to English Premiership matches and Manchester United matches in particular (as England's biggest club) could lead to unaffordable match access for fans, whether it be actual attendance or vicariously through live broadcasts.[3] SUAM was formed by high profile Manchester United share-holders and made a formal case against the merger to the MMC (Crick 2001: 65). Following the MMC's prevention of the merger, SUAM became a supporters' trust, Shareholders United, its formation directly inspiring Supporters Direct's establishment in 1999.

A manifesto was drawn up for this new perspective on football, revital-ising the nineteenth-century co-operative concept of 'mutualism'. 'Mutualism', as an alternative to 'socialism', is defined as the 'doctrine that mutual dependency is necessary to social well-being'. Full 'mutualism' would entail supporters' collectively owning a club, but supporters' trusts could be a significant initial step, gradually translating support into material ownership through share purchase. Trusts would be a defensive reaction to club flotation which, despite 'the language of "people's capitalism"' used to justify them, are means of extracting money from the game (Michie 1999: 9). In shareholder trusts, dividends would be pooled to purchase more shares, so providing increased club capitalisation and justifying claims for supporter trust representation on club boards of directors. Seventy-one trusts were established by January 2003, though largely at smaller clubs facing financial crisis. The trusts are progressive and communitarian in encouraging translation of economic support into influence over club deci-sions, mediating between passive 'consumption' and actual ownership, though currently two clubs, Lincoln City and Chesterfield, are under the full ownership and control of trusts. Expecting a complete supporter takeover of the game and 'returning' football to communal propriety would be idealistic at best. Football trusts will not change sport in a way that will satisfy Marxists. It is unlikely that sport could be radically transformed without other fundamental changes to the economic relations of society (see the related discussion in Chapter Six). However, such initiatives do offer an encroachment upon the subsuming of sport into big business and hyper-commercialism. They represent a limited form of guild socialism consistent with Hoggart's social democratic vision of culture, and go some of the way towards Williams's democratic socialist vision.

Williams would likely see the football trusts as a positive development within the practical building of a 'common culture'. Though some evidence indicates a preponderance of 'new middle-class' activists at their forefront (Nash 2001), football trusts nevertheless exemplify necessary collective action at local community level to assume a degree of cultural sovereignty from concentrated economic interests. As Williams was aware, common culture is not pre-given; it has to be worked for in an ongoing historical struggle (see the discussion of cultural materialism in Chapter Six). Indeed, from Williams's early position, such partial democratic intrusions into the realm of culture would be seen as occurring within the process of 'the long revolution'. Limited democratic intrusions into cultural arrangements need to be valued if more significant intrusions are to be made. Positive cultural progress cannot be taken for granted because complacency can undermine healthy working class scepticism and lead into self-defeating cynicism (Hoggart 1958 [1957]: 273–90).[4] Such an outcome leads to a retreat from genuine common culture (Williams 1961: xii). Although Williams, like Hoggart, had little to say about sport, it is clear that sport holds an intrinsic place within his purview of the common culture. Few other cultural forms have a closer relationship to the common people and Williams would surely encourage organisational endeavours, as romanticised as they are at times, to return sport to the community.

Notes

1   A most insightful case against the tendency within Cultural Studies to conflate the ideas of Hoggart and Williams has been made by Paul Jones (1994).

2   Gilroy (1996: 45–6) argues that Hoggart's preoccupation with class also overlooks racial division in Britain in the 1950s. Gilroy cites other relevant sociological literature published prior to *The Uses of Literacy* as evidence for the inexcusability of Hoggart's oversight. Gilroy's criticisms of Williams on race are discussed in the Connections section to Chapter Six.

3   BSkyB held exclusive rights to the live broadcast of English Premiership matches. Given the advent of digital broadcasting technology and the future unpredictability of the market, as BSkyB admitted in its submission to the MMC, its bid was a 'defensive' move to control access to England's leading club.

4   Hoggart's distinction between scepticism and cynicism within working class culture is interestingly applied to sport. Scepticism involves reflective criticism of the way that sport is played, for example, questioning rule changes introduced by sport's officialdom to supposedly 'modernise' sports, and, more generally, questioning the impact of the intrusion of corporate finance into sport. This scepticism involves a moral concern about *how the game is played*. Cynicism arises when the moral imperative of sport deserts the working class fan, and the interest becomes *winning the game at any cost*. To the cynical sports fan the deliberate foul aimed at thwarting a scoring movement (the so-called 'professional foul') is regarded as an acceptable part of the contest. Hoggart (2004: 184) raises this very issue in his current book with reference to the comments of a man speaking on radio in defence of such 'sporting' tactics. To Hoggart the man's insistence that cheating in sport is admirable as long as it is done successfully is indicative of a widespread retreat from ethical social behaviour.

CONNECTIONS

The supporters' trusts discussed in this chapter provide an interesting link between traditional and contemporary forms of fan culture. While appealing to a sense of the soccer team located within the community as traditionally perceived, the supporters' trusts evince a most contemporary form of collective fan activity. In their mobilisation and organisation of an often sophisticated critique of soccer club administration, trusts extend the role of more informal supporter fan groups such as those that have been behind the creation and distribution of fanzines. Fanzine culture mushroomed in the 1980s, usually without approval from soccer clubs and often in complete defiance of them, resulting in antagonistic relations between club and a rebellious minority of their fan base (Haynes 1998). As fans created their own media with limited resources and little or no commercial support, the soccer fanzines – a combination of 'straight' journalistic criticism, rumour circulation and speculation, parodic send-ups of club management, and often risqué cartoons – can be seen as a strange coalescence of the legacy of the 'punk' era in 1970s British popular culture and a 1980s 'Thatcherite' espousal of individual enterprise and invention (Haynes 1998). They also acted as an imaginative extension and refinement of the sense of fandom as community already present within football culture, giving a 'virtual' dimension, enhanced now through websites and chatrooms, to the traditional locality of the clubs, many of which were consciously established in the late nineteenth century by church and benevolent organisations as focal points for the fostering of community. As such they are indicative of the proto-communities referred to by Paul Willis (1990). See the related discussion in the Connections section following Chapter Three.

Fanzine culture more generally – in music and related forms of popular culture – has become an area of recent interest within Cultural Studies. This interest in fanzines has further elevated popular culture fandom onto the agenda of serious academic discussion. The emergence of fanzines lent weight to the claims of those academics within Cultural Studies that people are empowered by their engagements with popular culture (see the related discussion in Chapter Four). The emergence of fanzines also supported related claims that the lines are becoming increasingly blurred between popular culture consumption and production. John Fiske (1992; 1993) uses a corporeal metaphor, by depicting fans as hardworking cultural labourers whose works of creative interpretation and appropriation 'excorporate' cultural commodities, and so free themselves as consumers, from the 'incorporative' bodies of the cultural industries. They compete with the industries for the 'correct' or 'authentic' meaning of the products they consume (and in turn reproduce). The 'culture of defence' (Haynes 1998) of soccer clubs – as fans know and love them – in fanzine culture would appear to exemplify Fiske's metaphor. What is defended is the idea – whatever the messy history and actuality of private ownership and commodification may be – that the club is just that, a *club* rather than just another business, and that its authenticity as such lies in the *fans'* history of collective investment of time, emotion, imagination and money.

However, sports fans are always limited in the degree to which they can criticise and create their own cultural forms, because their cultural endeavours are tied to their sport in ways that fans of other cultural forms are not. Despite the familiar linguistic reference to 'we' when referring to the fan relationship with the team, fans do not 'own' their team in a way that gives them control over the team as a consumption item, despite considerable personal investment in match tickets and associated costs. However, although sports teams do not 'belong' to fans in a material sense, fans – through collective struggle – are able to secure the quasi-independence of their team from commercial corporate ownership. Such struggle can also thwart further corporate intrusion. The campaign against the Manchester United takeover bid from Rupert Murdoch argued that the appearance of an investment in the club belied a likely reality of expropriation of its value – economic value created through generations of fan investment – which would in turn affect its competitive status. It was an argument for the maintenance of the club as a quasi-independent entity (from owners and fans alike) whose symbolic representation of the fan community depended on its ability to compete unhindered by exterior, *selfish* financial interests. This is also why, as Brian Lomax (2001: 109) argues, supporters' trusts must remain independent of the clubs in which they invest. The symbolic status of a club depends on the idea – even if the reality is more complex – that the club is somehow independent of factional interests within or outside the 'community' it symbolises. The symbolic dissociation of clubs from particularistic interests also works towards reconnecting sport with a notion of 'public life'. This theme – the connection between sport, community and public life and culture – is at the heart of the next chapter, as we turn to insights from the American tradition of social and cultural commentary.

3

SPORT, PUBLIC CULTURE AND COMMUNITY

Letters from America

This chapter continues the discussion of sport and community by drawing on debates within American academe about the nature of public life. The chapter focuses specifically on literature within American sociology and American cultural criticism and from an engagement with this literature we expound our own preferred position on the relationship between community and sport. We commence by looking at how a distinctive take on community is developed within American intellectualism and how a tension between the themes of intimacy and impersonality is teased out within the literature. We are sympathetic to accounts contending that American society has witnessed a shift away from an understanding of community based on an acceptance of public commitment to an interest in so-called community based on an obsession with intimate knowledge of each other and of public figures. An influential work related to debates about community and public life is Richard Sennett's *The Fall of Public Man* (2002 [1977]). We address Sennett throughout the chapter giving particular consideration to the implications of his writing for the way that sport can be regarded as an aspect of public life. We compare Sennett with two key writers, Christopher Lasch and Robert Putnam, both of whom explicitly discuss sport in relation to community. In the discussion of Putnam we look specifically at his interpretation of 'social capital' and how it can be used to further the discussion of sport, community and public life. We conclude by reframing social capital through the lens provided by Sennett and argue that sport, unsullied by utilitarian interference, provides an arena of impersonality *par excellence*. Sport cannot be a model for public life but it might provide a lingering bastion of public life.

Democracy and culture: a continental critique

An underlying theme within American cultural debate is democracy. The key reason for this is that in the twentieth century the United States emerged as a nation most prominently disposed – at least rhetorically – to the extension of democratic principles of liberty, equality and fraternity to its citizenry. Accompanying the image of America as a democratic polity was the view of a culturally democratic nation. At a simplistic level this image is unproblematic, political democracy leads to democratic outcomes in other spheres. However, American intellectuals have never been willing to accept facile accounts of the democratic life in their country. First, it has long been widely argued that entrenched inequalities in American society give the lie to fundamental claims of the democratic polity. Gunnar Myrdal spoke of *The American Dilemma* (1962) to highlight the disjuncture between democratic pretension and the failure of the United States to provide anything like equal opportunity and life chances for its African-American citizenry. Although not an American – Myrdal was a Swedish academic commissioned to report on American society – Myrdal's study reflects criticisms that have been made in myriad other writings by American intellectuals, social critics and political and civic rights activists. Such criticisms of American society are highly pertinent to how sport is viewed within the context of the democratic polity and a number of polemically driven accounts take up these themes, the work of Harry Edwards (1969) being particularly important in this regard. At the level of political activism the so-called 'black power' salute given by athletes John Carlos and Tommie Smith at the 1968 Olympic Games provides a most enduring evocation of sporting rebellion against racial inequality in the United States. The demonstration successfully made a mockery of American democracy on the international stage.

As important as this level of social and political criticism is, our focus at this point is on cultural criticism that warns against the perils of democracy in the cultural realm. This often conservative form of critique is not so much concerned with questioning the existence of democracy at the political level or in society, but rather with the implications for cultural life within a democratic society. We have already looked at how critics such as F.R. Leavis feared the descent into a 'mass culture' in Britain under the influence of an inchoate globalising American popular culture in the 1930s. The mass culture debate had its own pertinence within the American context and, as indicated, it was bound even more directly than elsewhere to reflections upon democracy.

Particularly influential on the tradition of American cultural criticism is the writing of another visiting foreign critic, the French aristocrat and political thinker Alexis de Tocqueville (1805–59), whose voluminous study *Democracy in America* (1952 [1835; 1840]) was published after he had spent a year in the United States in the early 1830s. De Tocqueville was in many ways an admirer of the democratic polity in the USA, particularly the potential of corporate and communal forms of association to counter the dichotomous tendencies towards bureaucratic centralisation on the one hand, and atomistic individualism on the other. However, for de Tocqueville, democracy in practice carried its own tensions. Principally, he feared that the pursuit of equality would impinge upon the enjoyment of liberty. The American constitution embraced what de Tocqueville believed to be the 'tyranny of the majority'; a political situation in which the amorphous interests of the mass would hold sway over particular and legitimate minority interests (we can see the similarity here with Leavis).

This political shortcoming of democracy is accompanied by a moral one, which has implications for cultural life. De Tocqueville believed that the more equal men (*sic*) are perceived to be, the less importance is given to independent and privately considered judgement. 'Public opinion' becomes the accepted opinion and a socially meaningful sense of individualism is lost. A moral and intellectual laziness results, whereby people abdicate their responsibility of critical judgement by readily accepting the artificial public consensus. With regard to culture this results in the erosion of artistic taste and sensibility. De Tocqueville feared that democracy leads to the 'multitude of similar and equal people ... in search of petty and vulgar pleasures, with which they fill their soul' (de Tocqueville 1952 [1835; 1840]). Despite claims to freedom and pluralism, democracy threatens a cultural despotism in which fellowship is an illusion. People appear to stand together but, in reality, they stand apart, existing only for themselves. In such a situation community retains an appeal but in a phoney way, as what unites individuals is a quest for self-gratification. We can see here how, for Tocqueville – and this was a theme that pervaded subsequent cultural criticism within American intellectualism – democracy creates problems at the cultural level that are reflective of the political idealism of democracy: it is at the cultural level that we can witness the illusory appeal of community within the society given over to the democratic ideal.

Another influential foreign critic, the Spanish philosopher Ortega y Gasset (1883–1955), stretched the cultural criticism of American democracy to its logical limits by claiming that democracy establishes the cultural precondition for the emergence of totalitarianism in a society. In *Revolt of the Masses* (published in 1930 and translated into English in 1932), Ortega warned against the rise of 'mass man', seeing America in particular as 'the paradise of the masses' where the mediocrity of the 'commonplace mind' becomes the order of the day (Ortega 1961 [1932]: 18). This view of 'mass man' and the related critique of mass culture set the tone for a subsequent debate, following the Second World War, about the impact of popular culture on American society. During the anxiety of this early 'cold war' period popular culture was viewed by conservative critics as a form of contagion that would infect the cultural lifeblood of American society and leave the citizenry incapable of forming a discriminating opinion on all forms of cultural and social matters (Ross 1989). In a well known essay first published in 1953, 'A theory of mass culture', Dwight MacDonald (1957) presented a particularly evocative image of contagion by referring to the 'spreading ooze of Mass Culture'. MacDonald distinguished mass culture from folk culture, as the latter involved the people as the producers of their own cultural forms and artefacts. Mass culture on the other hand was mass produced by commercial industries and reduced people to cultural consumers. MacDonald also valued so-called 'High Culture' over 'Mass Culture' and rejected 'breaking down the wall' of cultural distinction (1957: 73).

Sport and the American way

In the next chapter we consider these types of criticism in depth as we return to address the cultural status of sport: sport in relation to other forms of culture and to popular culture in particular. This is to engage in an enquiry about sport and popular aesthetics. It also takes us further into considerations about the relationship between sport, culture and democracy. In the current chapter our focus is on sport as culture as a way of life, and we are particularly interested in how sport reflects what is, indeed, often referred to as the 'American way of life'. In popular parlance the American way of life conjures up an image of middle class America of a by-gone era: the white picket fence, a large detached house in a leafy suburb and a hot apple pie on the kitchen table. The 'American way of life' is also a phrase of political rhetoric used by American politicians and other public ideologues who want to valorise an American cultural and political superiority over other nations and cultures, especially those that come to be perceived in hostile terms. On the weekend following the terrorist attacks of 11 September 2001, President George W. Bush called on Americans to take in a ball game. Sport is a taken for granted dimension, or aspect, of the American way of life. The imagery and iconography of sport is ubiquitous within American film and television and politicians draw on sporting metaphors as a means of endorsing the American way within their jargon. It is, therefore, pertinent that sport should come under scrutiny when the critical gaze is placed more widely upon the facile notion that is the 'American way of life'.

A number of writers and filmmakers have, indeed, presented highly critical portrayals of American sport within their work. Some of this work is extremely popular and well known, for example the fairly recent blockbuster movie, *Any Given Sunday* starring Al Pacino, which presents a fictional exposé of the goings on within professional American football. Such work could be interpreted as a scathing attack on the institution of American sport at the highest professional level, and as suggesting that once sport is entirely penetrated by commercial interests that these interests hold sway over any others to do with sport being concerned with the nurturing of humanistic values. However, as we are constantly reminded by academics within media and film studies, movies – like any other texts – are open to interpretation both in terms of an intended meaning and in terms of meanings being made by the viewer at the point of reception. Without getting into this thorny issue of textual representation and interpretation, at this point allow us to suggest an alternative reading of a movie such as *Any Given Sunday*. While on the one hand we accept that the movie does call into question the commercial machinations behind American football and the effect that this has on the professional conduct of individuals within the organisation that is the football club, we do not believe that the movie offers a truly radical critique of sport and commercialism. Despite its superficial level of critique, *Any Given Sunday* comes to a resolution that is familiar in American cinema. While the capitalist intrusion into sport is seen to have given life to a corrupt and ruthless culture within American football, we are left with an image that individual determination and righteousness can prevail over this culture. The concluding message is not so much about criticism of the culture or system of professional American football, but about lauding those individuals who are able to overcome the deleterious potential of that system to crush those individuals who are not shrewd enough to learn how to play the system to their own advantage.

It could be argued that this focus on the power of the individual in *Any Given Sunday* is indicative of an American preoccupation with individualism, a preoccupation that is replicated within the various elements of American popular culture. For the remainder of this chapter we want to explore the implications of a culture of individualism in relation to sport, questioning the extent to which sport is caught up within this culture. We are interested in looking at the decline of a public culture in America and, as indicated at the commencement of the chapter, the demise of any genuine sense of community. If the critics are correct that appeals to a genuine sense of community in American society and culture are illusory, we are interested to consider what place sport might play in the purveyance of this illusion. After all, sport is commonly regarded as a cultural and institutional site through which a sense of community is fostered even in an increasingly atomised society such as the United States. Sporting clubs and associations still tend to be seen as tangible points of communal contact. Towards the end of the chapter we look at evidence – in the work of Robert Putnam – suggesting that formally and semi-formally constituted sporting associations are in decline in the United States, and at the attendant claim that this can be taken as evidence of the collapse of community. First, we want to more fully consider the view that American society and culture has drifted into a fascination with the individual to the extent that any meaningful interest in collective life has been lost. The most penetrating analysis of this trend has been provided by the sociologist Richard Sennett, particularly in his book *The Fall of Public Man* (2002 [1977]). Let us turn to a brief consideration of the central thesis of this book.

The fall of public life and the lost art of play

The Fall of Public Man was originally published in the United States in 1977. In this book, Sennett traces a decline in public life from the latter part of the 1800s until the time he was writing. The latter part of his book is concentrated on the United States and suggests that the historical trend has reached a point of maturity in that national context. Sennett decries what he sees as the dissolution of an appreciation of the public sphere in the wake of an encroaching private sphere. There are a number of familiar illustrations that we can bring to mind to highlight – if in a simple way – what Sennett is arguing. For example, we can readily recognise the tendency within contemporary politics for politicians to be highly aware of the personal image they present to the public. We might think of this in terms of the presentation of style over substance, and Sennett would be sympathetic to such a representation. Sennett argues forcefully that a healthy society should retain distinctive private and public realms, and that conduct within these realms should transpire according to natural demarcations. While the private realm is chiefly characterised by intimacy, the public realm is chiefly characterised by impersonality. Sennett claims that in a contemporary American society, obsessed with pseudo-, or at least, simplistic psychology, impersonality is expected to give way to intimacy in the public realm. To look back to our example above, politicians are expected to present a personal face – in keeping with the illusory notion of a collective personality – and the public demands knowledge of their private lives. This mentality extends to public decision making as 'therapeutic solutions' are sought for intrinsically social problems (Sennett 2002 [1977]: 12).

Sennett's critique explicitly follows de Tocqueville. Sennett (2002 [1977]: 31) notes de Tocqueville's concern that 'the intimacies of life would become increasingly important' in the public domain. A true sense of politics is lost as 'the engaging issues in life … become more and more psychological in character'. Once this occurs 'the pursuit of common interests is destroyed in the search for a common identity' (Sennett 2002 [1977]: 261). 'What is the problem with the desire for a common identity?', it might be asked. The answer for Sennett, as for de Tocqueville before him, is that the idea of a common identity stems from a mass mentality. Although not a cultural elitist in the manner of de Tocqueville, Sennett rejects appeals to mass sentiment that lead to the belief that public affairs should be based on commonly shared feelings and emotions. For Sennett, this represents the worst intrusion of intimacy into public life. Sennett is not hostile to the notion of the individual, but he believes that the essence of the individual as a public being resides within social relations, and that these relations are based on impersonality not intimacy. In a recasting of de Tocqueville's phrase 'the tyranny of the majority', Sennett entitles his concluding chapter 'the tyrannies of intimacy'. He acknowledges that the term can take on a number of meanings in relation to contemporary social life, but Sennett's (2002 [1977]: 338) stated interest and concern is in (what he believes to be) a subtle form of tyranny involving 'the measurement of society in psychological terms'.

The intrusion of intimacy into social life results in the disenabling expectation that public institutions should exhibit personality and that bearers of public office, particularly politicians, should be warm characters in the image of us – the public. It could thus be said that we get the politicians we deserve. At risk in all of this for Sennett is the important social experience of sociability. An 'intense kind of sociability' defeats the purpose of truly social sociability which is the outcome of social acts performed by social actors (Sennett 2002 [1977]: 339). Sociability loses its meaning when social action is reduced to individualised actions; the fall of the social actor is at once the fall of the public man. The tragedy in this situation occurs not just for society but for individuals as well, Sennett (2002 [1977]: 313) speaks of the 'actor deprived of his art'. For Sennett, social life involves artistry and this artistry is threatened when individuals are forced into contrived forms of social engagement. Artistry exists chiefly in 'playacting'; 'playacting in the form of manners, conventions, and ritual gestures is the very stuff out of which public relations are formed'. As the tyranny of intimacy encroaches upon social relations, individuals – as social actors – become 'inhibited from exercising the capacity to playact' (Sennett 2002 [1977]: 29).

Sennett (2002 [1977]: 315) supports his argument by declaring children as the masters of playacting. Through play children learn the 'expressivity of impersonal behaviour'. This is to say that in their play with others, children become aware of and accept the importance of conventions and rituals that govern the conduct of play. Against popular interpretations from psychology, Sennett sees rule bound play and structured play as natural, and he rejects the association of play with spontaneous impulses. Sennett's rejection of spontaneity is in keeping with his view of children as artists of everyday life. Importantly, children often create the rules of play themselves, through the invention of games, and more often through the adaptation of existing games to suit their own environmental circumstances. Play for children is, therefore, at once an inherently aesthetic undertaking and social activity; play is created through the natural sociability of children. Again, sociability depends on the acceptance of conventions and rituals, and in play children are most ready to call to account playmates who infract conventions of the game. Indeed, children tend to observe the rules of their own games without the authoritative intervention of a referee. Of course, arguments abound within children's play, but the arguments revolve around adherence to and application of rules in particular instances; rules that are unwittingly believed to be natural.

It tends to be in the adult world that play becomes detached from convention and the observance of associated rules. Adult play, referred to by Sennett (2002 [1977]: 315) as 'adult culture', has been infused with a different 'psychic principle' to that of children's play. While children remain concerned with play itself, adults have become preoccupied with uncovering the motives of play. This inquest into motives, ostensibly justified by a rationale to make play freer and more expressive of one's inner being, is ultimately bound in cliché and the type of 'stereotyped feelings' endlessly paraded in the confessions of participants on American television relationship programmes. Adults preoccupied with the quest – usually genuine – for 'deeper' meaning forfeit sociality and the fun of play. Sennett (2002 [1977]: 315) thus contrasts play with narcissism. Based on the mythological character Narcissus, narcissism describes the tendency towards self-absorption: the erasure of the line between self and other. For Sennett (2002 [1977]: 324) narcissism is the antithesis of sociability because in this condition the individual sees society and other people within his/her own image. Narcissism is also counter to civility because it involves individuals thrusting themselves into the social spotlight, effectively foregrounding their own personal interests. Sennett (2002 [1977]: 264) points out that civility – traditionally understood – is about respect for other people and not wanting to be a burden on them. It could be contended, from the position developed by Sennett, that a return to the impersonal world of play – as that of the child – might offer an antidote to the increasing incivility of adult society.

Narcissism 'rules'

Another landmark sociological critique of American society was published in the same year (1977) as Sennett's *The Fall of Public Man*. The very title of Christopher Lasch's *The Culture of Narcissism* indicates that he shared some of the concerns of Sennett. Like Sennett, Lasch discussed play and actually dedicated a chapter in his book to sport, based on his views of the degradation of play in contemporary society. He agrees with Sennett that play is an essentially social activity, one based on collectively observed conventions and rituals. He believed that, in a society where narcissistic tendencies come to the fore, conventions and rituals are forgotten and the drama of sports 'degenerate(s) into spectacle' (Lasch 1977: 194). He adopts a different, potentially contrary, emphasis to Sennett by insisting that part of the problem is not that sport is taken too seriously in contemporary society, but that it is not taken seriously enough. (Lasch (1977: 65–70) actually criticises an earlier version of Sennett's 'public man' thesis.) Lasch argues that sport in its most elementary form as play is a serious matter. According to Lasch (1977: 194), 'play at its best is always serious; indeed … the essence of play lies in taking seriously activities that have no purpose, serve no utilitarian end'. Lasch's comment prompts thoughts about the connection between narcissism and utilitarianism, and it could be surmised that in a culture where narcissism is prevalent the host of cultural institutions – including sport – set out to satisfy the goals of the self-absorbed.

From opposite standpoints Sennett (critical of play being taken too seriously) and Lasch (critical of play not being taken seriously enough) warn against the trivialisation of play and sport.[1] For Lasch a number of problems arise with the trivialisation of sport. To the extent that trivialisation relates to popularisation: the popularisation of sports to appeal to as broad an audience as possible leads to a lack of seriousness, due to the erosion of expert knowledge. In essence, Lasch has no complaint with commercial or professional sport, his problem is that, in the quest to establish large markets for professional sports, a crude utilitarian principle to satisfy as many people as possible comes into effect. Popularisation leads to a breakdown in the conventions of sport, the formal manifestation of which is the implementation of rule changes designed to simplify sports for the viewing audience. In the process, Lasch (1977: 192) believes, the importance of an expert knowledge that would be gained by fans after a considerable investment of time over years watching their favoured sports is abandoned to the rankest desires of the new audience: 'the sensation-minded and the blood thirsty'. Lasch cites ice hockey as an example of this cultural development in sport. This is perhaps a fairly extreme case in point but it does usefully illustrate Lasch's contention.

For Lasch, the trivialisation of sport undermines its key social purpose: the possibility of escape. For this consideration Lasch places sport under the more comprehensive rubric of leisure that allows him to view sport in relation to work. Lasch is opposed to sociological demarcations between the realms of leisure and work, believing that leisure – as a social category – exists 'purely' through a contrasting relationship with work. According to Lasch (1977: 216), leisure exists both in converse relation and 'organic connection' to work. It is only because of the organic connection between the two that leisure is able to offer people an escape from the rigours of their working hours. And like critics of both conservative and radical ilk, Lasch maintains, 'the degradation of play originates in the degradation of work'. This would be to agree that the contemporary world of work is diffused by a utilitarian ethos and that this has carried over into sport, at least at the level of professional sport. In the process the core play element of sport is marginalised, players are no longer play-actors and sport loses its quality of illusion. Lasch (1977: 215) suggests that the utilitarian ethos is met within mass mediated sport by an entertainment ethos that produces a spectacle devoid of illusion. Once illusion is taken from sport, sport loses its potential to provide individuals with a sense of escape, despite all of the smoke and mirror production techniques of contemporary mediated sport.

Lasch's comments about play and sports are focused on adults. In adult life play is constituted as leisure in direct relationship to work. Children – in contemporary Western societies at least – do not work, are not involved in the institutions of business, industry and labour, and therefore do not need an escape from these institutions. Work is of primary importance to adults as the institutional means through which they earn the means of subsistence, and it also provides the possibility of creativity and intellectual expression for many people. However, no matter how fulfilling work might be it is widely believed that work must be accompanied by the tandem institution of leisure in which people engage in purely recreational activities. In providing a forum for play, the escape that leisure offers to the adult is one to childhood. By devoting a chapter in his book to sport, Lasch recognises the prominence of sport as an institution of leisure within contemporary society. Sadly, from his perspective, the degradation of sport – as discussed above – at once involves the dissociation of sport from play. Lasch is on similar ground to Sennett when the latter insists that play and narcissism represent opposing 'psychic principles', one pertaining to children, the other to adults (at least in contemporary times). If sport has become an institution pervaded by narcissism then – according to this logic – it must be removed from play, and although providing adults with leisure it does not offer them escape: the return to childhood.

Both Lasch and Sennett are difficult to peg in relation to schools of sociology and we are not interested in buying into debates about such characterisations here. However, it is reasonable to say that both exhibit sympathy to functionalist sociology with regard to the importance of social institutions, the social roles occupied by individuals as social actors, and, most significantly, the connection between community and public life. The underlying linkage here is a belief in the idea of the organic society, a belief that also betrays a tacit association with culturalist intellectuals in Britain. Although – and, importantly – both Sennett and Lasch hold a considerably less romanticised view of community than the view of community held by English culturalists. Both Lasch and Sennett believe that the contemporary drift to narcissism, to the obsession with self, marks a retreat from any genuine ideal of communal life and from an organic society based on public engagement. According to Sennett (2002 [1977]: 314), 'there has been a movement from the idea of human nature to belief in human natures, a movement from the idea of natural character to that of personality'. Lasch is worried about the break-up of the natural order of and relationship between institutions. The degradation of work results in the degradation of leisure and the degradation of sport as an institution of leisure. The degradation of these institutions and their elementary principles of sociability must in turn degrade community life. The natural link between sport, as play, and community is most explicitly expressed by Lasch (1977: 216): '[play] retains an organic connection with the life of the community by nature of its capacity to dramatise reality and to offer a convincing representation of the community's values'.

The country and the city

Within much functionalist sociology there is a tendency to associate community with rural rather than urban social existence. The tendency can be traced back at least to the late nineteenth century in the work of the German sociologist Ferdinand Tonnies (1955 [1895]), who distinguishes between *Gemeinschaft* – social relations of an organic kind found in community – and *Gesellschaft* – social relations of a mechanical kind found in society. Tonnies then, clearly distinguishes between community as small scale social existence and society as large scale social existence. Tonnies associates community with intimate ties between individuals and believes that such relations occur only within geographical localities. With the impact of industrialisation local communities are broken up and the intimate relations that they foster are fractured. The division between community and society has been taken up in subsequent sociological writing characterised particularly in relation to rural and urban life respectively. In some cases, sociology has duplicated the readiness of cultural writers of the eighteenth and nineteenth centuries to romanticise the organic life of the pre-industrial country town. This served – within cultural criticism at least – as a useful rhetorical means of illustrating the deleterious social impact of industrialisation to accompany the easily made contrast in aesthetic imagery between the country and the city. Sociologists such as Simmel (1950 [1903]) appeared to accept the underlying view of anti-urban cultural critics that cities were the physical manifestation of inhumanity. From this perspective, the highly impersonal and, in turn, alienating relations of the city could be precarious for the individual and might ultimately lead to a breakdown in mental health. Importantly, however, this emergent sociology of the city was concerned with examining the decline of communal relations within the city rather than condemning the growth of the city (this emerges as a central understanding in Sennett's sociology).

Urban sociology became particularly prominent at the University of Chicago, and one of its key members was Louis Wirth. In his 1938 paper, 'Urbanism as a way of life', Wirth set out to show that the various sociological components of city life, high population and the demographic segregation of neighbourhoods, overcrowding and geographical density, an occupationally diverse but loosely structured labour force, resulted in a corresponding segmentation of human relations. For Wirth (1938), the differentiated and segmented group of the city replaces the unified community of the rural town. In another well known American study, published some ten years before Wirth's, Robert and Helen Lynd (1929) turned sociological attention to life in small regionally located cities. Their study *Middletown* was based on observation and survey analysis carried out in a small Midwestern American city. The Lynds' study suggested that the depersonalised way of life of the large cosmopolitan city had extended to cities and towns with moderate sized populations that had previously been culturally homogeneous. They were particularly interested in the cultural aspects of small city and town life and concentrated much of their discussion on leisure activities. The Lynds compared leisure activities of the late nineteenth century with the 1920s, noting particularly the impact of significant changes in technology and communications. Mass production and the availability of the automobile meant that people were able to travel between towns and cities in a hitherto unknown manner. This mobility affected communal activities, church attendance being one aspect noted by the Lynds. Cars also loosened family relationships as youths preferred to spend time in the cars of their friends rather than those of their parents.

The Lynds also noted the considerable impact of the emergent forms of mass media on communal life in Middletown. The biggest fear of adults within the town was that through exposure to radio and cinema in particular, young people were growing up too quickly and losing touch with the values they received from family and community life. F.R. Leavis delighted in his reading of *Middletown*, taking it as an endorsement of his own views about the breakdown of the 'organic community' and, further, that the breakdown could be traced to the mass culture coming from the United States (Leavis and

Thompson 1933: 3). Importantly, the Lynds' position is not as moralistic as Leavis's or those of the American cultural critics of mass or popular culture. They write as sociologists from a more distanced moral standpoint, and actually worked with a form of ethnographic method whereby they allowed Middletown residents to speak for themselves, thus giving the reader insight into how the people under study experienced and made sense of the cultural changes occurring in their lives (Inglis and Hughson 2003: 81). This is not to say that the Lynds remained neutral in their assessment of the cultural changes that beset Middletown in the 1920s. They noted with concern that previous types of association and communally organised leisure had weakened or disappeared as the new cultural forms took hold. Overall, the arrival of mass media such as the cinema had resulted in leisure becoming much more passive. For example, people would choose to watch a film on the screen or listen to a play on the radio rather than to maintain involvement in a community theatre association (Inglis and Hughson 2003: 82).

Importantly, however, the Lynds indicate that sport provided a renewed means of associational engagement. There had been a significant change in the culture of high school sport from their initial period of study in 1890 to the time of writing in the 1920s. Most remarkable was the unparalleled popularity of the emergent sport, basketball. By 1924 basketball had surpassed all other cultural activities to the extent that it 'dominate[d] the life of the school' (Lynd and Lynd 1929: 213). Whereas other cultural traditions in Middletown subsided in importance in the wake of cultural change, basketball rode on the crest of the wave. It benefited particularly from travel by automobile, as the high school team was able to compete in the widely celebrated state championship. Basketball was able to gain popularity with youth and also respectability with adults, as it was located within the traditional institution of the school. Thus the high school 'platform' heralded in the weekly newspaper included the call: 'Above all to foster the real "Bearcat" [name of the basketball team] spirit in all of Central High School.' From a more contemporary critical sociological approach we might be inclined to see this incorporation of basketball into the official school culture as indicative of an incipient phase in the social control – by cultural means – of youth. However, from an early functionalist viewpoint the Lynds offer a rather different analysis. They speak of basketball functioning as a 'more widespread agency of group cohesion'. Furthermore, 'more civic loyalty centres around basketball than around any other thing' (Lynd and Lynd 1929: 485). Basketball, according to the Lynds, became a unique form of social cement, drawing town people together across suburban, class and religious divisions. A series of quoted statements from a variety of residents supports the view that the spirit of 'the Bearcats' had permeated the town's cultural life.

The portrayal of basketball in *Middletown* gives an early insight into how sport can be characterised as a purveyor of community relations. Such a view has been transmitted from functionalist sociology to social policy. For example, in a number of national contexts sport is incorporated into programmes to assist with the re-socialisation of disadvantaged youth. These ambitions need not necessarily be criticised, but the rhetoric on which they are pegged should not be taken for granted. For example, in their excellent study of ice hockey culture in Canada, Gruneau and Whitsun (1993) maintain that the celebration of community within sport tends to 'romanticise the past' as well as misrepresenting the true relations of sport in the contemporary urban context. With regard to the former point, Gruneau and Whitsun (1993: 203) warn that sport can work against as much as it creates a sense of 'belonging' in small town life. The authors note that 'visible minorities' are sometimes ostracised from social life in small towns because they do not become involved in sporting activities. In such cases sport provides a social norm of inclusion for those who play the game, and one of exclusion for those who do not. In a related example from an ethnographic study of Australian small town life, Ken Dempsey (1992: 57) found that 'an ability to play sport' provided a means for newcomers to be warmly accepted into the social fold. Indeed, sport provided the strongest marker of masculinity in the town studied by Dempsey. Not to be able to play or have an interest in sport was likely to result in a man, newcomer or otherwise, being labelled pejoratively as 'a bit of a poof' (Dempsey 1992: 58). These observations in relation to sport reflect a concern that Sennett has with the insistence upon 'community' and the desired extension of the intimate relations of community into urban life. Sennett (2002 [1977]: 324) claims that 'community becomes a weapon against society', by which he ironically accepts the distinction between the rural and the urban and suggests that a continued preoccupation with the imagined social life of the former will do little more than inhibit an understanding of relations in the latter.

While holding reservations about the urban sociology of the Chicago School, Sennett regarded their work as seminal. He praised Wirth's work for providing the first coherent and systematic account of the division of labour in the American city (Sennett 1969: 16). He followed Wirth's interest in how segmentalisation, the new structure of social relations of the city, could result in orderly work and leisure relations. Importantly, while acknowledging increasing segmentalisation, Sennett (1970: 32) does not accept Wirth's neat distinction – the two poles – between the community (of the village) and the group (of the city). This is because Sennett does not accept the depiction of community primarily in terms of proximity and space. For Sennett community in the contemporary context is more likely to be based on shared identities between groups of individuals. From this perspective people do not need to live near to each other to share community. According to Sennett (1970: 31), 'the feeling of community is fraternal, it involves something more than the recognition that men need each other materially. The bond of community is one of serving common identity a pleasure in recognising "us" and "who we are".'

It seems to us that sport provides an interesting example of these two understandings of community working in tandem. Sport is certainly indicative in many cases of different parts of a geographical community coming together for a common purpose, even if it is to pursue a conflicting goal. A baseball league can bring together two groups of young people from neighbourhoods of different class status, the game being the common purpose, the desire to win the game being the conflicting goal. Sport provides a shared social experience and, often in team sports, a feeling of shared identity. This will be particularly the case where sporting affiliation is directly or indirectly connected to another form of social affiliation, ethnicity being a very good example. The conflicting goal of sporting victory mixed with extraneous rivalries brought into sport in connection with social affiliations such as ethnicity might be seen as a source of social disorder. However, from Sennett's discussion of urban communities this need not be something to worry us. Sennett ultimately rejects a liberal functionalist interpretation of urban life that emphasises diversity based on the continual toleration of difference. Sennett (1991: 198) takes what we would refer to as a *cosmopolitan realist* approach, recognising that there will be conflict between differences but that conflict does not necessarily translate into social breakdown. Conflicts between different social groups will be channelled – often unintentionally – through various formal and informal social mechanisms. Sport can function as one of these mechanisms and in so doing provide a very telling means of communal existence in the contemporary urban context.

Bowling alone?

Another prominent contemporary scholar who addresses similar themes to Sennett, to do with the decline of civic engagement in American society, is Robert Putnam. Putnam explicitly discusses sport and leisure in relation to the viability of community in contemporary society, as the title of his well known recent book, *Bowling Alone: The Collapse and Revival of American Community* (2000), indicates. Putnam (2000: 111–13) uses the example of bowling to illustrate a widespread, indeed national, decline in communal based activities and collective interaction. Unlike many books discussing culture and popular culture, Putnam's book is thoroughly and meticulously researched, and unless one were to find flaws in the accuracy of his statistical data it is difficult to criticise the quantitative dimension of his study. Accordingly, we will accept his facts and figures and look to critique his analysis of the trends he discusses. In relation to the example of his book title, Putnam (2000: 111) indicates that indoor bowling is currently the most popular sport in the United States and that unlike other sports it has experienced an upsurge in participation rates. What worries Putnam is that, although more people than ever are bowling, they are not doing so in competitive leagues. According to Putnam (2000: 112), 'between 1980 and

1993 the total number of bowlers in America increased by 10 percent, while league bowling decreased by more than 40 percent'. The title of Putnam's book gives the impression that people are now going to bowling alleys on their own but, as Putnam (2000: 113) admits, this is not really the case, as people usually play with friends or in other informal groupings. Putnam takes 'poetic license' to characterise a decline in competition bowling as 'bowling alone', and this, we believe, betrays the problem of his overall analysis.

Putnam's position is based on the view that going bowling with friends or playing in 'pick-up' games with strangers at the bowling alley does not constitute communal relations. Putnam prefers to relate community to formal and semi-formal types of local association. Putnam's understanding of community resides in an appeal to neighbourhood ties and related references arise throughout his lengthy book. Rather than discussing community in explicit detail, Putnam (2000: 21) prefers to deal with what he refers to as its 'conceptual cousin', social capital. As Putnam indicates, the term social capital has a number of interpretations. His preferred interpretation – although not definitively stated – is in accordance with an American 'progressive' intellectual tradition, which sees social capital as a necessary resource that is nurtured within neighbourhood networks through various forms of social intercourse. From this perspective, social capital involves volitional reciprocity whereby individuals contribute to the community in the knowledge that they will benefit in kind. Contributions and benefits will vary from individual to individual, and the ideal result is a balance between 'private good' and 'public good' (Putnam 2000: 20). This is an ideal-type and Putnam acknowledges that in the real world of community relations the 'positive consequences' of social capital – mutual support, co-operation, trust, institutional effectiveness – need to be 'maximized' against parallel 'negative manifestations': sectarianism, ethnocentrism and corruption.

Sport contains the seeds of both the positive and negative elements of social capital identified by Putnam. Putnam's view of social capital suggests an implied sociological functionalism; there is a functional side and a dysfunctional side. We can see this in a functionalist approach to sport sociology. On the one hand functionalists praise the capacity of sport to be character building, to develop teamwork, to foster an appropriate attitude towards competitiveness through fair play. On the other hand they recognise the dysfunctional possibilities of social inequality being reproduced in sport and of corrupt practices developing in the organisation and practice of sport. Unlike conflict sociologists, who believe that unequal power relations are systemically imbedded within sport, functionalists believe that dysfunctional tendencies are aberrational and can be corrected through appropriate institutional and organisational adjustment. For example, should it become apparent that a high school football programme is operating with an ethnocentric selection process, the problem can be overcome initially through an admission that it exists and through follow up remedial action. Such action could include a course of tuition in diversity issues for all staff involved in the programme. In the case of corruption creeping into sport, at whatever level, the functionalist position would generally maintain that, as long as ethical standards and fair codes of practice exist within the structure and culture of the particular sport, then the corruptive influences – usually corrupt individuals – can be weeded out. In this case dysfunction can even be turned into positive function as the corruptive sports official or administrator is publicly identified and paraded as a deviant whose misdeeds should not be repeated.

For Putnam the advancement of the positive consequences of social capital over negative manifestations comes back to his belief in community relations being based on volitional reciprocity and mutual obligation. If these core values are uniformly respected then we can be confident that social capital will be wielded and deployed in a positive manner. If this is to happen, individuals must be prepared to become civically engaged and welcome the extension of social networking across the community. To provide a clearer conceptual understanding of public spirited social capital, Putnam (2000: 22) distinguishes between *bonding* social capital and *bridging* social capital. Bonding is primarily an exclusionary form of social capital based in homogeneous group identity. It can be related to community understood as shared identity. Bridging is primarily an inclusionary form of social capital based not in group identity but on a desire for overcoming the narrow limits of such identities. It can be related to community understood more conventionally in terms of place, as it proposes that people living within proximity of each other work towards a common set of interests. Bridging social capital promotes reciprocal and mutual obligations and, therefore, is the form of social capital preferred by Putnam. However, as Putnam (2000: 23) says, bonding and bridging are not 'either or' forms of social capital but 'more or less' forms. Both will appear at once and be involved in the unfolding of social relations in particular social contexts. Sport is one such context where these forms of capital will simultaneously circulate.

We mentioned earlier the example of sport teams that have a primary affiliation in ethnicity. This can be interpreted as a practical manifestation of bonding social capital, whereby the identity of the sport team is drawn from a shared social identity in ethnicity. In some cases the lived experience of the sporting engagement might be kept within the limits of bonding social capital. This would be the case when an ethnic community within a city, or perhaps a wider geographical region, administers its own sporting competition to draw together people of the same ethnic background in a form of intra-group social networking. Bonding social capital connects with bridging social capital when the team affiliated to or representing a particular ethnic community competes in a broad based competition, for example against the schools within a particular region, or in a competition based on suburban locations within a city. Geography is the underlying organisational rationale in such sporting contexts and the competition provides the bridge that links people already bonded together within their sporting teams and clubs. The rather facile, but nevertheless understandable, analogy used by Putnam (2000: 23), 'bonding social capital constitutes a kind of sociological superglue, whereas bridging social capital provides a sociological WD-40', can be used to describe the process at work. The process can be observed in social settings characterised by multicultural life. For this reason it is particularly pertinent to the United States as well as other countries that have experienced large scale migration. Of particular interest is how migration experiences intersect with sporting cultures. A highly pertinent example is the social organisation of the sport of soccer in Australia, and we turn to consider this example.

A number of writers within sport sociology and history have discussed the way in which soccer competitions within Australia have comprised teams affiliated to different migrant communities. It is generally recognised in such commentaries that the soccer club has been a key point of social contact and bonding for members of these communities. The promotion of shared ethnic identity through soccer participation and support can be characterised, in Putnamian terms, as bonding social capital. For some writers (e.g. Mosely 1994) the expression of ethnic identity through soccer support has resulted in social conflict marked by collective violence. This has been particularly the case when the expression of ethnic identity is closely linked to declarations of national sovereignty, such as in the case of Croatian and Serbian communities. Looking at the same example, Hay (1994) has concluded that the very fact that the Croatian and Serbian communities have been drawn together by sporting competition into social engagement requiring co-operation and a degree of mutual respect is an illustration of the ability of sport to at least limit, if not overcome, the hostility nurtured within insular communal life-worlds. Hay accepts that physical confrontations have occurred between the members of these communities intermittently at soccer matches over the years, but contends that the lack of full scale violence at more regular intervals is the more remarkable observation for a sociological onlooker to take in. To apply the Putnam model of social capital to this example from Australian soccer as depicted by Hay, we would conclude that the formation of soccer clubs by the Croatian and Serbian communities is an illustration of bonding social capital at work, and that their relatively peaceful co-existence within the lived organisational context of soccer competition is an illustration of bridging social capital at work. From this fairly stark example, one where bonding social capital is a potential source of extreme social conflict, we can see the positive potential – through sport – of bridging social capital as a means of working towards harmonious communal relations.

Sport and the return of public man

While we would acknowledge the conceptual merit of Putnam's interpretation of social capital as an explanation of the aforementioned example, we have reservations about a thoroughgoing endorsement of bridging social capital as we have discussed it here. We accept that bridging social capital understood as some form or another of social connectedness – through sport or other organisational means – based on mutually accepted relations of reciprocity does genuinely serve a common good. However, we believe that the currency of bridging social capital cannot be imposed artificially by political decree or through social engineering. Bridging social capital will accrue as individuals and groups seek out contact with others for whatever social reasons or through whatever institutional means. In many situations this will involve sport, as sport, undoubtedly, holds interest to individuals and groupings across social boundaries. In the most simplistic way, sport typifies common culture. However, the connections sought out through sport by individuals and groups cannot be presumed to arise from altruistic concerns, and this is where Putnam's interpretation of social capital becomes tenuous. Individuals and individuals in groups, certainly by adulthood, engage in competitive sport because they enjoy it and because it provides certain kinds of perceived rewards. They do not generally engage in it for the primary purpose of wanting to improve broader community relations. Improving community relations might be an outcome of collective sporting engagement, but it is not an initial incentive to compete.

We therefore need to think about social capital and sport in a somewhat different way from the formula that would enhance community in the manner desired by Putnam. Putnam's hope for community is explicitly based on a desire – invoked with reference to democratic American statesmanship of the early nineteenth century – for intimacy in social relations (Putnam 2000: 23). Against this we would argue for a position on social capital and social relations more in keeping with Sennett, with an emphasis on impersonality. With regard to the example of Australian soccer discussed above we have accepted that the soccer competition serves as a means of bridging social capital for the two ethnic groups primarily engaged in sport as a result of bonding social capital. The bridging social capital developed through soccer might extend beyond the sports field and help the groups to come to terms with living together in Australia in other social arenas. Importantly, however, we do not accept that this development of bridging capital is, or need be, accompanied by social intimacy. Indeed, the two ethnic groups discussed are likely to come together into the public domain of sport in a rather impersonal way. The agreed purpose of their interaction is to play sport and the spirit of reciprocity is likely to extend only to this end. The communitarian might hope that some further goodwill will extend from this engagement but cannot presume that a mutual relationship of shared interest will develop beyond the soccer. Such an expectation is ultimately narcissistic; it is expecting others to conform to one's own image of good citizenship.

The most important communal aspect of sport is that it brings people together – as individuals and groups – in a leisure context providing a means of escape from work and other onerous aspects of everyday life. Through engagement with sport people observe the rules of conduct of the game; sport is a form of social theatre in which the social actor engages in the art of playacting. As Lasch has warned, sport should not become hostage to utilitarian desires. To the extent that it does, it loses its capacity for playacting. People certainly bring emotions and feelings based on bias and prejudice into sport. But ultimately they have to give themselves over to the game. We are clearly referring here to cases where people hold animosity towards their sporting opponents, but the argument also applies to situations where people know and are fond of their opponents. Indeed, if the very contest of sport is to be upheld, it is necessary for fondness, familiarity and intimacy to be suspended. Sport should be defended as an important public domain based on social relations of impersonality. Contrary to those who maintain that public discourse should be free from sporting metaphor and analogy, we contend that it should be replete with such reference. From sport we can be reminded of the rules of playacting and the underpinning codes of civility. The resurrection of public man might be some way off, but we can be sure that he lurks within the shadows of the sports arena.

Note

1   The respective positions of Sennett and Lasch on play (and the corruption of play through sport) are based partly on their different interpretations of Johan Huizinga's account of play in *Homo Ludens* (1955 [1950]). For Lasch (1977: 195), Huizinga understates the seriousness of play in childhood and, therefore, the essential seriousness of play. For Sennett (2002 [1977]: 323) Huizinga correctly disassociates childhood and play from the serious adult world of business. Turning to the source, Huizinga (1955: 5) explicitly states, 'play is the direct opposite of seriousness', and, therefore, his position is more directly supportive of Sennett's than Lasch's position.

CONNECTIONS

In this Connections section we consider theoretical means for further exploration of the connection between sport and community in contemporary social life. In particular we look at concepts proposed to account for new forms of communal association that arise in relation to sport. For example, how do we account in community terms for the possibilities that arise in conjunction with emerging trends in globalised sport fandom and internet technology? Paul Willis (1990: 141) uses the term 'proto-communities' to describe communal affiliations that develop through dedicated, if sometimes transient, commitment to contemporary leisure and consumer activities. People in proto-communities so-named may not actually meet but are increasingly developing virtual bonds through the internet and electronic communications. Sport fan groups are a key

69

example of communality formed through such electronic means. It is useful at this point for readers to think of and examine relevant examples of proto-communities based in virtual sport supporter cultures. How might social capital develop in such contexts? How do proto-communities measure up to the definitions of community presented by Sennett and Putnam? How does the notion of proto-communities compare with that of neo-tribes, as discussed in Chapter Five?

A related term to community is *communitas*. The term is derived from the work of Victor Turner (1969), and describes a state of affairs whereby individuals are able to establish a feeling of group bonding. Communitas occurs beyond and often in seeming defiance of the strictures of structured social life, particularly those associated with work. Communitas involves affective bonds of shared identity focused on ritualised objects and customs and is not based in geographical community except in a highly symbolic and ritualised way. The support for sport teams and major sporting events can be seen as indicative of communitas so understood. Within academic writing, communitas has been viewed both positively and negatively, and sport provides examples of these varying interpretations. John Fiske (1993: 69) believes communitas occurs as individuals form loose and often unintentional alliances in cultural consumption and use, alliances that challenge 'imperialising power', because they are based on creative cultural use and do not submit to the dictates of the marketplace or to officially prescribed uses of culture. Fiske (1993: 85) regards collective forms of celebration devised by sports fans as indicative of communitas expression, for example the spontaneous emergence of the 'Mexican wave' in sports stadiums and 'high fiving' following a touchdown or some other highlight. Of course, the 'Mexican wave' has been incorporated into a sanitised form of sporting culture encouraged by sports officialdom, and it is difficult to sustain an argument about the radicalism of such practices. Seemingly more important for Fiske (1993: 86) is the 'power of fan knowledge', because such knowledge 'is effective only within its own communitas'. In this context, fans create their own discourse on sport and in so doing challenge the official discourses and knowledge that come through the sport media. This type of communal experience is rather different from the understandings of community discussed in Chapter Three. It involves privileged access to shared knowledge but does not evince a shared sense of identity in keeping with sociological understandings of community.

As well as thinking of communitas as a form or variant of community it is appropriate to consider it as something removed from or even oppositional to community. The latter position is taken by Ingham and McDonald (2003) in a recent paper on the relationship between sport and community. The authors contend that in contemporary society (their focus is on the United States) community representation through sport has broken down meaningfully in both 'geophysical' and symbolic terms. This is aligned with the social fact that communities – physical and symbolic – have become increasingly fractured in late modern times. A semblance of community is mustered through the supporting of sport teams, but such support is largely manufactured by sports entrepreneurs in the endeavour to maintain social legitimacy for their particular sporting enterprises. Ingham and McDonald (2003: 28) contend that 'die-hard fans' will decrease in number as fans become more fickle in expectation of spectacular results. In such circumstances the community link is further eroded and communitas comes to the fore as fans are drawn together in spontaneous celebration of the mega-event and the mega-victory. Importantly, as Ingham and McDonald (2003: 28) point out, spontaneous communitas is fleeting and cannot be the basis for community and the development of related forms of social capital. On the contrary, expressions of sporting communitas will be manipulated to serve particular interests, those of business and civic planners. This recognition pertains to the increasing incorporation of sport into future 'visions' for cities and their regeneration through culture. Sport continues to provide a potent ideological support for the notion that 'community' remains at the heart of civic virtue. The link between sport, community and the city is further discussed in the Conclusion of this book.

4

SPORT AND POPULAR CULTURE

We concluded the previous chapter with a discussion of Robert Putnam's interpretation of 'social capital' in relation to sport. We commence this chapter with further consideration of Putnam, looking more into the cultural implications for sport that appear in *Bowling Alone* (2000). In the previous chapter we were interested chiefly in developing a position on sport and public life via an engagement with American social commentators, including Putnam. In this chapter we are interested in further developing our understanding of the cultural status of sport, more specifically how we might discursively locate sport within popular culture. We noted early on in the last chapter that the notion of democracy underlies the debate about culture within American intellectualism. This applies very much to Putnam, whose negative prognostications on cultural life in the United States are explicitly related to a decline in civic engagement and political interest. For Putnam a healthy democratic polity depends on people being actively involved in public affairs, not only taking an interest in politics but pursuing active involvement in community matters at the local level, in one way or another. This might involve a formal community engagement with sport as a participant or in an organisational capacity. For Putnam, then, the political merges into the cultural and the activity of people is vital for both political and cultural life.

Sport, popular culture and democracy

Putnam's democratic approach to cultural life places him at odds with the cultural elitist strain of cultural commentary – in the United States and elsewhere – that feared the extension of a democratic spirit into the cultural realm. There is no pejorative reference in Putnam to mass culture. His grassroots approach to cultural engagement militates against such characterisation. However, upon inspection, Putnam does ironically have something in common with mass culture critics. The position of mass culture critics is ultimately a paradox. They fear the intrusion of the so-called masses into the cultural domain on the grounds that they believe the masses to be incapable of coming to decisions based on cultural discernment. The masses are believed to be inert; their digestion of unworthy popular culture is put down to their intrinsic passivity. So while their passivity is abhorred, their activity – intrusion into culture – is feared. For Putnam the position is somewhat less tangled. It is passivity that he disdains and decries, and activity that he lauds. It is no coincidence that Putnam uses a sport related metaphor for the title of his book, *Bowling Alone* being intended to illustrate that people are retreating from active engagement in sport with each other. While some people might be bowling alone, others have resigned from sporting participation altogether, opting for a vicarious engagement with sport. Putnam (2000: 113) sketches a neat and simple distinction between active and passive relations to sport, referring to '*doing* sports' and '*watching* sports'.

Putnam taps into an anti-elitist temperament within American sociology that laments the decline of widespread public participation. For example, the prominent Chicago School sociologist Robert Park (cited by Putnam 2000: 377) believed that sport – as well as politics and other areas of cultural life – had been taken over by professional representatives who acted as proxies, participating in place of the average person, 'the great mass of men [*sic*] are no longer actors, but spectators'. Putnam (2000: 113) believes this trend has persisted to the present day. Furthermore, he suggests that it has increased exponentially since the 1960s. He notes a rapid rise in sports spectatorship in the United States, both in terms of television viewing and attendance of live events, from the 1960s to now. He also suggests that the abdication of sporting participation to professional proxies has afforded proxies – athletes – in the most popular sports extremely inflated incomes and inordinate rewards in public status. Putnam admits that sports spectatorship is not a complete 'dead loss' to social capital, acknowledging that it does generate communal gatherings; for example, people coming together to watch football matches. However, *watching* sports can only result in limited forms of community, it is *doing* sport that promotes the bridging social capital that is so important to Putnam.

The distinction drawn by Putnam (2000: 113) between 'active participation' and 'passive spectatorship', intentionally or otherwise, expresses disdain towards popular culture. This comes back to the similarity, mentioned above, that Putnam shares with cultural elitist critics who also associate popular culture with passivity. The difference is that cultural elitists regard the mass audience of popular culture as intrinsically passive and popular culture merely exacerbates this trait. Putnam's view is more benign; he believes that all people have active and passive dimensions to their personae. The problem with popular culture is that it triggers the trait towards passivity and once people become enculturated into passivity it is difficult for them to revert to being active. Putnam's position is largely driven by a familiar conservative concern with the technologies – principally television – that carry popular culture. Accordingly, he refers favourably to the claim by T.S. Eliot that television is, 'a medium of entertainment which permits millions of people to listen to the same joke at the same time, and yet remain lonesome' (Putnam 2000: 217). Television promotes entertainment in private, at low cost, therefore undermining traditions of public entertainment, sport being particularly affected in this regard. Again, from Putnam's view, people are not only 'bowling alone', they are watching sport alone on television. For him this provides the starkest possible picture of the atomised state of contemporary society. Sport should be the most active dimension of our cultural life. Instead, for Putnam, it serves to illustrate our increasing passivity and retreat from public engagement with our neighbours.

An oppositional view of popular culture in America – to that followed by Putnam – was declared by the sociologist Edward Shils in the early 1960s. Shils (1961) explicitly rejected the view that the emerging popular culture was undemocratic. Indeed, Shils maintained that by its very appeal to a large number of people popular culture was pluralistic and socially inclusive. Popular culture provided people with a new means of self-expression, not in a way that isolated the individual but one that opened channels of social communication. Rather than reducing people to cultural dopes, new forms of popular culture provided people with new and relevant means of critical reflection as well as enjoyment. Shils writes from the perspective of a functionalist sociologist whereby popular culture is seen positively, functioning to the benefit of society by providing the average person with films, television shows and other mediated offerings that are of interest to them. He rejects the negative portrayal of communication technologies favoured by critics of popular culture, instead preferring to focus on the democratic possibilities that a medium such as television opens up. Shils is also positive about the relationship between popular culture and capitalism. Here he is pointedly taking on Marxist critics from the Frankfurt School who claim that popular culture is merely part of the ideological armoury of the capitalist system (see the discussion of ideology in Chapter Six). Instead, while acknowledging the existence of class stratification in society, he claims that markets for popular culture will develop in accordance with 'taste cultures' pertaining to different class groupings and resulting in the production and dissemination of the cultural items that people – across society – want.

Putting sport in its place: taste cultures and taste publics

The idea of 'taste cultures' was developed further by another American sociologist, Herbert Gans, in the 1970s. Gans (1974) claimed that 'taste cultures' develop in connection with 'taste publics', which result from combinations of social factors such as ethnicity and class. This enhances a pluralistic view, that people have a democratic say in the popular culture they consume. Like Shils, Gans challenges the notion of mass culture, arguing that the production of popular culture is driven by a commercial interest to satisfy a differentiated consumer market. However, this differentiated market is hierarchically structured, principally in accordance with class background. Gans offers a six-tiered model comprising the following categories: creator orientated high culture; consumer orientated high culture; upper middle culture; lower middle culture; lower culture; and lower lower culture. Gans eliminates the familiar aesthetic dichotomy between high and popular culture to put all forms of culture into a sociological framework. This is useful for considerations of sport as culture, because rather than tending to think of sport as popular culture and, therefore, apart from high culture and the arts, we are able to consider how class-based taste publics might include particular sports within their range of cultural interests.

From this perspective sport can traverse all levels of the cultural hierarchy. At the top levels of Gans's hierarchy are the groups of people, first those who produce the fine arts, and second those who consume them in art galleries, concert halls or other such venues. The sporting interests of this class category (our thoughts here based in the British context) are likely to extend from arcane sports such as foxhunting and polo to sports based on a public school background such as rowing, cricket and rugby union. At the other end of Gans's scale are people within two working class categories, an upper level educated working class and a lower level poorly educated working class. Both levels are inclined to lack cultural sophistication and to be disinterested in the fine arts. Their cultural interests are likely to be in various aspects of commercially produced popular culture, although some members of these groups will have interest in traditional folk arts and crafts. Sporting interests are likely to be associated with popular sports of working class origin. Baseball in the United States and soccer in Britain are prime examples. At the lowest end of the taste hierarchy where sensationalism holds particular appeal, the pseudo-sport of professional wrestling has come to enjoy widespread popularity. Within academic writing, the success of professional wrestling has been viewed negatively on the one hand as indicative of the spread of 'trash culture' (Twitchell 1992) and, on the other, positively as a contemporary expression of working class 'carnival' (Fiske 1989: 69–102).

From Gans's sociological perspective the point would not be to judge the cultural merits of professional wrestling but to recognise its existence at the lower end of a taste hierarchy as evidence of the diversity of cultural interests across society. In a cultural democracy so-called 'low-culture' interests should not be discredited but given avenues of expression. If professional wrestling provides such an avenue, so be it, it serves a cultural purpose. It is also important to note that Gans is offering an analytical model to help us understand the social location of cultural tastes. He is proposing rather loose boundaries and in no way suggesting that people are rigidly locked into immutable taste publics. Class does structure cultural taste, but people have cultural interests that overlap the cultural categories sketched by Gans. There are a number of ways in which cross-category cultural interests can be explained. The Swedish sociologist Mats Trondman (1994) refers to 'class travellers' to account for individuals who experience mobility across classed cultural groupings. This applies particularly to people who start life in the working class and improve their class position by educational attainment and vocational success. As people move up the class ladder their rise is matched by an upward shift in cultural tastes. In music this might be from heavy rock to jazz to classical music. In sport a progression might work from football to golf to yachting. Of course, the trajectory is unlikely to be this neat and Trondman does not suggest that people leave their old cultural interests entirely behind them. Old rockers rarely die and personal affiliations to football teams, whichever the code, are mostly life-long.

Richard Peterson (1997) provides an even less linear view of cultural mobility by identifying individuals with highly eclectic cultural tastes as cultural 'omnivores'. Focusing on music Peterson is referring to people who might attend a jazz concert one evening, a symphony performance the next and a country music show the night after that. These musical interests are so diverse that they would almost completely traverse the class based cultural categories identified by Gans. The cultural omnivore appears to have broken free of class moorings entirely. However, Peterson is not proposing that class has become unimportant in cultural selection. Indeed, the cultural omnivore is almost invariably a person of middle class background who, owing to a loosening of cultural customs and formalities in the middle classes, has experienced exposure to a range of cultural activities. The young upper middle class person will be trained into classical music but is not as likely to be prohibited by his/her parents or schoolteacher from enjoying contemporary popular music, as might have been the case a generation or so back. Such a person will develop cultural competencies in different forms of music, in some cases becoming an aficionado in forms that would be located at different ends of the cultural hierarchy. The working class person is not as likely to be culturally omnivorous, as his/her interests will remain fixed at the lower end of the taste hierarchy. An interest in classical music might be sparked by exposure to a related television programme – i.e. high culture coming to the general public through a popular culture medium – but without an educational background in this area the person is unlikely to become an aficionado.

Acquiring cultural competency or 'expert' knowledge in 'high' culture is difficult without a formal background, but education into popular culture is much more accessible and available to anyone willing and able to put the time into television watching, radio listening, magazine reading, etc. The degree of competency and knowledge in popular culture will range from the aficionado to the dilettante, and this is nowhere more apparent than in sport. Some people are walking encyclopaedias of sporting facts and some, through years of watching a particular sport, have developed an analytical knowledge of the tactical play relevant to that sport. Other people are sport generalists who spread their viewing across a number of sports and might be inclined to watch highlight programmes rather than matches and meets in full. Sporting omnivores exist in both aficionado and dilettante forms. Aficionado sport omnivores are likely to come from higher class backgrounds. This is because they have developed competencies in sport associated with the middle classes through their social background in connection with family and school, while they have developed competency in sports associated with lower class categories primarily through contact with the media. As indicated above, sport aficionados will exist in the working classes but they are unlikely to be omnivores. Their expert knowledge is unlikely to extend upwards into middle class associated sports. Dilettante sport omnivores are again more likely to come from middle class backgrounds or from achieved middle class station, as omnivorous cultural interests always tend to work downwards. So, for example, a middle class sport dilettante may take a superficial interest in both equestrian events and football, whereas the interests of the working class sport dilettante are more likely to range from football, to boxing, to horse racing. Such an example shows a diversity of sporting interests, but the working class sport dilettante with these interests is not an omnivore because each of the interests is located towards the lower end of the cultural taste hierarchy.

However, we need to be wary of rigidity and to allow for seemingly anomalous expressions of sporting interest. In Australia in 1983, twelve-metre yachting, both an arcane and an extremely elite sport, captured widespread popular interest when an Australian crew defeated the American crew in the seven race America's Cup tournament staged in Rhode Island (McKay 1991). It was the first time in the over-100 year history of the event that the Americans had been beaten, and the Australian victory was feted as an extraordinary achievement given that the first of the three races of the series had been lost. The victory was greeted as an occasion of national celebration with the Australian Prime Minister declaring an impromptu and unofficial public holiday on the morning of the final victorious race. It can reasonably be said that interest in the event had built to fever pitch, people who had never been anywhere near a yacht were spending a good part of their time, both in their leisure and at the workplace, discussing the Australian revival. People spoke from a lexicon of yachting terminology that would have been completely unfamiliar to most of them prior to the event. So, from this example, we can see an upper class sport becoming popular to people of lower class station; yachting captured the interests of sport dilettantes across class groupings. Sport is probably unique in this way. It is unlikely that any other area of cultural achievement stemming from upper class origin could have gained such broad based popularity. This probability arises because of the unique relationship between sport and nation. Unlike other areas of popular culture sport offers a collective celebration of national identity. This can occur in relation to almost any sport, across class categories and groupings. Sport dilettantism finds its ultimate expression at the level of national celebration. A very recent example of a somewhat elite sport gathering widespread dilettante appeal in conjunction with national celebration occurred with England's victory in the 2003 Rugby Union World Cup.

Birmingham bound – subcultural elitism and the marginalisation of sport

Popular culture had come onto the academic agenda within American sociology by the 1960s; it made an appearance within the British academy at around the same time, but through a somewhat different avenue. In Chapter Two we noted the institutional emergence of Cultural Studies at the University of Birmingham in 1964 with the opening of the Centre for Contemporary Cultural Studies (CCCS) under the Directorship of Richard Hoggart. In disciplinary terms Cultural Studies was an amalgam of English studies (Hoggart's own domain) and sociology, initially marrying the humanistic concerns of the former with the analytical concerns of the latter. The work of Hoggart and Williams (and E.P. Thompson) provided the foundational inspiration within Cultural Studies to elevate the study of the everyday cultural practices of working people into academic research. As we have seen, both Hoggart and Williams believed that working class culture merited the attention of intellectuals and Hoggart provided a forum for this to occur at the CCCS. As we saw in our discussion of *The Uses of Literacy* (1958 [1957]), Hoggart's interest in working class culture focused on communal traditions of leisure and pastime, and in the second part of his book he wrote critically about emerging trends in popular culture in post-war Britain which he associated with the shiny barbarity of American entertainment industries. However, Hoggart had put the wheels of an academic juggernaut into motion and, in the hands of a cohort of young post-graduate students at the CCCS, Cultural Studies quickly came to be equated with the study of popular culture.

Indeed, young scholars at the CCCS effectively inverted the traditional and, in their view, stuffy attitude towards culture. For them it was popular culture, not so-called 'high' culture, that was socially important and in need of serious academic attention. Paul Willis (1979: 185–6), one of the CCCS luminaries, describes the Cultural Studies approach to culture as: 'not artifice and manners, the preserve of Sunday best, rainy afternoons and concert halls. It is the very material of our daily lives, the bricks and mortar of our most commonplace understandings.' The 'bricks and mortar' interpretation of culture certainly draws inspiration from Hoggart and is an evocative metaphor for the no-frills ethos of working class culture. It also illustrates the ordinariness of that cultural life spent in working class homes and neighbourhoods without the affected air of importance that usually accompanies bourgeois leisure activities. While a number of the studies at the CCCS focused on 'ordinary' aspects of working class cultural life in keeping with this mood, much of the work – as previously noted in Chapter Two –

became preoccupied with what have been referred to as 'spectacular' cultural activities. This was particularly the case with work focused on youth, which exhibited a preoccupation with youth subcultures such as mods, rockers, skinheads and, later on, punks. Willis himself contributed studies of this kind to the CCCS programme, culminating in the publication of his comparative study of the biker and hippy subcultures (Willis 1978). The concentration on spectacular youth subcultures, to some extent, severed the study of popular culture from its roots in working class ordinariness and meant that certain aspects of popular culture, more than others, found their way into Cultural Studies analysis. This early direction in the study of popular culture within Cultural Studies has implications for the subsequent treatment of sport as culture within the academy.

The work by CCCS researchers on youth subcultures offered a different approach to the analysis of popular culture than that found in the work of the American sociologists, such as Gans, discussed above. Gans was interested in looking at how popular culture is located within an overall classed hierarchy of cultural tastes, and at how popular culture is functionally beneficial to a democratic society because it provides a meaningful cultural outlet for people located at the lower end of the class hierarchy. Although considering popular culture sociologically, the CCCS academics have nothing to do with functionalist explanations. They adopt a conflict sociology approach that – unlike Shils and Gans – is inherently critical of capitalism. They are not interested in looking at how popular culture, produced within capitalist industry and sold in its marketplace, services social cohesion, but in the way that people – mainly young people – use the objects of popular culture profanely as a means of social transgression. Accordingly, they focus on the style of youth subcultures, clothing, hair fashion, argot, every aspect of the embodiment of rebellion and radical possibility. Resistance became the key term used to describe youth usage of popular culture, as highlighted by one of the best known published collections from the CCCS, *Resistance Through Rituals: Youth Subcultures in Postwar Britain* (Hall and Jefferson 1976). From the perspective of these writers, resistance exists in the symbolic use of culture by youth 'as a source of collective power struggle', not only against the capitalist system but also against more immediate institutions of authority such as the family and the school. Theoretically the work displayed an emerging British version of cultural Marxism drawn from Gramsci's account of hegemony (see the discussion of Gramsci in Chapter Six). Subculture youth were seen as being at the forefront of a battle to claim a collective cultural independence and integrity over a system innately geared to cultural incorporation. Methodologically a number of the CCCS researchers favoured ethnography, and actively undertook participant observation fieldwork, providing them with an intimate knowledge of the subcultures they were studying. Such intimacy also promoted sympathy for the research subjects and a championing of their perceived struggle.

The CCCS research did not see youth upturning the social order; this was a view more common within radical American sociology. For example, in *The Making of a Counter Culture* (1970) Theodore Roszak believed that the collective radicalism of youth would ultimately usurp the ruling elite of our 'technocratic society'. While the counterculture was about changing the world, subculture was about making do within it; it was a limited politics that, at best, offered a poke in the eye to social conventions and authority relations. Sport has little place within either of these conceptions of youth rebellion. The image of counterculture youth was that of the hippy, and the college sports jock was regarded as too conservative to be at home in such company. However, occasional overlaps did occur, particularly when the counterculture found unlikely support for its causes from prominent sports celebrities. Most notably Muhammad Ali became an icon of the counterculture when he resisted the draft for the Vietnam War in the late 1960s. Within the more limited politics of the subculture, sport is even less likely to feature and it finds little mention in the CCCS analyses of youth, popular culture and subcultural resistance. Music was both a source of status and a means of communicating a distinctive subcultural ethos and, unsurprisingly, it was music that preoccupied much of the attention of the subculture researchers. Sport, on the other hand, appears almost antithetical to the politics of the subculture. Given its links to formal institutions of adult authority, particularly the school, sport represented the type of cultural conformity that rebellious youth wanted to be freed from (Rowe 1995: 10). By implication sport was a cultural activity to be associated with ordinary conformist youth rather than resistive subculture youth and, therefore, of limited importance as a form of popular culture (at least from the perspective of subculture researchers).

An exception is the work of CCCS scholar John Clarke (mentioned in Chapter Two) on the subculture of London skinheads. Clarke (1973; 1976; 1978) discusses football as an integral aspect of the subcultural milieu of the skinheads. However, football and its paraphernalia are not an obvious part of the skinheads' 'stylistic ensemble'. Their exaggerated masculinity was paraded in a braces and boots fashion that parodied the working class generation of their fathers. Football support provided a means of group identity in connection with neighbourhood and the football stadium provided a public gathering place where the subcultural style was collectively displayed. The football stadium also provided a social arena for the enactment of violent or, at least, highly boisterous behaviour through which the skinheads attempted to claim kudos within the stakes of masculinity. One skinhead group would target another on match day and to successfully penetrate the rival or 'home' end of a football ground with your own number was regarded as an ultimate victory for the invading skinhead group. The confrontations between subculture groupings such as skinheads are somewhat analogous to sport teams which – even in the professional realm where prize money is involved – are competing against each other for cultural status. A key difference is that skinheads, and other hooligan elements, are understandably accused of using the sports arena for deviant social activities, whereas the sanctioned sport confrontation enjoys public legitimacy.

Sport, then, does find its way into the subculture work at the CCCS, not through a consideration of sport as such, but via a discussion of the appropriation of a sporting domain by a subcultural group for the enactment of deviant ends. Clarke's interpretation does not make this judgement. As discussed in Chapter Two, he sees the skinheads involved in a lamentable attempt to 'magically recover community', and football is an aspect of working class life connected to this recovery. Like his fellow subculture researchers, he relates skinhead cultural activities to a 'resistance through ritual', in so doing setting the minority of youth in subcultures apart from the majority of non-subculture affiliated youth. Through Clarke's study sport is brought into Cultural Studies, but in a very particular way that evinces an interest in the spectacular aspects of sports fandom. Clarke's study can hardly be taken — nor does he suggest it should be — as representative of the majority of football fans who do not engage in unruly behaviour at or in association with football matches, but who enjoy football support as a key component of their cultural lives. Cultural Studies, concentrated on routine cultural practices, should be as interested in the ordinary displays of sports fandom as it is in the spectacular. Sarah Thornton (1995: 93) has referred to an elitist tendency within the subcultural studies of the CCCS and subsequent work on youth subcultures to tacitly disparage an assumed but, necessarily, abstract mainstream of youth. Thankfully, this tendency has been avoided in some of the fairly recent writing on male football supporting subcultures in Britain. For example, both Armstrong (1998) and Giulianotti (1996) take care to examine, albeit briefly, the nature of the distanced relationship between the 'hooligan' groupings they are studying and the larger fan base of the clubs featured in their research. Although particular 'hooligan' groups remain the focus of their studies, fans that we might call ordinary are depicted not in abstraction but in material reality.[1]

Cultural Studies and the 'mystery' of sport

For the reasons discussed, it is not surprising that sport did not feature in the subculture studies at the CCCS. However, given the prominence of sport within working class culture at large, it could be expected that sport would receive attention within the broader agenda focused on the study of popular culture. Such a case was made for sport in the early 1980s by the now prominent British sport sociologist Jennifer Hargreaves. However, Hargreaves's (1982: 17) point was made in critical reflection upon what she perceived as the 'dearth of studies' about sport within academic Cultural Studies. Indeed, she refers to the 'silences' about sport as a 'form of cultural chauvinism' that ranks sport lowly within the domain of popular culture. One reason offered by Hargreaves for this chauvinism is that Cultural Studies academics, despite their iconoclastic pretence, operate with a traditional intellectual mindset that dichotomises mind and body. Hargreaves's suspicions are probably correct, but beg a further question as to why an emerging area of academic enquiry that gave so much thought to how cultural styles were embodied by people would give little consideration to highly visible and energetic bodily practices within sporting cultures. Before giving further attention to the failings of Cultural Studies in relation to sport, it must be noted that work on sport did emanate from the CCCS and associated scholars. In a paper partially aimed at countering Hargreaves's accusation, Andrews and Loy (1993) suggest that to ignore the limited work on sport that occurred within Birmingham and related Cultural Studies would be to create another silence hindering the critique that must necessarily be made of the marginalised place of sport within that field.[2] Chas Critcher was one CCCS scholar who appeared particularly interested in the cultural significance of sport. Interestingly, his writing on sport reflects the theoretical developments that occurred at the CCCS. His paper 'Football and cultural values' (Critcher 1971) presented a Hoggart-like discussion of soccer within the cultural heritage of the working class. He followed this culturalist offering with a paper attacking the masculine hegemony over sporting culture that effectively subordinated women (Critcher 1974). A few years later Critcher (Critcher *et al.* 1977) connected the CCCS interest in subcultures with sport by presenting a case study of skateboarding subculture. This paper can now be seen as a pioneering work on what are variably termed alternative, extreme (in some cases), fad or whiz sports (Rinehart 2000). These sports are usually portrayed by their adherents as being opposed to the customs and formalities of conventional sport. However, many extreme sports have become highly professional and commercial, as well as financially rewarding for their participants. Nevertheless, the faddishness, style and mere mention of radical ethos are likely to draw the attention of contemporary Cultural Studies scholarship to these sports. Sport Studies is also turning attention to these sports; an impressive collection of case studies can be found in a recent volume edited by Rinehart and Sydnor (2003; see the related discussion in the Connections section following Chapter One).

Despite the potential for sport to grow in stature within Cultural Studies, it is hard not to be pessimistic about this potential being realised. Andrew Blake (1996: 17–18) has trawled through the pages of dedicated Cultural Studies journals to find very little mention, let alone specific treatment, of sport in featured articles. Not too much has changed since Blake was writing, although two of the present authors have had papers published on the aesthetics of soccer within the Cultural Studies journals *Cultural Values* (Inglis and Hughson 2000) and *Space and Culture* (Hughson and Inglis 2000). Rhetorically, Blake refers to the absence of sport within Cultural Studies as 'a mystery': why has sport remained relatively invisible within an academic enterprise concerned with popular culture when sport is such a highly visible aspect of the lived experience of popular culture for many people around the world? We have partially answered this question above, agreeing with the earlier point by Hargreaves that Cultural Studies has reproduced its own form of cultural elitism, leaving sport on the margins. Again, as Rowe (1995: 10) has suggested, sport suffers from an image problem in an image obsessed academic environment. Put simply and colloquially, sport is just not cool enough to count for a large number of Cultural Studies academics. It is somewhat galling that an academic profession that has spent so much time berating the elitism of Leavis – and even Hoggart – has unwittingly nurtured a research culture that has de-privileged a major form of popular culture.

To be fair, we must also consider the institutional circumstances of sport in the academy to understand why sport has largely been left off the Cultural Studies agenda. Sport has become a prominent area within university curricula in North America, Australasia and Europe. This trend has fitted within the shift of the educational profile of universities towards vocational preparation. Sport Studies programmes are variously based within university faculties, primarily constituting the physical education organisational component of education faculties. Sport Studies programmes have brought together academics from a number of disciplines incorporating the physical and social sciences with coaching and other sport specialisms to produce a relevant course of studies. Sociology has been the predominant discipline from the social sciences and humanities to gain a formal foothold within Sport Studies programmes and a matching staff representation within sport departments in universities. This has resulted in the sociology of sport becoming a fairly well established sub-field of sociology with internationally constituted bodies of scholars. Sport sociology has at least two dedicated journals – *International Review for the Sociology of Sport* and *Sociology of Sport Journal* – published quarterly. This means that scholars writing on the social and cultural aspects of sport have established publication avenues to which they can submit their papers with some assurance that the content will be regarded as relevant to the charter of the journal. Cultural Studies has not developed a profile within Sport Studies departments in the way that sociology has, rather Cultural Studies has become almost totally aligned with another vocationally based area in the academy, media and communication. However, given that disciplinary boundaries are rather flexible these days, particularly with regard to sociology and Cultural Studies, the cultural study of sport has found its way into sport programmes under the umbrella of sociology. The point we are leading to is that much of the academic writing on culture and sport will follow the same path as writing on the sociology of sport, i.e. into dedicated sport journals. While it is good to have a publication outlet for work on the cultural aspects of sport, we would hope that the existence of sport specialist journals does not work to prevent sport intruding into the Cultural Studies mainstream more than it has done thus far.

'Common culture' or 'cultural populism': accounting for the uses of sport

Blake also notes that sport has not received reasonable coverage in Cultural Studies textbooks, readers and broad based monographs analysing trends within popular culture. A book of the latter kind that he criticises is *Common Culture* by Paul Willis (1990). This book is based on ethnographic fieldwork examining the cultural practices of youth living in the Wolverhampton area of the English Midlands. While acknowledging that *Common Culture* discusses sport amongst a range of cultural practices observed in relation to youth, Blake (1996: 19) suggests that the treatment is too cursory to be of consequence. This is not a view we particularly share, as Willis is clearly casting a very wide net across youth cultural activities, and sport is adequately tied in with the theoretical discussion of the various other examples addressed in the book. Indeed, it is the theoretical discussion in *Common Culture* and its implications for sport as a form of popular culture that attract our interest. We would describe Willis's theoretical orientation, developed in *Common Culture*, as *radical culturalism*. This is because Willis inverts the credo of conservative culturalism – culture as that which makes life worthwhile – to an understanding that everyday life actually makes culture. Furthermore, Willis goes beyond Williams's interpretation of culture as a 'whole way of life' to propose that art itself is nothing more than everyday activity. Willis (1990: 2) recognises a 'symbolic creativity' in the everyday practices of ordinary people: art is to be seen in the way that people 'humanize, decorate and invest with meanings their common life spaces and social practices'. Willis completely rejects the traditional view from cultural appreciation that works of art carry an intrinsic value. For Willis, art value occurs as people invest meaning and worth into objects through usage. From this understanding Willis (1990: 21) refers to 'grounded aesthetics': 'the creative element in the process whereby meanings are attributed to symbols and practices ... grounded aesthetics are the yeast of common culture'.

Willis recognises sport in both participative and spectator modes as an important site of symbolic creativity. Through sports participation young people – and older people for that matter – gain a sense of identity based on a 'complex articulation of meaning and practice', in the process connecting an expression of 'the self' with their social world (Willis 1990: 110–11). Sport participation offers the development of a 'bodily grounded aesthetic'. Willis illustrates the term with reference to a research participant Jane, and her experience of playing netball:

> Jane takes a pride in her ability to make her own body move as she wants it to and for as long as she wants. Not everyone's body has these qualities, so it is a comparative pride and distinction too; a social as well as a bodily quality.
>
> (1990: 111)

The 'bodily grounded aesthetic' is developed not through the rigours and discipline of training or coaching techniques but through externalisation and performance of naturally embodied talent; art being brought to the surface, as Willis might have it. This view allows us to see sport even in formal and semi-formal settings as a cultural arena through which individuals can engage with others in self-expressive and liberating forms of bodily conduct. From this understanding organised sport does not necessarily impose conformity on the participating individual. As a site of artistic possibility, participative sport steps out from its conservative image and should become of interest to Cultural Studies.

The idea of the 'bodily grounded aesthetic' is also of relevance to under-standing the experience of sport spectators. Willis (1990: 112) comments, 'though the movement and control of one's own body is not important for the spectator, its sensuous and communicative presence within an immediate mass social spectacle is of the essence'. Willis provides examples from inter-views with supporters of the Wolverhampton Wanderers soccer team to support his point. The fans emphasise the importance of the match day 'atmo-sphere', being at the ground and sharing the physical camaraderie of their fellow supporters. A powerful 'symbolic communication' is at work in the football stadium as people enjoy a cultural unification in the imagined community of Wolverhampton, in a manner unavailable through other dimensions of social contact. The collective expression of the 'bodily grounded aesthetic' can, thus, serve a socially purposeful function by bringing together, in common cause and celebration, people who might otherwise remain divided by neighbourhood or other social barriers. Sport can be one of the sources for the development of what Willis (1990: 141) refers to as proto-communities. Willis (1990: 104) recognises that not all expressions of bodily aesthetics will be socially positive, and provocatively discusses the 'dramatic grounded aesthetic' of fighting. In relation to football support this conjures an image of the hooligan element, and fighting is indeed a bodily expression carrying cultural kudos within football hooligan subcultures (Armstrong 1998; Hughson 2000). We should be careful though not to over-state the occurrence of actual fighting by so-called football hooligans; much of the confrontation between rival groupings involves a macho bravado of posturing, goading and imprecation, moving to the edge of violence but not crossing the line. The bodily aesthetic of pseudo-violence involves a more dramatic performance of 'symbolic creativity' than could ever be the case with violence proper.

Willis is also interested in more private expressions of sports fandom, the ways in which young people invest meaning into their lives through personal usage of the cultural paraphernalia of sport. He notes the case of a young Wolverhampton Wanderers supporter whose bedroom is decked out as a virtual shrine to his beloved team (Willis 1990: 114). From the description given it appears that the young man has mixed items such as team flags and scarves with newspaper clippings and photographs to create a particular world of meaning in his own bedroom. This prompts us to think about the place of 'official' sports merchandise in the cultural practice of supporting teams. Willis would oppose the common sense criticism that people who purchase items such as soccer team strips are being swindled by avaricious sports marketing branches of sporting clubs, well attuned to the possibilities of making money from the blind faith of loyal followers. Such an assumption fails to recognise the awareness that people have of their own place in the cultural economy of sport. Most consumers of sports attire are aware that they could buy a shirt of similar quality for a much cheaper price than the 'official' home or away top of their favourite team. However, consumers sanction the cultural value of objects and give them legitimacy over apparently similar items for the purpose of being able to hold kudos with other individuals on the basis of mutual ownership of the legitimised item. Such is the case with sporting paraphernalia like soccer shirts (see the related discussion in Chapter Five).

Some fans will entirely shun official merchandise. In the case of soccer fans in Britain this trend commenced in the 1980s with the emergence of the 'casuals', groups of young men who discarded all apparel identifying them with particular teams (Giulianotti 1993). However, this stylistic development had more to do with young men of hooligan ilk wanting to remain inconspicuous to increased policing at soccer matches than it did with a shunning of the commercialism of soccer clubs. Indeed, the 'casuals' favour expensive designer clothing and accessories to signify a lifestyle of consumer excess. Other fans will engage in activities of 'bricolage' (Hebdige 1979: 106) whereby they combine items of commercial production with those of their own making to produce 'secret' meanings in their sport supporting experiences. Hughson (1997: 256) discusses this in relation to the Bad Blue Boys soccer supporter group in Australia who developed a stylistic ensemble combining team colours with icons, badges and banners identifying their Croatian parentage. In this way these young men were able to subvert the authority of Australian soccer officialdom, which had prohibited soccer teams and their supporters at matches from identifying with ethnic nationalisms. One BBB member spoke of 'keeping ethnicity in on the sly' (Hughson 1997: 255). For Willis (1990: 23) this would display a 'collective awareness of the ability to control symbols and their cultural work'. This potential stems from the cultural marketplace of capitalism and the availability of items that can be put to profane use. Willis (1990: 27) declares that the 'genie of common culture' has been let out of the bottle by commercial carelessness and warns against stuffing it back in. Cultural analysts, he believes, should be more interested in examining what people do with cultural items and in cultural places. No more so with other cultural things than with the items and places of sport.

Willis goes on to provide the ultimate statement of the non-passive use of popular culture when he refers to 'production in meaning': the imaginative uses to which people put cultural products turn 'creative consumption into production' (Willis 1990: 135). For Willis the 'circuit of culture' (Johnson 1986) spins full circle as consumers become producers. This relates not only to the uses of tangible cultural items but also to uses of media. In this regard Willis (1990: 135) speaks of 'made messages', suggesting that the messages of media texts are made wilfully upon reception by their audience either in disregard for or blissful ignorance of the messages intended by the senders. John Fiske, another well known Cultural Studies academic, has argued a similar position. Fiske (1987: 311) contends that to fully overcome the elitist idea that the majority of people are cultural dopes mindlessly consuming the media that come into their homes, we must accept that popular culture operates within two distinct, if parallel, economies. First, there is the financial economy where popular culture is commercially produced and, in the case of mediated culture, transmitted to an audience. At this level of economy popular culture is treated as an exchange commodity, an item designed for making economic profit. In contrast there is the cultural economy where people actively create popular culture as they give their own meanings to mediated products. It is through actual use by the audience that popular culture assumes status as a cultural commodity. Although the forces within the financial economy attempt to control the cultural economy, they are ultimately unable to do so because a knowing popular culture audience is able to resist opinion forming from above. From Fiske's position, the cultural uses of sport are, then, to be understood in relation to their circulation within the cultural economy. For example, he suggests that televised American football only becomes popular culture through the viewing process as fans apply their 'expert' knowledge and consume the product in a manner both meaningful and enjoyable to them. The commercial producer is unable to reclaim economic capital from the cultural value created *in situ* by viewing fans (Fiske 1993: 84–6).

Jim McGuigan (1992), a key critic of Willis and Fiske, has referred to their positions on the uses of popular culture as 'cultural populism'. He claims that both of these authors too readily accept the power of the audience and the consumer, without critical reflection upon the social relations of cultural consumption and production. He insists that both incorrectly assume that the positions they advance are politically progressive. Indeed, McGuigan (1992: 159) is particularly scathing of Fiske's reference to the 'semiotic democracy' of media consumption, likening the term to the marketing terminology 'consumer sovereignty'. The suggestion is that while claiming to advance a position that is subversive in its interpretation of consumption, Fiske is actually presenting a position that supports the production practices of capitalist media and culture industries. McGuigan proposes a return to a political economy understanding of popular culture, explicitly rejecting the idea that cultural consumption can be considered separately from cultural production. Similarly, Golding and Murdock (1991: 15) have rejected Fiske's twin economy analysis, suggesting it invents a false dichotomy. The cultural economy does not operate apart from the financial economy, and, accordingly, they argue for the reconnection of the 'symbolic and economic dimension of public communications'. Only by viewing the overall media process can a consideration be made of the 'wider economic formation' within which purchases and uses of popular culture take place. An emphasis on the economic circumstances of consumers becomes more pronounced as the increasing privatisation of television transmission through pay-per-view cable and satellite channels and particular broadcasts defines, to some extent, who gets to watch what according to the ability to pay (cf. Golding and Murdock 1991: 29). The restriction of sports events to pay-per-view channels and broadcasts is indicative of a decline in the democracy of popular culture.

While accepting Golding and Murdock's critique of Fiske's notion of twin economies, David Rowe (1999: 93) argues that cultural factors are increasingly impinging upon economic factors within the decision making of media and popular culture producers. Rowe (1999: 173) refers to a process of 'culturalisation' whereby culture 'become[s] increasingly central to all social institutions, including the political apparatus and economic structures'. In this process culture takes on an enhanced commodity status as media executives seek to extract as much value as they can from the symbolic goods that they have at their disposal. Sport features significantly in this development, especially because of the global appeal of a number of sports and sporting events. Sport is so valuable to the major media owners that they have established interlinking ownership into leading international sports organisations: sport as culture and media as business presently exist in symbiotic relation. However, the relationship does not go unchallenged, as the cultural status of sport is a matter of some passion, more so than most other forms of popular culture. Some sports have cultural heritage status – particularly in countries such as Britain and Australia – and carry a matching expectation of public broadcast accessibility (Rowe 1999: 88). Whether this is to be via free-to-air or pay-per-view televisual transmission is a matter for debate. But the fact that this debate is so crucial requires us to consider its terms and conditions of reference. With regard to the latter it is undeniable that questions of media ownership, production and broadcasting must be addressed if we are to make any sense of the cultural conditions of mediated sport consumption. Willis and Fiske have usefully placed emphasis on the uses of media and popular culture, but in a way that risks closing off the analysis both of how cultural goods and messages come to people and of the economic relations and circumstances in which people put them to use.

Maintaining distinctions: sport as 'popular art'

In conclusion we consider a position on popular culture advanced by Stuart Hall and Paddy Whannel in their 1964 publication *The Popular Arts*. The book draws on the culturalist influence of Hoggart and Williams and is critical of the cultural elitism of Leavis and other dismissive accounts of popular culture. Nevertheless, Hall and Whannel do not propose a relativistic approach to cultural analysis in the manner of Willis and Fiske. They contend that all popular culture need not be deemed of equal cultural worth or value and offer a means of discernment intended to avoid arbitrary aesthetic distinction. While their approach has been criticised (Turner 2003: 60) for retaining the subjectivism of Leavis, we believe that the distinction Hall and Whannel (1964: 66–85) draw between popular art and mass culture provides a simple analytical means of approaching the evaluation of forms of popular culture in a way that combines considerations of cultural production with those of cultural consumption. Hall and Whannel (1964: 66) speak favourably of *popular art* as popular culture that arises in some way from folk art and tradition and retains an intensity of feeling and a 'genuine contact' with its audience. On the other hand *mass culture* is commercialised and operated to a utilitarian rationale aimed to please the audience without extending them emotionally or connecting with them in a genuine way. The artist or performer within popular art is a truly public figure as his/her personality is located within the artistic performance. Mass culture involves 'personalisation', whereby personality becomes an external prop, merely another aspect in an artificial performance designed to please.

Hall and Whannel set up a dichotomy that appears passé within contemporary Cultural Studies. We do not suggest that analyses of popular culture work with a rigid distinction between popular art and mass culture, but we are attracted to the idea that there is an intangible element within some popular culture that arouses feeling and suggests a depth of relationship between performer and audience. In contrast, some aspects of popular culture are undoubtedly contrived for utilitarian purpose and, even if deemed artistic, must be so by some other criteria. If we are to accept that people do engage creatively with popular culture it is useful to have a basic means of making distinctions within popular culture, otherwise all uses of and relationships with popular culture are reduced to a common denominator: rather unfertile grounds for a *common culture*. Such distinctions are usefully drawn within the cultural study of sport, otherwise we are unable to differentiate culturally between sports and to identify cultural changes within particular sports. A distinction between popular (art) sport and mass (culture) sport provides a useful construct to locate related considerations and debates. For example, it could be proposed that amateur and professional sport align respectively to these categories. However, some professional sports with traditional links to working class communities, such as association football, can certainly be thought of as popular (art) sport. A related point of enquiry is to look at how some sports have shifted from the popular (art) sport to the mass (culture) sport category as utilitarian and commercial forces come to bear. Sports contrived entirely as business entertainments would be in the mass (culture) sport category; professional wrestling provides an obvious example. Although we accept that professional wrestling affords a certain feeling of pleasure to its fans, we believe that this pleasure is qualitatively different from the fan experience pertaining to popular (art) sport. We accept that these categorisations are contestable; the point is that it is a debate worth having. We need to discuss the cultural distinctions in and between sports in order to be able to make sense of the cultural uses of sport.

Notes

1   For discussion of the ethnographic contribution in Giulianotti and Armstrong's studies of football supporters see Chapter Eight. For a critique of Giulianotti's depiction of post-fandom within football supporter culture refer to Chapter Five.
2   Pertinent here also are the media studies contributions by Hall (1978) and Whannel (1979), using content analysis of press coverage on football hooliganism to show the creation of a media generated 'moral panic'. Poulton (2004) argues for the continuing relevance of such models in her analysis of the media amplification of contemporary football fan violence.

CONNECTIONS

One of the key areas of Cultural Studies to be explored within academic work on sport is subcultures. A key contributor to the discussion of 'sport subcultures' is Peter Donnelly, who, over a lengthy period, has discussed the conceptual and definitional issues surrounding the use of the term subcultures in relation to sport (1981) as well as providing ethnographic insights into rock climbing subcultures (2003). In his early writing Donnelly (1981) contended that sport offers up particular forms of 'achieved subcultures' that display a number of characteristics indicative of distinct group bonding. He suggests that as the institutional significance of work decreases as an identity marker, many people seek out an alternative identity status through sport, and in the process form subcultural allegiances with other people who share and actively engage in the same sporting interest. He notes that studies of sport subcultures will be undertaken via ethnographic research enabled by the fact that many researchers will have an established participative involvement in the sport subcultures they study. For further discussion of sport and ethnographic research, refer to Chapter Eight.

Donnelly (1981: 578) also notes that a number of case studies of sport subcultures focus on deviance within sport and associated with sport. His emphasis is on sociological studies, but this mention of deviant subcultures prompts thoughts about the Cultural Studies work on subcultures done at the CCCS, work later referred to by Donnelly (1988). While the CCCS subculture researchers spoke of resistance rather than deviance they were ploughing a similar, if more overtly political, field to the earlier American sociology researchers of subculture, both seeing subcultural activities emerging in converse relation to a dominant culture or dominant cultural

---

patterns. In a more recent paper reviewing the work on sport subcultures, Crosset and Beal (1997) focus on the dominant culture/subculture tension to contend that what are often taken to be sport subcultures are better described as sport 'subworlds'. Crosset and Beal (1997: 82) note that subcultural analysis looks at structurally subordinate groups and at how new modes of cultural expression and in-group relations emerge through negotiation with the dominant culture and its value system. In contrast, subworld analysis does not presume conditions of dominance and subordination, but is concerned with examining specific cultural processes, which unite people in the creation and use of particular 'social objects'. Subworlds exist below and in direct relation to overarching 'social worlds' that pertain to key areas of social and cultural life: sport, the arts and various forms of leisure pastimes. These social worlds 'produce' social objects of both symbolic and material kind: works of art and exhibitions and sports teams and events are examples of social objects in this sense. As indicated, social worlds give life to subworlds, which bear resemblance to, and in some cases correlation with, subcultures. Punk rock in relation to rock would be an example of a subworld and also a subculture, at least in some of its manifestations. The chief contention of Crosset and Beal is that sport is less likely to give rise to subcultures because subgroup social relations in sport do not, on the whole, evince a subordinate/dominant culture relationship. Subgroup relations in sport are better analysed, in most cases, as subworlds.

This does not mean that subcultural analysis becomes irrelevant to sport studies. The increasing interest within sport studies in alternative and extreme sports has tended to keep usage of the term subculture in vogue. For example, in her case study of windsurfing, Belinda Wheaton (2003) specifically refers to a subculture of windsurfers that rejects values consistent with a dominant sporting culture. *Inter alia*, the windsurfer subculture is hedonistic and rejects 'combative competition' and tough masculinity (Wheaton 2003: 78). Wheaton's study alerts us to the important ways in which relations of gender and sexuality can be challenged within particular social contexts of sport, and she makes a compelling case for the reconsideration of subcultures in this regard – primarily in terms of gender rather than class. Nevertheless, Crosset and Beal do well to warn against over-readiness to define any sport related social grouping as a subculture, and their introduction of the term subworld to sport studies opens a range of possibilities for the study of ordinary and non-spectacular social group relations in sport. They also note, quite interestingly, that sport subcultures turn into subworlds in circumstances where they are 'incorporated' into the dominant culture in one way or another (Crosset and Beal 1997: 82).

For a further discussion of sport in relation to the notion of 'social world' – specifically drawing on Howard Becker's sociological concept of Art Worlds – see the introductory chapter to Maguire *et al.* (2002) *Sport Worlds: A Sociological Perspective*. These authors recognise that sociologists tend to avoid aesthetic judgements in relation to culture, whether to do with the arts or sport (Maguire *et al.* 2002: xvii). Sociologists do this in order to be able to make dispassionate assessments of social life in both theoretical and empirical terms. Accordingly, they are concerned with examining the social circumstances within which art and sport are produced as forms and objects of culture, rather than with what – from a social scientific viewpoint – might be regarded as an indulgence in arbitrary judgement. However, some sociologists are prepared to argue the case for the existence of purely aesthetic value (Barrett 1999: 105). Michele Barrett (1999: 107) contends that in the endeavour to rid the sociology of art (and related fields such as Cultural Studies) of romantic and bourgeois notions of artistic value, the aesthetic dimension of art has been displaced altogether. In some ways this has suited sport as a subject of sociological and Cultural Studies interest because by leaving questions of aesthetic standards aside all dimensions of culture can be regarded as being of equal analytical merit. Within contemporary sociology of culture and Cultural Studies art and sport should occupy a similar footing. However, once the notion of a pure aesthetics is introduced to social and cultural analysis the ground shifts – the sociology and cultural study of art adjusts to take on board questions of aesthetic judgement and value, but what about sport? Where is the aesthetic value in sport?

Of course, we are being somewhat rhetorical as academic discussion about the aesthetics of sport is not unfamiliar. Scholars in the philosophy of sport have investigated the possible intrinsic connections between art and sport. For example David Best (1995) argues that sport has inalienable aesthetic qualities but that it is not art. Art, unlike sport, is non-purposive, and the aesthetic qualities in art reside in its non-purposive nature. The result orientation, or purposive nature, of sport undermines the possibility of an aesthetic essence. Importantly, however, there are degrees of purposiveness in sport – think of soccer compared with synchronised swimming – just as there are degrees of non-purposiveness in the arts. The commissioning of paintings and entry into Eisteddfod competitions can hardly be regarded as non-purposive. Surely if we are to consider the existence of aesthetics within sport we need to focus on the stylistics of play and to consider whether certain sports players exhibit true artistry. Two of the current authors take up such considerations in a paper published in the journal *Cultural Values* (Inglis and Hughson 2000): the paper discusses a naturally gifted category of 'star players' (within soccer), artists in possession of the 'silky touch'.

A particularly bold and persuasive claim for seeing sport as art is made by C.L.R. James in *Beyond the Boundary* (1983 [1963]). Indeed, James does not claim that all sports can be equated with art; it is only certain sports, his particular claim is made for cricket, that exhibit pure aesthetic qualities. James makes aesthetic claims for cricket in both its performative and imaginative dimensions. With regard to the former, James contends that the essential component of artistic performance is drama. This prompts thoughts of the dramatic element within all sporting contests, the build up to a dramatic result. But James (1983 [1963]: 196) sees this as drama in a 'superficial sense' rather than drama in a deeply aesthetic sense. True drama is actually embedded within the game as a whole and in the beauty of how every component of the cricket game contributes to a 'structural perfection' (James 1983 [1963]: 197). For James (1983 [1963]: 197), cricket is the most dramatic of sports even though the end result, in distinction from other sports, 'is not of great importance'. James (1983 [1963]: 199) also regards cricket as a 'visual art'. He accepts the contention from art criticism that great works of art are not great due to representational value but that they are great because they exhibit 'significant form'. James is particularly drawn to the views of Bernhard Berenson who sees significant form in paintings that evoke 'tactile values' and 'sense of movement'. Berenson believed that great figurative painters such as Masaccio and Raphael gave the viewers of their paintings 'the imaginary experience of certain complicated muscular movements' (Collingwood 1958 [1938]: 147). For James (1983 [1963]: 202) the greatest of cricketers offer the same heightened aesthetic possibility; in the truly great player 'the significant form in its most unadulterated is permanently present'. In cricketing terms the significant form – of tactile value and sense of movement – is referred to more simply as 'style'. James's elevation of cricket onto a lofty aesthetic plane is, of course, contentious, and Berenson's position on aesthetics is used for convenience as much as it is with conviction. Nevertheless, James takes us into provocative territory on sport and art, a far more interesting territory than that offered by much of the contemporary academic writing on culture, that tends to shy away from making such connections on aesthetic grounds.

5

SPORT, POSTMODERNISM
AND CULTURE

The term 'postmodernism' has gained currency over the last twenty years within discussion about culture. Within the arts and related areas from film to architecture, postmodernism is referred to as an artistic development that has superseded modernism. All areas of culture are assumedly impacted upon by this trend, which not only extends but also makes irrelevant distinctions between high and popular culture. If we do live within a post-modern culture, then how do we explain sport in relation to postmodernism? We address this question in this chapter looking critically at the postmodern characterisation of sport by some writers. While we accept that cultural life in Western societies has undergone significant changes, we do not accept that these changes are so profound as to speak of the arrival of postmodernity and the need for a radical means of analysis to explain the accompanying cultural changes and trends. Indeed, it is our contention that older forms of cultural analysis, adjusted to the times and phenomena at hand, provide a more reliable means of understanding what is going on in the realm of culture today.

Sport provides a particularly interesting contemporary example of cultural study, as contemporary sports have undergone significant cultural changes over recent years. While some of these changes might appear indicative of the postmodernising of sport, we believe that, upon sober reflection, the cultural relations of sport – in terms of both production and consumption – can be seen to occur within a framework that postmodernism is unable to account for. Postmodernism is often referred to as playful, and by this very description holds an immediate appeal in relation to sport considered as play. At an aesthetic level, as with dance and other forms of performance art, as well as the visual arts, there is a tendency for sport to be described as postmodern. A discussion of postmodern sport from the aesthetic standpoint is taken up in the Connections section following this chapter. In the chapter itself we focus on postmodernism as a form of cultural theory. We look at how postmod-ernism has been lifted from the realm of aesthetics and into that of cultural analysis, and into the academic areas of Cultural Studies and sociology. We contend that danger arises as postmodernism obscures more than it elucidates, and the true nature of the relations of culture – in sport as well as other areas – are hidden beneath a layer of often impenetrable jargon.

Postmodernism: the Gallic roots

Before discussing postmodernism in relation to sport, we need to get a handle on how postmodernism can be understood in theoretical terms in relation to culture and society. This is a potentially difficult task, as postmodernism is a fairly broad church and a number of writers from the social sciences and humanities could be cited as key figures. The Gallic heritage of postmodernism is especially pronounced and it is to two well known French theorists – Jean François Lyotard (1924–98) and Jean Baudrillard (b.1929) – that we turn to establish our bearings. Lyotard, a philosopher and prominent figure within French intellectual life throughout the latter part of the twentieth century, was originally inspired by Marx's political thought. However, by the 1980s Lyotard's work had exhibited an 'extreme break with Marxism' (Lechte 1994: 246) and his best known book, *The Postmodern Condition*, published in 1979 (1984 in English), became a seminal postmodernist text. The break with Marx was exhibited by Lyotard's attack on what he referred to as 'meta-narratives', totalising theories that claimed to explain the way society works. Accordingly, Lyotard was not only critical of Marxism; his broadside was intended for countervailing theories such as liberalism. As contrary as they are, from Lyotard's perspective both Marxism and liberalism are modernist theories that offer an erroneous critique of society, both of how society is and how it should be. For him they are nothing more than grand stories falsely promising to cast light on an illusory good society. The core idea of postmodernism as a social theory is that there is no such thing as the good society, and, therefore, no sensible or honest means of describing the path towards it. Lyotard maintained that the best theory can do is to recognise that knowledge is always particular and subjective rather than universal and objective. From this perspective, theory is not interested in 'meta-narratives' but in the 'mini-narratives' through which people explain their particular experiences of the world; each mini-narrative is valid in its own right.

This position has profound implications for how we view the truth. Indeed, for Lyotard truth is an unstable concept when understood in the conventional sense of one truth pertaining to certain instances of reality. Lyotard, like most other postmodernists, accepts the simultaneous existence of multiple truths; accordingly there is no social reality to which we can claim certainty. Lyotard contends that this has always been the case, but in contemporary society people – without announcing it in theoretical terms – generally have become disillusioned with the search for a social truth and for this reason have turned away from political ideologies (reflected in a widespread disinterest in formal politics). This is the postmodern condition to which the title of Lyotard's book refers. The general social attitude reflects a retreat from modernist complacency, and this requires a whole new approach to political action. Lyotard (1984: 82) concludes *The Postmodern Condition* in aggressive fashion by declaring: 'Let us wage war on totality ... let us activate the differences.' Lyotard will only condone political action based on an understanding of the 'absolute difference' between human beings rather than a presumed humanistic unity. The social unity assumed by humanism is, for Lyotard, chimerical, and when pursued through politics downright dangerous, in the worst instances resulting in fascism. Being opposed to universalistic ideas and projects Lyotard encourages a limited form of politics geared to the expression of difference. In this sense postmodernism becomes pertinent to questions of cultural identity and race, and ethnicity in particular. It promotes a controversial politics by foregrounding the notion of difference over sameness, disputing the idea that all people share a common humanity. Sport becomes a highly pertinent social arena from which to view this politics being played out. Within the modernist tradition sport, principally through the Olympic Games, has been used to actively parade the idea of a humanity in common. However, sport has also been used as a form of identity politics in both protest and celebration of racial and ethnic identity. Such striking expressions of difference through sport are taken by some writers to indicate the emergence of a postmodern politics into the realm of culture. As the chapter concludes we consider the relevance of such claims.

The other key French intellectual figure we discuss in relation to postmodernism is the sociologist Jean Baudrillard. Like Lyotard, Baudrillard was initially inspired by Marx's writing on culture and society but was drawn to the poststructuralist trends in French thought during the 1970s. From there he came to reject Marxism because of its structuralist theoretical underpinnings. For Baudrillard (1975) Marx's focus on the relations of production as the predetermining aspect of social affairs had become increasingly irrelevant. This was particularly so, he believed, in the realm of contemporary culture where the main commodities of cultural production were not objects as such but signs. For Baudrillard, cultural objects themselves do not possess value; value resides in the signs attached to objects. This claim can be illustrated in relation to clothing. There is no intrinsic value in a pair of jeans. One pair of jeans takes on a greater exchange value than another because it carries a designer label. The label working as a sign confers value on objects, such as jeans, and establishes value distinctions both in terms of cost and cultural kudos. A similar example from sport is the football top of British soccer clubs: the so-called 'replica' shirt. At the time of writing 'official' replica shirts – those manufactured by the sport clothing company licensed by the football club – sell at a retail cost of around £40. However, 'counterfeit' versions of these shirts are usually available from markets or even less formal retail sources for no more than £10. However, despite the availability of an alternative product that might be only marginally inferior in quality as a garment, many fans would prefer to purchase the perceived real item – the officially sanctioned shirt – than to save a considerable amount of money. Many fans are also concerned to obtain the latest available version of the team shirt, usually released for purchase in the summer prior to the soccer season and often featuring the logo of a new commercial sponsor. The value of the shirt is thus conferred by the sign, in this case the official stamp of approval by the football club and its financial backer.

Baudrillard extends these ideas on the commodity value of signs into a sweeping critique of the mass media in Western society. He believes that we live in an age dominated by the proliferation of signs and that we experience a production of meaning best described as 'simulation' (Baudrillard 1983). By using this term he does not suggest that signs create false meaning, because – in accordance with Lyotard – there is no such thing as an ultimate truth for signs to convey. Reality is but an illusion and signs function to fabricate a reality that does not exist apart from the process in which it was fabricated. The images that we receive from the media are not generated by reality – as we are led to believe – but actually create the reality we come to know. Baudrillard thus refers to 'hyperreality' – beyond the real – as a means of explaining how the contemporary media works according to a system of changing and unstable signs. From this perspective, the cultural analyst should abandon any interest in the representation of reality, as there is no reality to be represented. The 'crisis of representation' requires a shift of interest to the examination of the sheer significance and meaning of signs. However, this is not an uncritical endeavour, and part of Baudrillard's intention is to provide an updated understanding of the mass media so that a relevant analysis to the times can proceed within sociology and related areas of study. The whole thrust of Baudrillard's position suggests a shift away from Marxist analysis where the media is seen as an agent of capitalist ideology. For him the problem is not to be reduced to a question of ownership and subsequent ideological promulgation in the interests of media owners. Of greater concern is the very working of a mass media system that has taken on a life of its own in the realm of consumption, beyond the processes of ownership and production.

The oppressiveness of the mass media occurs not through the pursuit of self-interest by media owners or their managerial representatives but through the 'code' embodied in the very function of the media. The 'code' to which Baudrillard refers is basically a dominant mode of logic to which mass media forms operate in the interests of themselves as media of communication. This is a deterministic view that sees interests detached from human controllers and embedded in the mass media as a social entity in their own right. The code ensures that the transmission of signs is unidirectional, as media of mass communication send messages out to an audience but do not allow an audience response, despite some illusory gestures to audience participation on television and radio (Baudrillard 1993). Once caught in the mass media vacuum even events supposedly based in reality are reduced to simulations. Sport again offers an example, as recognised by Baudrillard (1990: 79–80) in his book *Fatal Strategies*. He refers to a European Cup soccer match that was played behind closed doors, excluding spectators from the arena because of crowd violence experienced in a previous match between the two teams involved. The match was broadcast on television despite the non-attendance of spectators in the stadium, thus transforming the match into a purely mediated spectacle. For Baudrillard, this provides a glimpse of the future of sport, the social dimension of sport disappears and the sporting event becomes nothing more than a series of 'synthetic images' deprived of meaningful cultural referent. The sporting audience becomes part of what Baudrillard (1983) refers to in earlier work as the 'silent majority' of media consumers. An unintended 'counter strategy' eventually unfolds as the 'silent majority' become increasingly 'indifferent' to the signs they are offered by the array of available mass media. The point will come, Baudrillard (1983: 11) muses optimistically, when people stop listening and watching altogether.

Postmodern pessimism: a new way of seeing?

While calling for a new analytical means of examining contemporary culture in Western societies, both Lyotard and Baudrillard are dissatisfied with the cultural life they observe. Lyotard (1984: 76) expresses irritation with what he refers to as the 'eclecticism' of contemporary popular culture. The eating of 'McDonald's food for lunch and local cuisine for dinner', the wearing of 'Paris perfume' and 'retro clothes', the acquisition of knowledge about 'TV games' are hallmarks of what Lyotard dismisses as the 'kitsch' of popular culture. Although Lyotard criticises the 'academicism' of aesthetic distinctions of high and low culture, he is troubled that commercialised popular culture has no 'aesthetic criteria' existing beyond the capitalist marketplace. He betrays a 'mass culture' phobia somewhat reminiscent of criticisms discussed in other chapters, and he holds, at the very least, an anti-populist view of popular culture (Hebdige 1988: 184). John Docker (1994: 111) argues that Lyotard's dismissal of popular culture is authoritarian and puritanical and that his mode of criticism is indicative of a lingering modernist temperament. Docker (1994: 105) characterises Baudrillard in similar terms. In describing how the simulacrum comes to replace the real in contemporary culture, Baudrillard offers a 'classic modernist narrative', presenting a linear history of mass communication. Ultimately, we are not that far from a 'mass culture' interpretation of the audience, and as Swingewood (1998: 171) claims, for Baudrillard, so-called postmodern culture is a 'culture of passivity'. Seemingly, with Lyotard and Baudrillard in mind, Paul Willis (1990: 26–7) refers to 'postmodernist pessimism' obfuscating the creative possibilities of popular culture. For Willis (1990: 139) postmodernism declares 'defunct ... those modernizing forces' that popular culture has given life to.

But need a postmodernist account of popular culture presage doom and gloom? Some theorists offer a completely contrasting vision of contemporary culture viewed through a postmodernist lens. For example, Iain Chambers (1986) discusses the validation given to popular culture by the creative uses of people as evidence of the existence of postmodernism, with the resultant flattening of distinctions between high and low culture. Another well known Cultural Studies academic to offer an optimistic take on postmodernism is Dick Hebdige. In his 1988 book *Hiding in the Light*, Hebdige presents a collection of essays, a number of which rely on a postmodernist interpretation of the production, representation and popular use of a variety of cultural artefacts. In one example, Hebdige studies the 1950s 'pop art' of the London based Independent Group, taking a particular interest in their fascination with the iconography of post-war American popular culture. Hebdige regards the aestheticisation of readily accessible and disposable items of culture as an important early example of a postmodern sensibility (see the following Connections section for a related discussion). Hebdige (1988: 74) refers favourably to a similar usage of items of American popular culture in everyday consumption. Contrary to the anti-American tradition in British cultural commentary, Hebdige sees American popular culture adding richness and possibility to cultural life. Hebdige imagines British youth in their use of American popular culture as postmodern bricoleurs who 'assemble and re-assemble' symbols and items of culture into a dizzying array of self-constructed semiotic combinations. Hebdige also applies a postmodern interpretation to a number of British popular culture texts, including Biff cartoons and style and design magazine *The Face*. By blurring the boundaries between popular music, fashion, politics and cultural commentary, *The Face*, for Hebdige (1988: 156), is most relevant to youth living in a 'postmodern world'.

The Americanisation of culture issue is taken up later in the chapter when we consider the impact of globalisation on sport. For now the point to recognise is that postmodernism is used as a frame of cultural analysis by both pessimistic and optimistic observers of contemporary popular culture. Within the cultural study of sport we can find examples of both, which we will now view in turn. From a pessimistic perspective Harriss (1990) identifies a number of changes within the sport of cricket as being indicative of the intrusion of postmodernism. Harriss refers mainly to rule and format changes introduced to speed cricket up, to make what is undoubtedly a rather arcane game accessible to a broader audience on television. Many of the changes occurred in tandem with and following the promotion of the one-day cricket match, a variant of cricket that was popularised following the formation in 1977 of World Series Cricket, a breakaway tournament of leading international cricketers bankrolled by the Australian media mogul Kerry Packer. The subsequent tailoring of the sport to suit a mediated package was decried by traditionalists as a sell-out to commercial interests, but came as little surprise to cultural observers aware of the 'corrosive sea mist' (Jenks 1993: 136) of postmodernism. Thus Harriss (1990: 118) contends that cricket became 'a postmodern, decentred spectacle that emphasises a glossy surface without depth'. He likens this to other developments in television production and programming, with cricket blurring into a pastiche of melodrama and soap opera. From this perspective not only is the distinction between high and popular culture broken down but also the genres of popular culture are blended and imbricated by the television camera.

The changes brought to cricket are a matter of debate and Cashman (1995a) has actually argued that the conventional form of cricket has benefited from the shake-up following World Series Cricket. However, contention notwithstanding, even if we accept that cricket has been trivialised through the media process, this does not necessarily mean that we must explain its plight with reference to postmodernism. Indeed, Harriss's critique suggests that he and other like-minded watchers of cricket demand something more than the flashy excess and gimmickry that he believes cricket has been reduced to. In essence, what is being lost for Harriss is realism, and his complaint in this regard suggests a different form of viewer to the one conjured by Baudrillard's postmodern pessimism. Of all audiences of mediated popular culture the sport audience remains the most demanding of realistic representation. Sport may have its melodramatic elements, but of ultimate interest to the sports viewer is the reliable representation of what is going on in a genuine contest between participants. This is, after all, the difference between 'real' sports and pseudo-sports such as professional wrestling – the ultimate soap opera. Some of the major changes brought to games such as cricket are entirely concerned with a rationalist quest for realistic representation and getting a true result from refereeing decisions. Video camera umpiring based on the viewing of several replays of an incident may upset traditionalists because it interferes with the natural rhythm of the match as a reflection of life's uncertainties and unfairness, but this is in keeping with a humanistic understanding of sporting culture rather than one based in postmodernism.

Authenticity and post-fandom

The desire for realism within culture hinges on a belief in authenticity, a term of some contestability within contemporary Cultural Studies. Authenticity implies purity and immaculate origins (Barker 2000: 381), and is an ideal familiar to conventional aesthetics. However, within popular culture the commercial commodity nature of the artistic product makes considerations of authenticity problematic. In an interesting discussion of country music, Richard Peterson (1997) argues that even performers usually associated with the genre's grassroots traditions styled themselves as cowboys or hillbillies with a view to audience appeal. He thus speaks of the 'fabrication of authenticity' within country music. One of the best known discussions of authenticity, emerging from leisure studies, is Dean MacCannell's work on tourism. Writing prior to the postmodernist boom within social science and humanities academe, MacCannell (1976) identified a trend within the contemporary tourist industry that he referred to as 'staged authenticity'. MacCannell was concerned that commercial tourist sites ostensibly based in heritage were little more than a rip-off designed to exploit the alienated suburbanite in search of a genuine leisure experience. From a functionalist sociology perspective this is a worrying cultural development because the person already alienated through work and the routine of everyday life is likely to become more socially alienated as they are unable to find authenticity through leisure. However, from an optimistic postmodernist interpretation this concern is ill founded, all aspects of contemporary cultural life are inauthentic and the important thing is to gain an awareness of this and to play ironically with the inauthenticity of various cultural offerings.

Grossberg (1988: 41) has provided a related theoretical explanation with reference to the seemingly self-negating term, 'authentic inauthenticity'. He believes that an awareness of the inauthentic nature of culture is at the heart of a 'popular sensibility' that allows people to revel in their engagements with popular culture without expecting too much from it. Importantly, Grossberg (1988: 43) refuses to privilege any categories of cultural consumers in relation to this sensibility. 'There are no hidden truths within authentic inauthenticity' according to Grossberg, and it should, therefore, be an awareness available to all. However, Grossberg's democratic intentions have not been sustained in some related celebratory accounts of postmodern consumers. We can see this in regard to sport with the creation of the post-fan in the writings of Giulianotti (1999) and Redhead (1997) on British soccer supporters. The idea of the post-fan is an adaptation from John Urry's (1990) discussion of the post-tourist. The post-tourist is a shrewd contemporary cultural consumer who enjoys a variety of tourist experiences in the knowledge of their superficiality. Freed from a search for truth in his/her travels the post-tourist is able to enjoy tourism without modernist cultural anxieties (Urry 1990: 100). The post-tourist sees through the illusion of cultural barriers and is able to experience the museum and the theme park on an equal footing of cultural evaluation. The artificiality of all tourist sites is recognised by the post-tourist as they look beyond the conventional 'tourist gaze'.

The post-fan possesses a similar clarity of vision. For Redhead (1997: 29) the post-fan is a self-conscious, reflexive, artistic and style surfing popular culture polymath with interconnected interests in soccer, music and fashion. The post-fan approaches fandom with irony, knowing it is 'just a game' (Redhead 1997: 30), assumedly unlike other fans that take the supporting experience with complete seriousness. The post-fan is attuned to the mediated nature of contemporary football and is not obsessed with live attendance at football stadiums. Indeed, the post-fan makes the most of the satellite television intrusion into football broadcasting and avoids the inconvenience of inter-city travel to watch the favoured team. According to Redhead (1997: 29), 'the post-fan – does not have to leave the home or the bar to see the object of the gaze because television and video provide endless opportunity for 'grazing' and 'channel surfing'. Giulianotti (1999: 148) agrees that the post-fan has become past master in the consumption of contemporary media. Post-fans are able to deconstruct moralistic media portrayals of football fan identities, particularly the re-stereotyping of the hooligan menace. Post-fans maintain a reflexive distance from the clubs they support, are ironic in their idolisation of players and critical of the decision making of soccer authorities. They sometimes find voice in alternative media and have been responsible for the proliferation of fanzine culture. For Giulianotti (1999: 148) post-fans reflect the breakdown of the traditional class structure in the leisure domain. Post-fans are likely to be tertiary educated and employed in 'knowledge industries'. They eschew bourgeois cultural elitism while bringing middle class discernment to their engagement with popular culture. Post-fandom is the epitome of active cultural consumption (Giulianotti 1999: 148).

While we agree that new dimensions of fan culture have taken place in response to the changes in mediated sport we want to question whether this is best described as post-fandom or in terms of post *per se*. The entire assumption about the post-fan, or the post-tourist, possessing a reflexive knowledge about the inauthentic nature of organised and commercial leisure suggests that there is a truth to be ascertained about leisure experiences. The reinstatement of a knowing subject potentially contradicts the challenge that postmodernism seeks to pose to modernist theory. From the depiction of post-fans as reflexive, self-conscious social actors we might, indeed, be more inclined to think of them in relation to modernism. We are reminded of the *flaneur* discussed by the modernist cultural analyst Walter Benjamin (1892–1940), a detached and anonymous character who strolls the streets of the modern city all the while subjecting it to an inquisitive gaze (Benjamin 1973). The *flaneur* remained indifferent to the changing modernist city much in the same way as the post-fan remains indifferent to the changes wrought to contemporary culture by postmodernist influences. Was the *flaneur* an earlier incarnation of the post-tourist (post-fan) and, if so, how could a postmodern sensibility exist prior to postmodern times and the cultural dynamics that are ascribed to the arrival of postmodernism? We are disinclined to answer this question because we do not accept that there is a distinctive break within the history of culture warranting such a radical form of cultural analysis as postmodernism. And by taking such a position on theory we are dubious about related terminological ascriptions such as post-fandom to describe contemporary forms of cultural engagement with sport and other types of popular culture.

Enter the neo-tribe

Nevertheless, we remain open to discussion about renewed forms of cultural identity exhibited through sport fandom, and particularly in the social relations of culture that accrue around such formations. This involves examining collective modes of fandom, looking at how fan groups are constituted, at their points of gathering and at the ontological nature of their constitution. Although wary of postmodern epithets we are attracted to Maffesoli's notion of the neo-tribe to consider collective sport fan identity. We find the notion of neo-tribe more fruitful than Bauman's (1992: 198–9) related notion of the post-tribe because the former notion lends more possibility to sociological considerations with regard to class, gender and ethnicity. Maffesoli (1996) believes that within contemporary societies the basis of cultural identity has shifted from rational to emotional commitment. To explain how this works collectively, Maffesoli (1996: 12) retrieves Weber's term the 'emotional community'. The neo-tribe is depicted by Maffesoli as a contemporary form of sociality based in informal associations of cultural expression reflecting free choice, affectual commitment and transient membership. However, as Hetherington (1998: 53) notes, the sentiments and shared experiences of neo-tribal members are often derived from deep social affiliations such as class and, therefore, the emphasis on choice must be measured against the continuing importance of structural factors in collective cultural identity – another warning against the overly optimistic tendency within postmodernist theory for individual choice and action. However, by discussing cultural groupings in terms of neo-tribes we are able to consider the ritualistic dimensions of the cultural life of the group in relation to matters of social structure. For example, by looking at how class is manifested into cultural expression and lived out in contemporary collective metropolitan guises.

The notion of neo-tribe provides a means of looking at class, not in a static and deterministic sense, but in a dynamic way, from a view of how people make sense of class through expressions of cultural identity. Both Armstrong (1998) and Giulianotti (1996) take such an approach in their ethnographic studies of soccer hooligan subcultures. While both authors point out that football hooligan culture cannot simplistically be attributed to lower working class men, they show how the culture reflects changes in the urban class structure and provides young men with a relevant – if anti-social – means of ritualistic engagement with other men of similar cultural ilk. Armstrong (1998: 306) refers to the temporary nature of the parochial football supporter neo-tribe, maintaining that commitment and membership are dependent on the longevity of cultural attraction. Age and related responsibility could be one factor to draw an individual away from the neo-tribal milieu. Neo-tribes will vary considerably in terms of patterns of gathering, and sport neo-tribes offer examples of these differences. If we consider web-based supporter groups as neo-tribes then the supporter space is predominantly a virtual one, but a lived and occupied space nonetheless. In Armstrong and Giulianotti's studies, neo-tribal activities were mainly carried out in physical spaces that served as performance sites. Most obviously, the football ground provided a key gathering point, but once policing measures made it difficult for the routine conduct of neo-tribal rituals – confrontation with other fan groups – other spaces such as pubs on city outskirts became key sites to which the conduct of neo-tribalism shifted. As well as occupying key sites in a physical way, neo-tribes evince a metaphorical occupancy through the development of a 'critical spatial awareness' (Hughson 1999: 15) via which they find room for the construction of a collective cultural identity.

As indicated above we prefer not to describe the neo-tribe as a post-tribe, and would contend that the very reference to tribalism suggests a state of collective being more pre-modern than postmodern. The ongoing collective expression of emotion was anticipated in the sociology of Durkheim, who realised that the rationalist approach to social order, that would increasingly come to bear in industrial society, could not satisfy all dimensions of the human spirit. We do not accept that the move into an advanced stage of industrial society has been accompanied by a collapse of rationalism. Indeed, rationalism in the workplace has become so intensified in a number of contemporary work domains – including those often referred to as post-industrial – that emotion has been squeezed out altogether. Not surprisingly, people seek emotional outlet through experiences of leisure and culture. Sport is particularly important in this regard because it provides not only situations given over to high emotion, but also attachments to tradition through the support of teams on a perceived basis of personal history; for example, the team from my neighbourhood, or the team from my country. However, as work has become more rationalised so too has leisure, and this is especially the case with sport as the corporate ethos extends from the boardroom onto the sports field. Accordingly, sport is a domain of social control as the organisations that run sport impose discipline on the professional sportspeople who are essentially their employees and also the spectators within sports stadiums. Increasingly, the terms of spectatorship are dictated to people who pay considerable amounts of money to watch live sports events. Some of the control measures are justifiably couched in terms of safety, such as all-seated accommodation within British football grounds. But other measures, in a number of sports, restricting the ways in which people can support their teams (for example the prohibition of home made banners from Australian soccer matches) have as much to do with rationalising sport fandom as they do with public safety. John Clarke's prediction, noted in Chapter Two, regarding the imposition of 'disinfected commitment' and 'contained partisan-ship' on British soccer supporters has broad relevance within the rationalised stadia of a number of contemporary sports in Western societies.

Neo-tribalism offers a means of considering collective modes of resistance against the rationalisation of sport. Hughson (1999; 2002), drawing on Hetherington's (1998) interpretation of Maffesoli, has referred to 'expressive fans' who defy the dictates of sports officialdom with regard to behaviour in the stadium and also the general attempt to prescribe appropriate fan identities. Hughson's study focuses on soccer supporters in Australia, a case specific context that is highly politicised due to attempts by Australian soccer officialdom to sever the nexus between soccer clubs and migrant communities, and to ban the display of allegedly nationalistic paraphernalia and symbolism from soccer grounds. In this example groups of young fans that attempt to subvert authority by continuing to display 'ethnic' insignia are at the same time refusing to relinquish their sovereignty as supporters. They maintain within their soccer support *the expression of identity*. This characterisation of fans is not exclusive to extremely parochial contexts of the kind studied by Hughson. Fans refusing to purchase official merchandise or partake in forms of supporter conduct that they deem to be handed down from above may be described as expressive fans. Expressive fandom can be an individualistic matter and need not be conducted in the context of a neo-tribe. The categorisation of expressive fans suggests a binary opposition and, accordingly, Hughson (1999; 2002) has referred to 'submissive fans'. Submissive fans are inclined to go along with whatever is asked of them by sporting authority. This is not to suggest that they do not enjoy their sport supporting experiences, but that such experiences do not involve practices indicative of social resistance. In this way their fandom does not express an identity of their own making but offers affirmation of the sporting culture encouraged by sport officialdom.

There is a danger, however, that such binary characterisations confer privilege on one group over the other. To distinguish between expressive and submissive fans risks reintroducing the distinction between the active and the passive audience. A similar implication lurks behind categorisations of the post-fan, although the post-fan's chief profilers, Redhead and Giulianotti, avoid explicit construction of a binary opposite. They nevertheless privilege the post-fan over an assumed category of other fans, those fans that do not have the pop cultural savvy of the post-fan. Redhead's hedonistic post-fan who is able to enjoy watching a soccer match on Sky television as much as being at the ground is distinguished from supporters who resent the shift away from live attendance that the proliferation of satellite broadcasting of football portends. The implication is that these latter fans are stuck in their ways and unable to embrace the possibilities of mediated culture in the way that the post-fan is able to. Giulianotti concentrates more on the cynical character of post-fandom: the post-fan constantly deprecates and remains aloof from the official culture of soccer. However, those soccer supporters who are not post-fans remain within the realm of conventional fandom and are implicitly attributed an inferior cultural status for their lack of critical engagement and reflexivity. Post-fandom as discussed by Redhead and Giulianotti does little to encourage faith in the postmodern 'popular sensibility' promised by Grossberg. Although anti-institutional and anti-authority the post-fan is nevertheless an elitist within the realm of popular culture, elevated by the cultural analyst to a position of cultural superiority. Furthermore, there seems to be an epistemological inconsistency within the category of post-fandom itself. Postmodernist theory disputes the notion of progress, but the idea of the post-fan hinges on an implicit understanding that the post-fan has progressed to a stage beyond conventional fandom. Criticism of elitism notwithstanding, we accept that critical and alternative forms of sport fandom have emerged in recent years but, again, we question whether these forms are best explained in terms of post-fandom.

Postmodernity or late capitalism: accounting for sport in the global age

The core of our criticism comes back to a debate with postmodernist theory, not only to the description of contemporary life and related social and cultural practices as postmodern, but also to the very reference to contemporary times as postmodernity. We are more attracted to positions that recognise the inexorable penetration of culture into the realms of economy, industry and politics but stop short of declaring epochal change. From a Marxist perspective Frederic Jameson (1992) claims that society has moved into a multinational or consumerist phase of capitalism, best described as 'late capitalism', but not a new epoch of postmodernity. The cultural industries continue to operate within a capitalist economy, on an increasingly global scale. Jameson accepts that culture has become postmodern, but within the societal frame of capitalism. A related non-Marxist riposte to the idea of post-modernity has been proffered by Anthony Giddens (1990). Giddens sees contemporary Western societies in a condition of 'late', 'high' or 'radicalised' modernity, as opposed to postmodernity. Late modernity particularly features transformations of time and space, and individuals experience a sense of immediate global connection through mediated technologies and also – for some – the possibilities of frequent international travel. The sense of place becomes confused as the local is impacted upon significantly by the global. However, 'detraditionalisation' does not bring the disintegration of the local, and the intrusion of global culture is invariably unraveled and made sense of in local contexts. Although such conditions can increase feelings of unease and dislocation, they are also potentially empowering, as they provide individuals with the possibility to reflect upon and question what is occurring in their cultural world. It is this reflexive possibility that Redhead and Giulianotti recognise in the cultural awareness of post-fans. Less cliquishly – but also betraying a postmodern optimism to which we recommend wariness – Rowe and Lawrence (1998: 162) announce the arrival of the 'global' sports citizen, who retrieves from the sports spectacle 'new meanings and identities in information flows, media images, communication networks, cultural forms and aesthetics'. However, Rowe's own discussion of the political and economic aspects of media sport, as adumbrated in the previous chapter, alerts us to the limited possibilities of global sports citizenship. Rowe (2003) has also recently argued that the notion of globalisation is incapable of accounting for the heightened sentiments of national and regional identity that not only linger but also become reconstituted within sport supporting cultures.

106

A theme related to globalisation is Americanisation; indeed, it might simplistically be presumed that globalisation is tantamount to Americanisation. As discussed in previous chapters the Americanisation of culture has been particularly feared in Britain, a fear voiced over the years in both popular and intellectual discourse. Hebdige (1988: 73–4) argues that predictions of creeping cultural homogenisation have proved wrong. Although American popular culture has been highly influential in Britain, it has invariably been drawn upon in imaginative ways and blended into homegrown cultural forms. This is certainly the case with youth culture and music, but sport provides something of a different example, as sport cannot be hybridised in the manner of music. Nevertheless sports steeped in local tradition are not impervious to American cultural influences. Giulianotti (1999: 143) notes that the rules of soccer, pertaining to throw-ins, back passing and other aspects of play, have been altered to speed the game up in keeping with the American epithet that a fast game is a good game. Importantly, however, this change is indicative of an intrusion of Taylorist time and motion principles into sport, a rationalistic and, therefore, modernist rather than postmodernist intrusion. However, Andrew Blake suggests that the intrusion has been minimal not only in terms of Americanisation impacting on established sports, but also in terms of the ability of American sports to penetrate sporting cultures beyond North American boundaries. Admittedly, some American sports have been absorbed into foreign cultural landscapes, for example baseball in Japan. However, Blake (1996: 110) contends that American sports such as gridiron football, baseball and even basketball have remained on the 'the fringes of popularity' on an international scale. American sport has tended to push inwards not outwards as exemplified by the heralding of its national baseball play-offs as the World Series.

Australia provides an interesting national context to examine in regard to Americanisation. In his famous ironically titled book, *The Lucky Country* (1964), Donald Horne refers to Australia as a vassal state that, following the Second World War, has become subservient to the United States as it once was to Great Britain. The subservience is manifested in politics and economics and also reflected in culture. In the cultural realm the fear is that having, to some extent, overcome the 'cultural cringe' towards Britain, Australian culture has been given over to the same American influences derided by English critics (Bennett *et al.* 1999: 203–4). Richard White (1980: 284–5) has noted a tradeoff between politics and culture, whereby promise of military support during the 'cold war' meant a welcoming, albeit begrudgingly, of America culturally. However, White (1983: 108) maintains that such tacit agreement does not portend cultural imperialism. Americanisation is experienced by 'no two cultures ... in quite the same way'. Australians might experience American popular culture in its 'purest form', in that we do not have 'a rich cultural tradition of [our] own' (White 1983: 109), but American culture is, nevertheless, adapted by Australian people to have relevance to the local cultural setting.

This is certainly the case with sport, as sport more than other forms of popular culture has established a strong historical footing in Australia which is not easily displaced. As Cashman (1995b: 162) argues, even if Australian sport becomes more American in tandem with globalisation 'it is unlikely that the Australian sporting map will ever be the same as the American'. In Australia, American sports and affectations of American sporting culture become '[local] variants of global sports' rather than a transposed cultural form in its own right. Therefore, even if American sport and sporting culture increases in popularity, these forms of sport and sporting influences will be reconfigured through the cultural uses to which Australians put them. As observed by McKay *et al.* (1996: 216–17), 'Australians from Broome to Cooktown wear T-shirts displaying images of American teams' such as the Chicago Bulls, and related stylistic practices, such as the 'wearing of baseball caps, the selling of sports trading cards and the adoption of American names for Australian teams', have become 'pronounced'. But this does not mean that American sporting culture has been passively incorporated into Australian sporting culture, or local traditions sold out. After all, the notion of a homogeneous Australian sporting culture is a mythology, and so are notions of national sporting cultures in general. Sporting cultures can be so fragmented – for example, different codes of football predominating in different states or regions – that it makes more sense to address the aspects and features of sporting culture within nations than to speak of holistic national sporting cultures. From this starting point more sober assessment can be made of the impact of globalisation on national and local sporting contexts.

From post-fans to post-heroes

David Andrews *et al.* (1996) refer to two camps of globalisation interlocutors, one being the homogenisers, the other the heterogenisers. From the discussion above we can understand this dichotomy and the attribution of pessimism to the former camp and optimism to the latter. These two camps may be matched to the respective camps of pessimistic and optimistic postmodernists. However, a cultural analyst may also take either position on globalisation – and, in themselves, they are not mutually exclusive – without any adherence to postmodernism. We are likely, however, to find optimistic interpretations of globalisation being explained in postmodernist terms. Accordingly, the post-fan is also a global sports citizen. The globalisation of sport has assumedly also impacted on the way we perceive prominent sports people or sports stars. In Chapter Two we looked briefly at Hoggart's comments on the sports hero, which reflected a view common in cultural commentary at the time of the moral purpose of the sportsperson, exemplifying the heroic possibilities of life to his/her adoring audience. Even though Hoggart may have been referring to sportspeople of national fame, there is something quaintly local about the reverence in his attribution. In a global sports world heroes appeal to a wider audience and possibly serve an even higher, albeit secular, purpose. But in being asked to be many things to many people, the social and cultural role of the idolised sportsperson becomes blurred, and postmodernism has been offered as theoretical deliverance from confusion. Indeed, through the postmodernist lens the sportsperson may be seen in montage as star, hero, villain, celebrity, icon and deviant all at once.

In his 1961 book *The Image* Daniel Boorstin witnessed a cultural shift from hero to celebrity. Boorstin (1961: 48) suggests that celebrities are manufactured while heroes are natural: 'We can make a celebrity but we can never make a hero.' For postmodernists this distinction is passé. Cultural consumers can make what they please from the iconography of popular culture, including sport. Again in reference to soccer, but with general implication, Giulianotti (1999) proposes a typological extension (cf. Critcher 1979) to accommodate sport stardom to contemporary times. He sets out, in historical trajectory, three analytical categories: (1) the traditional 'working class hero'; (2) the modern professional sportsperson who becomes a celebrity; and (3) the postmodern sports star. In a subsequent paper Giulianotti and Gerrard (2001) discuss the England international soccer player Paul Gascoigne in relation to this third category. The paper is in two halves, the first presenting a waggish account of Gascoigne's exploits on and off the field as portrayed by the media. We are left with an undeniable image of Gascoigne as a brilliant footballer and artiste – as recognised by no less than Germaine Greer – but also as a high profile deviant from the standpoint of conventional judgement. The second part of the paper exposes Gascoigne to a postmodernist assessment and in the process frees him from the moralistic gaze to which he might otherwise be subjected. We are prompted to accept with irony and glee the incoherence of Gascoigne's divided self. The shifting dimensions of his identity: 'alcoholic, philanthropist, jet-setter, local boy, wife-beater, sex object, athlete, slob, offender, victim' (Giulianotti and Gerrard 2001) are but 'discontinuous discourses' (Andrews and Jackson 2001: 13) that heighten the appeal of the elusive rogue that is Gascoigne. According to Giulianotti and Gerrard (2001: 134), Gascoigne finds ultimate rapport with the 'masses' that, in Baudrillardian style, embrace him because they unwittingly make sense of and warm to the mediated meaninglessness of his persona. Gascoigne as post-hero is a resource for post-fandom: fan and hero united in playful enterprise.

The main attraction of the postmodernist position on sports stars is that it does afford critical reflection upon the popular tendency, spawned by media editorialising, to moralise about their lives. This is increasingly the case as sports stars are simultaneously sucked into the vacuum of celebrity while being reminded that they are role models for youth, and are thus burdened with a presumed greater moral obligation than that pertaining to music and soap opera stars. However, we do not propose a retreat from moral judgement altogether, and reject postmodernism because of its intrinsic amorality. Sports stars should be held to some moral account, particularly with regard to behaviour directly related to their sporting persona. Sport rules, modes of conduct and convention are underpinned by notions of morality, and without this sport would simply not function in an organisational context. The public life of sport hinges on morality and sports stars subscribe to a moral game by their very participation in sport. Moral interpretations and evaluations are, of course, contestable, but without morality we have no grounds for decision making about such matters as the use of drugs in sport or about how to punish violent conduct on the sports field. Morality not only underpins the rules of the game but also attunes the conduct of sport to wider social mores and expectations. In a celebrated case in Australian rugby league in the late 1990s, prominent Aboriginal player Anthony Mundine accused a rival player of racial vilification and put in train a set of proceedings that led to the establishment of legislation within the sport outlawing this type of conduct. Mundine's protest was based on a widely shared assumption that racism is morally unacceptable on the sports field as in other areas of life. The problem with postmodernism is that by evacuating a moral position it is unable to support the type of claim made by Mundine. And even more worryingly, by giving life to such categories as the post-hero it potentially provides refuge for the racist scoundrel in sport whose behaviour cannot be judged by any humanistic standards.

Sport and postmodern identity

A theme that remains to be discussed in conclusion is identity, a theme that has gained simultaneous prominence with postmodernism within sociology and Cultural Studies. Stuart Hall (1992: 276–7) points to three conceptual versions of identity that have emerged over time within social and cultural theory. First, identity may be related to the self, explored through psychoanalysis and interpretative sociology. Second, identity has been considered in a more pure sociological sense as the outcome of the connection between individual subjectivity and social structure. The related agency structure debate, which remains at the heart of contemporary sociology, is largely a debate about identity. Although different positions and emphases arise from the debate, depending on the theoretical leaning of the interlocutors, the notion of identity at issue is a stable one, identity is perceived as being constructed via an ongoing process of reciprocation between the individual and the social forces they encounter. Contrasting with the sociological notion of identity is postmodern identity, a view of identity severed from notions of social structure. For Hall (1992: 277) postmodern identity is a decidedly cultural identity composed of a multiplicity of cultural images, icons, and influences on which an individual draws. Postmodern identities tend to be contradictory and unresolved, complimenting the postmodernist understanding of the unfinished human subject. To the modernist mind this depiction of a 'fragmented' identity could seem schizophrenic, but from an optimistic postmodernist outlook it is life affirming for the contemporary individual. Hall (1992: 277) likens the postmodern identity to a cultural smorgasbord; it is a veritable 'moving feast' from which individuals can construct identities at their choosing.

In conclusion we want to consider the implications of the postmodern notion of identity in relation to sport, specifically with regard to the expression of race and ethnic identity through sport. When race and ethnicity are discussed in relation to postmodern identity the term hybridity usually arises. A hybrid identity is a loose construction of mixed 'cultural elements' put together in a strategic manner by individuals to create new and unexpected meanings (Barker 2000: 385). A number of studies have looked at how young people from non-host country ethnic backgrounds draw on aspects from both their parent culture and the host country culture to create collective identities that are relevant to their own perceptions of their cultural world (for an example see Dwyer's (1998) study of young Asian women in London). This was the basis of Hughson's (1997) study of young males in Australia of Croatian background who used their supporting of the Sydney United (formerly Sydney Croatia) soccer team as a means of establishing a subcultural identity, through which they enmeshed a vigorously declared affinity to their parent culture with contemporary youth fashion and the stylistic trends in international soccer support. At the hub of this interpretation of identity is a shift from an essentialist to a non-essentialist understanding of ethnicity (Woodward 1997: 11). In the case of Hughson's study there is a denial of an essential Croatian identity in Australia. The young men were able to construct their own hybrid identity from the range of cultural insignia and practices that were familiar to them in their lives as the progeny of Croatians living in Australia. Given the prominence of soccer as a cultural form within 'a Croatian way of life', it was not surprising that the sport and its associated imagery became the key cultural element around which the young men's identity was based.

It seems to us important to retain a non-essentialist understanding of ethnicity (as opposed to humanity; see the Connections section of Chapter Six) if we are to guard against the worst forms of chauvinism for which sport all too often offers an arena of promulgation. Most problematic is the representation of nations in sporting teams, with soccer again providing some deplorable examples of what sport can achieve in the name of country. Of course, sport in the form of national teams gives opportunity for the display of multiculturalism – through the selection of players from different racial and ethnic backgrounds – in turn a tacit recognition of a non-essentialist notion of nation. Again, however, caution is advised, as Gilroy (1996) alerts, when multiculturalism becomes institutionalised it reclaims from ethnic groups the notion of 'solidarity' and dampens the politics of ethnicity. Sport is perhaps the cultural arena where this is most likely to occur, as the old saying 'sport and politics do not mix' still has considerable currency in public discourse. However, a number of sport followers and sports performers refuse to be denied the expression of race and ethnicity through sport. Continuing with Australian examples, the defiance from supporters – including the young men in Hughson's study – towards the 'de-ethnicising' of Australian soccer is a claim to rights within the multicultural arena that is sport. Olympic athletic champion Cathy Freeman running her victory lap with the Aboriginal flag and the Australian national flag back to back is as much a declaration of a non-essentialist national identity as it is one of hope for the prospects of Aboriginal and white Australian reconciliation (Bruce and Hallinan 2001). Finally, we would contend that these expressions of identity in sport are not best understood in terms of postmodern identity. Whilst they are dynamic they undoubtedly stem from cultural relations arising from the structure of society: relations of race and ethnicity. Rather than speaking of postmodern identity we propose a return to the sociological identity in Hall's typology to explain the basis of the identity construction that occurs within and through the cultural arena of sport. Postmodernism acknowledges an interest in the superficial; if we are really to understand cultural identities we need to be concerned with revealing their foundations. In the next chapter we proceed to an examination of these foundations.

CONNECTIONS

Chapter Five concentrates on postmodernism as a theoretical orientation with a view to examining its adequacy as a means of explaining sport as a cultural phenomenon within contemporary society. We are clearly critical of postmodernism as a form of cultural and social theory but will not rehearse our criticisms in this Connections section. Here we want to look at postmodernism as an aesthetic temperament or orientation, or, put more simply, postmodernism as a form of or movement in art. From here we consider the relevance of this understanding of postmodernism to sport, and engage critically with academic positions linking sport to art.

We begin with a quotation from the English art critic and broadcaster Matthew Collings on what he refers to as the 'visual level' of postmodernism:

> Postmodernism is when modernism is no longer seen as a move-ment toward a refinement down to nothing, which is what it had seemed by the time it got to minimalism. With postmodernism, modernism is seen as just a lot of styles. None of them more important than any other. Not even cubism. So you could use any one you like, or mix them up.
>
> (Collings 1998: 170)

Collings, obviously enough, is writing for a general readership and he provides an elementary and useful distinction between modernist and

---

postmodernist movements in art. Collings's orientation is correctly historical; he suggests that postmodernism arrives as a logical consequence of
modernism at a point when modernism has exhausted its aesthetic possibilities. Wheale (1995: 43) claims that postmodernism works with a 'radical
eclecticism', challenging modernism's continuing attachment to the representation of meaning: meaning challenged and reinterpreted within the
various movements that make up modernism. Postmodernism is not so
much concerned with challenging conventional notions of representation
and meaning but rather with denying the possibility of meaning and representation altogether.

A commonly assumed key difference between modernist and postmodernist art is that while modernism remains elitist, postmodernism explicitly
seeks abolition of distinctions between high and low culture. Upon closer
inspection it is more the case that postmodernist artists draw from popular
culture for their art, rather than wanting to collapse art into popular culture.
The aesthetic debate can be traced to modernist art criticism. Writing in
the 1930s, the leading American art critic Clement Greenberg (1986
[1939]) distinguished between the 'avant-garde and kitsch'. By the avant-
garde he had in mind work within modernist art that had developed since
the First World War. By kitsch – derived from the German word for wasted
energy – Greenberg had in mind the mass produced art forms that had
mushroomed within popular culture: artwork associated with magazine
covers, movie posters, comics and advertisements. For Greenberg, although
aesthetically distinct from and vastly inferior to what he regarded as 'true'
art, these forms steal devices and ideas from avant-garde art and in so doing
risk sullying the inherent value of the latter (Inglis and Hughson 2003:
69–70). The 'pop art' that emerged as an identifiable movement in the early
1960s rejected the elitism of modernist art criticism and willfully incorporated the commercial artwork of popular culture into traditional art forms
such as painting and sculpture. Pop art is thus often equated with the arrival
of a postmodernist attitude to art, key figures include Andy Warhol and
Roy Lichtenstein in the USA and Richard Hamilton and Eduardo Paolozzi
in Britain. The intention of these artists was not necessarily to shock with
their usage of examples from commercial art and advertising but stemmed
'from an urge to exploit the formal [i.e. aesthetic] potential of brash
commercial graphics' (Read 1974 [1968]: 298). Although these artists are
interested in the objects and imagery of popular culture, their incorporation
of it into their artwork does not necessarily indicate a cultural levelling out
or breakdown of distinctions between high and popular culture. The art
world might have been invaded by items and aspects of popular culture, but
this does not mean that the art objects of postmodernist art assume the
same cultural status as commodified items within popular culture as such.

From here we are wary of attempts to draw parallels between sport and
postmodernist art. These attempts are usually made with reference to the

aestheticisation of sporting culture. For example, Rail (1998: 147) contends 'that sporting images and commodities are constructed in such a way as to reproduce postmodern aesthetics and facilitate their hyper-consumption'. Redhead (1997) refers enthusiastically to sport (English soccer is his example) entering 'pop time', whereby it has embraced the imagery and iconography of popular music and is marketed in similar terms. In a previously published paper (Inglis and Hughson 2000) two of the present authors are critical of the 'before and after' assumption that underpins these positions. Intentionally, or otherwise, these positions suggest that sport becomes aestheticised once it is penetrated by or absorbed into postmodern culture. These positions tend to overlook that even before the arrival of postmodern cultural influences sport is endowed with its own aesthetics in forms of embodied movement. Theorists who refer to the aestheticisation of contemporary sport tend 'to focus on aspects *external* to the game, to the detriment of recognising the fundamentally aesthetic nature of the *internal* dynamics of the game itself' (Inglis and Hughson 2000: 282). We believe – in keeping with the position on sport and aesthetics advanced by C.L.R. James (see the Connections section following Chapter Four) – that the term 'aesthetic' should only be applied to the internal workings of the game itself, not the external characteristics of sport. Even if we accept that sport has become postmodern, this has more to do with the socio-cultural and historical organisation, administration and marketing of sport than it does with aesthetics *per se*. 'What is happening is not that [sport] is becoming aesthetic but that its component parts, including its aesthetic aspects, are being packaged' (Inglis and Hughson 2000: 294). Essentially, we are talking about processes of commodification rather than aestheticisation.

To refer to the aestheticisation of sport can also imply a positive interpretation of current trends, similar to the positive interpretations that are made of postmodern art within some art criticism. To do so in regard to sport potentially detracts from the critical interpretation that can be made if we retain sight of what we are referring to as the commodification of contemporary sport. Namely, criticism of the way in which sport has been commodified for the pecuniary gain of advertisers, media conglomerates and other vested interests within sports franchises. Finally, we would reiterate the difficulty of equating a postmodern sport with postmodern art. Postmodern art, or its antecedent pop art, brings the imagery of popular culture into the actual work of art in a way that sport does not. Postmodern art involves a deliberate plundering of popular culture imagery by artists themselves for the express purpose of artistic creation. Sportspeople have no such *artistic* engagement with popular culture and, therefore, for cultural theorists to speak of the 'implosion of sport and art' is confusing at best. Postmodern artists – irrespective of how we might judge their particular works – have developed an aesthetic movement within art that warrants a completely different analytical categorisation to what has been referred to as the postmodernisation or aestheticisation of contemporary sport. If we must speak of the postmodernising of sport let us at least keep the discussion within the realms of socio-cultural theory and a related political economy and avoid lapsing into spurious connections with art criticism and appreciation.

6

SPORT, POWER AND THE MATERIAL RELATIONS OF CULTURE

Our criticism of postmodernism in the previous chapter is based on the concern that postmodernism, as a social theory, does not allow for the adequate study of social relations in culture and other realms. Some sociologists, including Bauman (1992), have argued that we can have a sociology of postmodernism, if not a postmodernist sociology. This is basically to recognise that society has moved into a stage of postmodernity and that sociology, as an academic discipline, is equipped to explain what is going on in contemporary times. This position is not dissimilar to that of Giddens (1990), except for Bauman's willingness to embrace the term postmodernity as an epochal characterisation. Although we are more in agreement with Giddens than Bauman, of greater concern to us are positions that imply a retreat from sociology altogether. Central to the discipline of sociology is the idea of 'the social'. Postmodern theory strikes at the heart of sociology by reducing this idea of 'the social' to the status of myth. From a postmodernist theoretical perspective there is no basis for a claim to know 'the social', such a claim rests on an erroneous 'foundationalist' assumption of the kind found within modernist thought (Owen 1997: 10–11). Postmodernist theory proposes the deconstruction of the sociological project, an assignment that has been described in practical and provocative terms as 'undoing the social' (Game 1991). Ultimately, it becomes oxymoronic to speak of postmodernist social theory. As this is so, we believe it is necessary to rely on more traditional approaches to social theory – and sociology – as we believe that a meaningful discussion of the material existence of culture can only be grasped by an understanding of the social relations within which culture and cultural practices transpire. By extension we believe that the link between sociology and a socially informed Cultural Studies is undoable (Inglis and Hughson 2003).

Culture and materialism

In the current chapter we attempt a reconstruction of the social to analyse the material conditions in the culture of sport. As indicated at the conclusion of the previous chapter, particular cultures of sport established in the context of localised settings and the individual and collective identities that are developed in these contexts of sporting engagement – of participation and spectatorship – cannot be understood apart from the social circumstances from which they arise. This is not to understate the importance of culture. As noted previously in the book, academic Cultural Studies emerged at the intersection of sociology and literary studies and steadily developed a critique of the tendency within sociology to underscore the importance of culture. This related particularly to Marxist sociology that prioritised the economic base as the determinant of outcomes in other spheres, including culture. Our aim is to examine this tension in relation to sport. We do this by a consideration of the key sociological dimensions, class, gender, and race. Class, of course, is the key issue stemming from Marxist sociology and became the dominant theme within early Cultural Studies, the latter taking issue not only with the economic determinist account of class within Marxism, but also the non-Marxist characterisation of class within culturalist writing. The young scholars at the CCCS sought to negotiate a position on class that was at once cultural and indebted to Marxism. They did so via referral to continental theorists such as Althusser and Gramsci, the latter being generally regarded as the key figure in the generation of culturally focused Marxist theory. Gramsci, indeed, became influential on the mid-period writing of Raymond Williams, who described his own homage to Marx as 'cultural materialism'. As we will see, this aspect of Williams's work has had considerable influence on scholars within academic sport studies in their attempts to describe the cultural power relations within particular sports and sporting episodes, and it is from a particular reading of Williams's cultural materialism that we derive the sociology of culture position advanced in this chapter.

Although Williams was not known for discussing gender and race, we will argue here that his cultural materialist position has great relevance to understanding the cultural manifestations of gender and race in a social context. Within the history of Cultural Studies, gender and race were put onto the agenda as scholars at the CCCS became disgruntled with the white British male centredness of the research work and associated publications that predominated in this supposedly pluralistic hive of intellectual activity (CCCS Women's Studies Group 1978; CCCS 1982). This response produced some interesting work that not only challenged the prioritising of class but also the sociological tendency to reduce gender and race to markers of social inequality. An emphasis on the cultural importance of gender and race illuminated ways of seeing how women and people from racial and ethnic minority groupings experienced gender and race relations dynamically rather than statically. It provided a means of stepping beyond the image of victimhood – sometimes inadvertently promoted by conflict sociology – by matching concerns of inequality with those of identity. Sport offers a particularly interesting arena of cultural activity where identities of gender and race are eked out. We further this discussion as the chapter proceeds, and in so doing hope to extend the relevance of a cultural materialist position on culture from class to gender and race and ethnicity. In the process we intend to establish an appropriate balance between the concerns of sociology and Cultural Studies. To commence we want to look at sport from respective positions within conflict sociology to establish how sport can be seen to, rather starkly, reflect the power relations that stem from structural inequality along the fault lines of class, gender and race. In each case we look at the general position and then discuss positions within the sociology of sport.

By way of leading up to a discussion of cultural materialism we want to consider the notion of materialism within Marxist theory and then look at how the material conditions of existence are explained by structuralist positions within sociology on class, gender and race. Marx (1818–83), as social philosopher, developed his notion of materialism in direct contrast to that of Hegel (1770–1831), a prominent thinker in Marx's youth. Hegel favoured an idealist view of the world whereby human life was to be understood in the realm of ideas; ideas exist prior to the material existence of life. This results in Hegel elevating culture – the artistic outcome of ideas – to a position of primary importance, standing above the political and economic aspects of social life (Inglis and Hughson 2003: 20). Marx believed Hegel's position to be a social abstraction, removed from the 'material conditions' that come to bear on individuals as they actually live their lives. For Marx, culture did not stand above society, but was created within society and shaped by the prevailing social forces: such is the basis of historical materialism. The economy is the most determinant force and for Marx (1977 [1859]) provides the 'material base', the structure which supports all other aspects of society. This is particularly the case in a capitalist society, where the relations of production inexorably favour the owners of capital and the other realms of society, the state and civil society, constitute a superstructure that effectively works in the interests of the capitalist class and reinforces the economic relations at the base level. Again, material factors are primary, cultural factors secondary, with culture tending to reflect the social relations from which it arises. Marx spoke of culture carrying the dominant ideology of the capitalist class and providing an ideational means of keeping workers in their place by subjecting them to 'false consciousness'. This theme of ideology, as we shall observe, becomes increasingly important for subsequent Marxian influenced sociology.

Sport and structured inequalities

The key term used by Marx to explain how the class inequality of capitalism impacts on the personal being of members of the working class is 'alienation'. Workers become alienated within the workplace as they are reduced to commodities in the production process and, in turn, are alienated from the creative element in their work. Marx (1981 [1844]) suggests that alienation is

118

reproduced within the realm of culture, as artistic works become cultural commodities, not so different from the commodities produced within factories; artists become alienated from their art. A related form of alienation arises in sport as a field of cultural production, according to Marxist sociologists of sport such as Bero Rigauer and Jean-Marie Brohm. Rigauer (1981 [1969]: 68) claims that the athlete is alienated at the point when their sporting performance is transformed into a commodity. The commoditisation of sporting performance necessarily quantifies the performance in terms of an exchange value and this is alien to the intrinsic artistry of sport. For Rigauer, sport in capitalist society is reduced to work, it takes on the same relations as the workplace and the sportsperson, like the worker, is dehumanised in the production process of sport. Brohm (1978: 175) agrees, claiming that the institutionalisation of sport in Western society coincided with the development of the capitalist mode of production, and that the production relations of the latter were infused into sport. Brohm (1978: 23) believes that the sportsperson experiences bodily oppression through the physical demands that are placed on them in training and in sporting contests. The inhumanity of this situation is itself, for Brohm, a form of alienation. He claims that sport has been developed as a 'technology of the body' exhibiting the 'structural reproduction' of 'capitalist repressive techniques'; the division of labour, ultra-specialisation, repetition, measurement and stop-watch timing are all aspects associated with sport performance (Brohm 1978: 50). In a further consideration about alienation in sport, Beamish (1988) argues that despite the availability of large salaries for many professional athletes they remain precariously placed in their relationships with sports promoters and clubs. Promoters and owners and controllers of sports clubs maintain control not only over the contracts of athletes but also over their working conditions. As the effective employers of athletes they determine the length of competition seasons, how and where matches will be played, the time and length of training sessions and pre- and post-season training schedules. In some team sports players may be loaned to other teams for indefinite periods of time in circumstances contrary to their own choosing.

Before moving to consider the Marxist position on the ideology of sport we want to continue with the materialist and structural determinist theme in relation to gender and race with application to sport. In relation to gender we need to consider the claim of feminist scholarship that men have subjugated women within society, and that these relations of subjugation extend to all areas of social life. Particularly relevant is the term patriarchy, literally meaning rule by the father; in societal terms patriarchy is used to define the 'power relations by which men dominate women' (Hargreaves 1994: 31). These relations stem from the domestic sphere and penetrate the public sphere where various institutions take on the patriarchal relations of the family, the primary social institution for feminists. Gender rather than class is, thus, regarded as the defining social dimension of inequality. Importantly, there are a number of feminist positions that coincide with different theoretical and, more obviously, political orientations: liberal, socialist and radical feminisms have been the variants most often cited (Eisenstein 1984). With regard to the current chapter, radical feminism is the most relevant because it sees gender as the material base of social inequality. Whereas socialist feminism is at pains to work through the complexities of the relationship between class and gender (Barrett 1980), radical feminism is focused on the primary importance of gender. However, radical feminists have maintained a discursive interest in socialist theory, Marxism in particular. Most notably, in *The Dialectic of Sex* (1971), Shulamith Firestone transposed the language of gender onto Marx's (and Engel's) theoretical framework to propound the view that the 'division of labour [is] based on sex' and that 'biological classes' are in struggle over the relations of 'reproduction' (Firestone 1971: 12). Firestone agrees with Marx's attempt to find a material basis – and scientific explanation – for social equality, but believes that he was wrong to recognise class rather than gender as the key to understanding power relations. Where Marx argued that capitalist class relations must be completely overturned for social emancipation to be realised, radical feminists argue the case in regard to patriarchal gender relations. This has led to the call by some radical feminists for 'separatism', women creating their own society apart from men. Sport has been included in the vision of a separate society, where women would reclaim control of sport from men and create an environment for co-operative rather than competitive relations in sport (Hargreaves 1994: 29–31).

Race is the third dimension of social inequality often discussed within sociology. It is difficult to attribute structural discussions of race to particular branches or theoretical perspectives within sociology. Sociologists who identify the foundational importance of race to social structure cannot be defined as Marxists or feminists in the same way as those who write on class and gender. Sociologists who have concentrated on race have been variously related to major theoretical perspectives. For example, Lloyd Warner (1936) discussed race in relation to 'social class' from a conflict sociological position that drew upon stratification theory familiar to structural functionalist sociology. Warner argued that American society was divided into a range of social classes that allowed for upward and downward mobility, but that a 'caste barrier' existed between 'white society' and 'black society', essentially restricting the class mobility of 'blacks' to their own social sector. In an early Marxist position Oliver Cromwell Cox (1970 [1948]) argued that social inequality is directly tied to the relations of the labour market and that inequality is, therefore, necessarily a matter of class. However, he noted that black Americans were overwhelmingly positioned at the bottom end of the labour market and were disproportionately unemployed. Race relations are at once class relations, according to Cox. What Cox more or less does is to integrally insert race into the relations of labour and, hence, production. Importantly, from Cox's perspective, race is a sociological determinant that impacts on the class structure differently across capitalist societies. Race is a key explanatory factor for why American capitalist society is different to others, although various studies have drawn on Cox's influence to show how race and ethnicity structurally intersect class (for example, Collins's (1991) study of labour market inequalities in Australia). Sport stands in interesting relationship to considerations about race and work and inequality. In American society sport has historically evinced the race barrier identified by Warner. As Coakley (2001: 258) notes, prior to the 1950s black Americans were excluded from white organised sporting competitions and set up their own leagues. The monumental changes that have occurred over the last few decades have meant that black Americans are proportionally over-represented in a number of professional sports, giving the false impression that sport is an arena that operates contrarily to the wider labour market. However, despite impressions, the labour market of sport is structured by race to some extent, as the limited number of sports in which black people predominate would indicate. The assumed good prospect for black Americans in sport obscures the materiality of race as a determinant of life outcomes. Ignorance about the material conditions of race in sport militates against awareness of the more general condition of race inequality. This leads us into considerations about ideology and the obfuscation of inequalities and the perpetuity of dominant power relations. Accordingly, the next part of the chapter turns to consider the ideological bases of class, gender and race and relevant discussions about sport.

Sport, ideology and culture

By the time Cultural Studies had established an institutional foothold at the University of Birmingham in the 1970s, Marxism was well established as the dominant intellectual paradigm within sociology and related disciplines in Britain. It was hardly surprising, then, that the cohort of young scholars working at the CCCS favoured a Marxist approach to the analysis of culture. However, the theoretical prioritising of economics in classical Marxism was seen as too deterministic and reductionist by scholars interested in the study of culture. For these theorists culture must be able to claim a theoretical independence, apart from but related to matters of economy. Neo-Marxist positions concentrated on ideology rather than economics held particular attraction, and these began to emerge in CCCS scholarship under the stewardship of Hoggart's successor as Director, Stuart Hall. Hall (1977) was particularly adept in explaining the relevance of the ideas of the Italian Marxist Antonio Gramsci to Cultural Studies. Writing from prison in the 1930s – as a communist Gramsci was imprisoned by Mussolini's fascist regime – Gramsci foresaw that rule within developing capitalist societies would occur through consensus rather than coercion, hence his interest in Marx's notions of dominant ideology and false consciousness. Gramsci (1971) used the term 'hegemony' to explain the way in which ideology would enable the ruling class to maintain power over the working class into the future. Ruling class ideology would pervade society through a host of informational outlets in both the public and private spheres. While formal education and the church would continue to have an ideological importance, Gramsci recognised the growing influence of the media by making reference to the impact of the press on 'public opinion'. Through the influence of key interpreters such as Hall, Gramsci's notion of hegemony was used to elevate the media to the forefront of intellectual debates about the nature of class rule in contemporary society. Importantly for Gramsci, hegemonic rule is never complete, as the dominant ideology system is prone to the sporadic distillation of counter-hegemonic ideas. In the contemporary sense we can recognise the penetration of alternative ideas into media discourses through rebellious journalists and the general inability of the capitalist owners and managers of media to control the voices that are able to gain access to their informational outlets. Gramsci was thus inclined to speak of a 'dual consciousness' rather than a 'false consciousness' and believed the potential for social resistance resided in the awakened second level of consciousness.

From this adumbration of Gramsci we can see that hegemony operates at the level of culture and it is pertinent to consider how various forms of culture in capitalist societies might function as a dimension of what Gramsci referred to as a 'hegemonic bloc'. Sport provides a most interesting example, as it tends to be an inherently conservative institution (as discussed in Chapter Four), one lending itself to easy promulgation of ideas conducive to capitalist rule. Sport is not generally thought of as a radical cultural terrain – certainly it is less so than other areas in the realm of popular culture such as rock music. The ideological impact of sport can be seen to work in the areas of both participation and viewing. Much has been written on sport as an institution of socialisation that works in tandem with other key institutions, particularly the school, to socialise young people into appropriate forms of conduct and an acceptance of the ways and norms of society. Functionalist sociologists value sport as an institution for these reasons, as a supplementary institution that guides young people into their responsibilities as good citizens. Marxist sociologists take an antithetical position, arguing that the socialisation of which functionalists speak is little more than an ideological manipulation of individuals into customs, mores and social ethics conducive to the interests of capitalist society. The good citizen for the functionalist is, for the Marxist, a compliant citizen who is socially conditioned into not challenging the inequalities of capitalist society. For Marx, the working class in capitalist society fundamentally exists as a 'class in itself'. To overcome its experience of exploitation the working class needs to become a 'class for itself', whereby members of the class will unite to take collective action. The ideological forces of capitalism work to prevent the unification of the working class and sport can be seen, from a Marxist perspective, to play its role in this regard. Sport in its participative form is seen as an ideological means of inculcating young people into the culture of the capitalist workplace. Slogans such as 'sport builds character' should thus be viewed with scepticism, and as ideologically loaded rather than value neutral (Sage 1990: 27). The character of a compliant worker is what is actually being developed, a Marxist would contend.

At the level of viewing or spectatorship, from the Marxist perspective, sport provides a different but no less potent ideological support for capitalist class relations. A chief influence here is the Frankfurt School, a group of German Marxist scholars displaced to the United States in the 1930s. The Frankfurt theorists, and most prominently Theodor Adorno, provided a politically converse cultural elitism to Leavis's rightist critique of popular culture. Adorno and colleagues were not worried about the intrusion of the masses into the realm of culture but about the quelling of potential dissent within the masses that emerging forms of moronic popular culture would bring about. Adorno (1996) wrote of 'culture industries' that had arisen within modern capitalism for the insidious purpose of chloroforming the critical faculties of the working class. Translated to the contemporary context, and put simply, the case would be that mindless television programmes, commercial and formulaic films and repetitive nonsensical music make people culturally dim-witted and unlikely to establish the collective momentum necessary to develop a working class cultural fraternity beyond work hours. If one is watching too much television soap opera, there is little time and incentive to engage in radical politics with one's exploited comrades. Adorno (1996: 78) included sport within his critical purview of popular culture to the extent of arguing that culture reflected the barbarism that was inherent in modern capitalist sport. From this perspective, popular culture not only creates a diversion from more serious affairs, but also increasingly promotes a ruthlessly competitive spirit that is concealed, at least in soap operas, by a flimsy veneer of lachrymose sentiment. The proliferation of reality television programmes and quiz shows promoting a crude 'survival of the fittest' mentality bears witness to the intrusion of hyper-competitiveness into popular culture.

Another key ideological function of sport, critically highlighted by Marxist sociologists, is the diversion from class solidarity to an illusory solidarity in nation. No other form of culture is as successful as sport in drawing people together in the celebration of national identity. The symbolic identification of nation with representative sporting teams and individuals intensified in the inter-war years and has continued since (Hobsbawm 1992: 143). This is particularly galling to Marxists who favour the idea of an internationalist working class movement. By encouraging people to focus on a classless national identity sport services the ideological needs of the capitalist system and its ruling class in the most reprehensible manner. The media generated frenzy occasioned by Olympic Games, World Cups and other sporting events based in national contest is unavoidable to most people in Western nations and irresistible to many. When Australia defeated the United States in the

1993 America's Cup yachting tournament even an arch-cultural critic (albeit non-Marxist) of chauvinistic Australian nationalism, Donald Horne, admitted being reduced to tears (McKay 1991). Sport seems able to bind the politically minded with the non-politically minded together into an imagined national community, where the nation does not exist beyond sport.

This bond is unable to exist purely on the basis of goodwill towards fellow nationals. The bonds of nationalism always contain a fear of what exists outside. Sporting nationalism is popularly perceived as an innocuous collective identity, but it too has xenophobic psycho-cultural roots. Indeed, the way in which national sporting contests are conducted, in terms of nation against nation, arouses the perception for participants and spectators of battle being waged against an imagined enemy. Indeed, according to critics, sport reproduces a particularly insidious variant of the patriotism mustered during time of war (Hoch 1972: 83). The 'sport is war minus the shooting' argument, persuasively made by George Orwell (1968 [1945]) amongst others (see also Alan Sillitoe's (1975 [1972]) essay 'Sport and nationalism') remains relevant today.[1] Orwell's criticisms were mainly targeted at on-field hostilities where footballers vicariously waged war – through violent tackling – as soldiers of nations on either side of the cold war. The mass media has repeatedly whipped up a fervour of nationalist enmity amongst sports fans when the occasion suited, most prominently in Britain when the England national soccer team has played major international fixtures against the teams of former wartime enemies Germany and Argentina. However, now that the traditional enmity of nation states has been unsettled by the emergence of de-centred international terrorism as the prime threat to security within national borders, sport potentially offers a somewhat different ideological function. More than ever, sport in the manifestation of the global tournament, such as the Olympic Games and the World Cup, provides opportunity both for parading the continuing relevance of the nation state and for the promulgators of nation states to unite in international sporting contest as a show of defiance against the terrorist threat. Marxists face further despair at this prospect, as class becomes further submerged under the ideological detritus of the reconstituted sporting nation.

The discussion thus far has concentrated on the ideological impact of sport in relation to class. Dominant ideologies of gender and race in sport have also been identified within critical social and cultural theory. For example, Bryson (1983) has argued that the oppression of women primarily works through ideological domination in a number of social arenas, including sport. With regard to sport, Bryson rejects liberalist type positions that argue for the equality of women in terms of equal participation numbers and the equalling of payment and prize money for professional sportswomen. For Bryson greater 'equality' for women on the playing field does not do anything to challenge the masculine ideology of sport and is likely to instil into women the competitive value system of masculinity. Sport, from this feminist perspective, is seen as an ideological prop for patriarchy by ensuring that women accept that they have to be like men in order to be successful. Women who are unprepared or unable to take on a highly competitive ethos will have limited success in sport and could be inclined to think that their appropriate role is in the domestic sphere as family nurturer. Bryson (1983: 421, 425) goes on to note the particularly insidious link between sport and violence. Sport has traditionally sanctioned male aggression, force and violence, and by ideological extension condones the conduct of male violence in public and private life, women often being the victims of this violence. Bryson thus implicitly rejects the familiar proposition that sport provides a catharsis, more commonly referred to as a 'safety valve' whereby the venting of pent-up emotions on the sports field works to prevent aggression and violence occurring elsewhere. Bryson suggests that sport enculturates men into violence that is inevitably inflicted upon women in some cases. Although she lauds the achievements of women in sport, Bryson (1983: 414) concludes pessimistically that feminist sociology should mainly be interested 'not in the liberating possibilities of sport for women, but rather in its potential to oppress'.

Sport has also provided an institutional channel for the purveyance of racial ideology. Sport was used by the Nazi regime in pre-war Germany to promote the superiority of the 'Aryan race', a myth shattered by the African-American athlete Jesse Owens with his record medal haul at the Berlin Olympic Games in 1936. In more recent times sport has not been used overtly in Western societies to propagandise racism, but sociologists of sport have argued that sport is one the main conduits for a continuing belief in physical attribution being determined by race (i.e. people of certain race backgrounds are naturally predisposed to be successful at particular sports). That black sportspeople are not known for success in swimming but are known for success in track sports is explained by physiological reference to anatomical make-up. Much work has also shown that the penetration of black athletes into professional sports has been accompanied by a racial ideology that permeates the culture of sport management and coaching. Coakley (2001: 248) argues that decision making within sport performance operates according to a 'race logic'. This logic crudely dichotomises white and black sportspeople according to the ascription of distinctive traits pertaining not only to physicality but also to intelligence and character. Principally, black sportspeople are perceived to be highly athletic, fast moving, quick of reflex and strong. Whites may have these traits but they are not pronounced within the 'race logic'. What race logic does pronounce for whites in sport is play making acumen, leadership aptitude and reliability. This has resulted in the institutionalisation of a process within sport known as 'stacking'. Stacking occurs within team sports whereby the field positions assigned to players by coaches and selection committees are affected by the ingrained stereotypes of race logic. A number of studies undertaken across a range of sports in different national settings – Hallinan (1991) on Australian rugby league, Maguire (1988) on English soccer and Curtis and

Loy (1978) on American basketball – have shown that black team members are assigned to peripheral running and receiving, and sometimes scoring, positions, whereas white players dominate positions in the centre of the field where the tactical course of the game is largely orchestrated.

Hegemony, counter-hegemony and sport

From the foregoing discussion we can see how dominant ideologies about class, gender and race permeate sport and how these ideologies function to reproduce the oppressive power relations of society at large. However, while ideological explanations move us beyond the rigidity of structuralism, they still tend towards determinism by emphasising the unidirectional impact of ideology. The explanations considered above do not approach ideology as a contested terrain and therefore do not allow us to consider how oppressions of class, gender and race in sport might be challenged. To open this ground we come back to the term hegemony, to establish that dominant ideologies are inherently unstable. They have hegemonic effect but, at once, produce counter-hegemonic tendencies. So while we can observe ideological forces of class, gender and race impacting oppressively on sport, we can also witness resistance against these forms of hegemonic power. That oppression is apparent along each of these sociological axes should not detract from an awareness that empowerment has also occurred. While it can be argued that sport in capitalist society does operate with a similar competitive ethos to the workplace, many working class people extract immense enjoyment from their sporting activities and, often unwittingly, resist the appropriation of sport to rationalistic ends. This can be done in the very course of sporting engagement, as individuals refuse to surrender fun from sport. This type of resistance would dissatisfy Marxists, as they would not regard it as class action. Similarly, Marxists would be sympathetic to but not convinced by campaigns to defend assumed working class community traditions in soccer. Their argument would be that any genuine working class action must be based in completely overturning the capitalist relations within which sport is embedded. However, this in itself is a rigid view and working class gains and challenges to the power relations of sport can surely be seen to have occurred in limited ways within sports from a democratic socialist if not a Marxist perspective.

Hegemony has also been used to define the masculinist ideology that dominates sport. Hargreaves (1994: 21–4), amongst others, recognises a male hegemony in sport to which many women unwittingly subscribe and in so doing are coerced into their own oppression. Importantly, however, and as illustrated by examples below, the male hegemony is not absolute and it offers up liberating potentialities which women are able to seize upon (Hargreaves 1994: 23). Many men are also oppressed by what writers within masculinity studies refer to as the 'hegemonic masculinity' of sport. Messner (1992: 18) – from an American perspective – contends that as the traditional masculinity of the middle class became threatened by modernisation and changes in the realm of work, sport became the key institutional forum in which classed male power could be maintained and have ideological input back into other areas of social life, including the workplace. To seek masculine kudos from sport, men from other class backgrounds have to subscribe to the hierarchical power relations of modern sport. For many men this will not be such a problem and they do, indeed, extract power benefits from sport to the disadvantage of other men and women. Men who do not benefit from hegemonic masculinity in sport could include: young men who are not good at sport but who are forced to partake in sport in institutional settings, particularly the high school; men who are good at sport but who are unable or unwilling to conform to macho team cultures; gay men who are alienated by and potentially at risk within the homophobic culture of sport teams. However, by very definition, the hegemonic masculinity is not all powerful, and men who do not subscribe to the values and culture of dominant masculinity can both enjoy aspects of their sport experience and challenge the power relations of sport. For example, Pronger (1990) notes a number ways in which gay men are able to find empowerment within sport in knowing resistance to the heterosexual expectations of masculine sporting culture. Feminist scholars have also pointed to the ability of women to find empowerment within the hegemonic context of sport. By moving from a discussion of male ideology (Bryson 1983) to male hegemony in a more recent paper, Bryson (1990) becomes analytically positioned to see ways in which the sporting engagements of women challenge the masculine power relations of sport. She believes that feminist challenges occur collectively within sport as an institutional site and at the personal level as women routinely take issue with masculine ideology in their sporting activities. Other feminist scholars have presented case studies that illustrate how women have challenged masculine hegemony by carving out their own space within sports that are bastions of masculinity (for example, Theberge's (2002) study of women's ice hockey in Canada) and in sporting territories largely of women's own making (for example, Markula's (1995) study of aerobics).

Race ideology may also be usefully considered to work in a hegemonic way. As we have seen, sport has served quite tellingly as a social arena for both the promulgation of blatant racial ideology and in recent times for the maintenance of unintended yet nevertheless prejudicial racial stereotyping. However, racial ideology and racism have not gone unchallenged in sport and, furthermore, sport has been appropriated by some sportspeople of colour for the celebration of race identity. A striking example of anti-racist resistance within sport in the 1990s occurred when Aboriginal Australian rules footballer Nicky Winmar responded to racist taunts from the crowd by lifting his shirt and pointing to his skin. Winmar went on to join other professional Aboriginal players to lobby the ruling body of the Australian Football League to take measures to counter identifiable forms of racism in the sport (Gardiner 2003).

As discussed in the previous chapter, the Aboriginal rugby league player Anthony Mundine turned an on-field dispute over racist sledging into a campaign for the elimination of such behaviour in the national competition of that sport. Campaigns against racism in sport have now found strong support within major sporting organisations, for example the support given by the English Football Association to the *Kick Racism out of Football* campaign. This is a significant breakthrough, but Giulianotti is sceptical about the attribution of blame about racism within British football (soccer). Giulianotti (1999: 162–4) points to the tendency within the media and football officialdom to associate racism with a deviantised hooligan element, but not the majority of football supporters. However, as Giulianotti suggests, racism in football is at once more pervasive and more subtle than such a characterisation implies, and if this is to be understood the dismissal of racism as the aberrant behaviour of the few is unhelpful and lets many fans out of facing difficult questions about their own complicity in racist culture. Giulianotti's scepticism surely has pertinence to other sports and other national contexts and points to the difficulty of mobilising counter-hegemonic strategies on a large scale and through official organisational channels.

Perhaps the most famous example of the celebration of race identity in sport were the 'black power' salutes given by the African-American athletes Smith and Carlos at their medal presentation ceremony during the 1968 Olympic Games in Mexico City. As recounted by Harry Edwards (1969) in *The Revolt of the Black Athlete*, this protest was part of a political strategy by black American athletes to extend the civil rights protests of the late 1960s into sport. The sanctions imposed on Smith and Carlos by Olympic officials were indicative of a hegemonic backlash which, while not necessarily racist, was intended to disallow sport to be opened to perceived controversies of race. The critical response by a number of athletes against these sanctions was indicative of counter-hegemonic action aimed at keeping sport open as a forum of protest. This was regarded as very important to black activists, including the academic Edwards, who believed that sport provided a prominent public platform for the symbolic display of civil rights protest. Even less provocative displays of race identity in sport are indicative of counter-hegemonic practice. Australian Aboriginal athlete Cathy Freeman seemed more intent on pure celebration and reconciliation of black and white Australians when she ran victory laps with the Aboriginal flag and the Australian national flag held back to back. Freeman came under considerable criticism from some conservative minded Australian sports officials and media commentators who insisted that to fly any flag other than the Australian flag when representing Australia in an international sporting tournament is a dereliction of national duty. Freeman's dignified response to these lingering colonialist visions of Australian nationalism was to repeat the twin flag display, most prominently on a victory lap at the Sydney Olympics in 2000. Freeman's particular celebration of identity might not involve radical race politics but it is counter-hegemonic in its challenging of the remnants of empire that still flavour the nationalist predispositions of many in Australia.

Sport and cultural materialism

At this point it is pertinent to reflect upon the way we have used hegemony in the above discussion in relation to ideology and power relations around class, gender and race in sport. We should reiterate that hegemony as developed by Gramsci is a Marxist notion concerned with identifying the nature of class power in contemporary capitalist society. Relating hegemony to gender and race involves a theoretical appropriation that has been criticised by some scholars, for example John Hargreaves (1992). However, while acknowledging the appropriation we believe, following feminists and theorists of race ideology, that both gender and race operate in a way that reflects and often materially intersects with the hegemonic power relations of class. We also believe, as we hope our discussion makes clear, that these power relations can be observed at work within sport. However, even if we are allowed this usage of hegemony, a further criticism from Marxists can be anticipated. While being concerned with explaining the oppressive ideological nature of power, hegemony is also about explaining how dominant ideologies are challenged and overcome. Importantly, however, from the Marxist perspective this challenge must be radical rather than reformist or socially transgressive, counter-hegemony is about completely over-turning hegemonic power relations. Most of the examples we have cited above in relation to class, gender and race in sport would not satisfy the requirement of radicalism, the examples cited in each category had more to do with reform and transgression than systemic change. To sustain our case we need to seek further clarification in the use of hegemony, and it is for this reason that we turn to Raymond Williams and his related notion of 'cultural materialism'.

Williams developed his position on cultural materialism in the 1970s, princi-pally in the book *Marxism and Literature* (1977) and in two essays 'Base and Superstructure in Marxist cultural theory' (1973) and 'Problems in materialism' (1978). These essays were both published in the *New Left Review* and later in the collection *Problems in Materialism and Culture* (1980). Williams's purpose in speaking specifically about cultural materialism was to highlight the relations involved in cultural production. This offered a decidedly sociological position on culture, a more sociological one than Marx's, in Williams's view. Williams was critical of the economic determinism of the classical Marxist base–superstructure formulation, which relegated culture to a secondary position whereby cultural outcomes result from economic prerogatives. Williams was also dissatisfied with Marxist positions following Althusser on ideology that saw the economy as 'determinist in the last instant'. The problem of these positions for Williams is that they reduce culture to a pure system of ideas divorced from 'the complex social relations' within which they are produced (Williams 1980: 245). For Williams (1977: 97) the Marxist economistic position is 'not materialist enough'

129

and, by implication, Althusserian ideology positions are not material at all. To overcome the analytical detachment of culture from materiality, Williams (1980) argued for a return of culture to 'the base'. He believed that such unification was demanded all the more in contemporary times as culture industries in Western society are too embedded within matters of economy to be consigned to a super-structural location. For Williams, Gramsci provided the best theoretical pathway to a materialist position on culture and, in Gramsci's debt, he set about outlining his own position on hegemony. For hegemony to explain dominant power relations in society, Williams (1977) believed that it needed to account for the range of pertinent and actually occurring societal circumstances. Accordingly, he designated 'dominant', 'residual' and 'emergent' forms of hegemony and created a further division of the residual and emergent forms into 'alternative' and 'oppositional' strands.

Williams's turn to Gramsci was itself a sign of the times, as Gramsci had by then become a theorist of enormous influence in Cultural Studies, sociology and political science. Williams realised that he had to move closer to Marxist theory if he was to avoid the criticisms of the academic left that had dogged his earlier work. Gramsci provided him a means of doing so in a way that satisfied his preoccupation with culture. The most troubling criticism of Williams's early works *Culture and Society* (1958) and *The Long Revolution* (1961) came from the Marxist historian E.P. Thompson. Thompson objected to Williams's reference to culture as 'the whole way of life', on the grounds that is was too similar to Eliot's usage of the same term. Thompson argued that a more appropriate term for the cultural life of the working class was 'the whole way of struggle' (Dworkin 1997: 102). Thompson was suggesting that Williams's humanistic interpretation of culture did not grasp the under-standing that culture was at the heart of the working class struggle. Gramsci's notion of hegemony allowed Williams to re-engage with Marxism in theoret-ically substantive terms that bypassed Thompson's comparatively atheoretical and historicist approach to Marxist cultural analysis. However, Williams's turn to Gramsci for his own progression as a cultural Marxist did not involve a complete retreat from his former culturalist position. The idea of distinctive cultural formations existing within particular historical periods, and in rela-tion to particular social and political arrangements, was loosely discussed by Williams in *Culture and Society*. Williams was always a cultural materialist, but given the theoretical monopolisation of the term materialism by Marxism, Williams had to explicitly show Marxist theoretical credentials to establish his claim to cultural materialism. His excursion into Gramscian theory enabled him to do this.

The formulation of hegemony offered by Williams also opened optimistic possibilities for the practical consideration of how the hegemonic power of culture within Western societies can and is being combated in a number of cultural sites: culture being won over from oppressive relations to democratic relations. Williams's categories of 'alternative' and 'oppositional' culture are particularly pertinent in this regard. Alternative culture seeks to operate within the dominant hegemony, making changes towards democratic culture where and when opportunities arise. Oppositional culture is radical in intent and concerned with entirely overcoming the dominant cultural hegemony (McGuigan 1992: 25). Williams seems to fudge the 'rules' of Marxism as his alternative formations of culture suggest cultural reform and transgression rather than cultural revolution and transformation. Pragmatism plays its part here, as Williams (1980: 41) recognised that the dominant cultural hegemony of the post-war period was more pervasive than it had been previously, and that incursions from below would be hard won and often limited. But in taking this position – in particular setting out a counter-hegemonic cultural route that is not revolutionary (i.e. alternative culture) – Williams removes hegemony from strictly Marxist moorings. In so doing his cultural materialism evinces a Marxist inspired humanism, a theoretical position that positively accounts for democratic cultural reform in the face of a continuing dominant cultural hegemony. Williams's account of hegemony failed to attract support from Marxist theorists within Cultural Studies, as they in turn sought a more sophisticated theoretical reconciliation of Althusserian and Gramscian positions on ideology (CCCS 1978). However, Williams's account of hegemony has found favour with scholars writing about resistance in relation to a number of cultural areas including sport. For example, Donnelly (1993) uses Williams to examine sport subcultures, as 'alternative' cultural formations in both residual and emergent contexts. Donnelly suggests that within sport, as with other forms of culture, there is a tendency towards incorporation into the dominant hegemonic cultural form. For sport this would generally involve patterns of high commercialisation, so-called professionalism and, as stated by Donnelly (1993: 120), 'Americanization'. Donnelly claims that incorporative tendencies will come to bear on sports in both residual and emergent contexts, but that sports within each of these contexts harbour subcultural elements that provide resilience against or resistance to the dominant incorporation processes. These subcultures provide counter-hegemonic alternatives in the manner of Williams's formulation.

The primary terrain on which hegemony is contested, certainly from the Gramscian Marxist position, but also in Williams's modified discussion, is class. Thus, in the case of sport, various aspects of sporting culture within both residual and emergent formations are subjected to hegemonic forces in the attempt to shape the overall sporting culture in accordance with requirements of capitalism. Counter-hegemonic struggle or conflict to resist and overcome the hegemonic influences of capitalism is, customarily, class based. However, Williams's cultural(ist) materialism potentially opens hegemony to association with gender and race. Even though Williams did not venture down this path in his own work, the humanist core within his formulation of hegemony enables thoughts about cultural domination and power to extend beyond capitalist ideology to patriarchal ideology and racial ideology. Accordingly, accounts of female resistance to the dominant male hegemony in sporting cultures may be regarded as episodes of counter-hegemony. Hargreaves works explicitly with such an understanding in her discussion of women's struggle over sporting culture. According to Hargreaves (1993: 180), 'sport is a site for freedom and constraint: It produces new opportunities and meanings for women and it reproduces prejudices and oppression'. Hargreaves notes that the opportunities occur within residual and emergent cultural contexts, and that oppression occurs within the dominant (patriarchal) cultural context. The resistive and trangressive possibilities to which she alludes are – within the Williams's formula – 'alternative' cultural forms that exist in tension with the dominant male sporting culture but do not seek to overcome it.

Resistance along the lines of race to the dominant white sporting cultures within Western societies may also be regarded as counter-hegemonic struggle. The position is taken by Carrington (2002) in his study of race and cricket culture in contemporary England. Carrington presents a study of a cricket club formed in Leeds in the 1940s as a social and sporting organisation for West Indian migrants. The club's senior cricket team became very successful over the years and by the late 1980s was elevated into a leading county league. Although the senior team now includes a few white players, it remains predominantly black in playing personnel and retains support from the British-Caribbean community. Carrington (2002: 146–147) refers to the club finding a 'Black social space', a space that serves as a 'cultural resource', where black people can express themselves in a manner of their own choosing, rather than according to the strictures of white society. That such a space has been claimed within the cultural bastion of white Englishness that is cricket is surely as indicative an example of a counter-hegemonic alternative cultural formation as we could find. The existence of the space occupied by the club is precarious and constantly under challenge, not necessarily in terms of its position within the cricket league but in terms of external reactionary forces that would implicitly undermine the cultural legitimacy of such a sporting organisation. For example, the Tory politician Norman Tebbit maintained that a true test of Englishness could be based on establishing loyalty for the England national cricket team. His point being that Britons of West Indian, Indian or Pakistani backgrounds who support the teams of these countries rather than the national team of England are guilty of disloyalty (Polley 1998: 135). Although his comments were not directed at local clubs existing on the basis of 'non-English' identity, the message clearly fits into a cultural context that reinforces a dominant cultural hegemony in sport in terms of race expressed as nation. Accordingly, Carrington (2002: 151, 143) makes explicit reference to cricket as a cultural arena of hegemonic contestation over racial identity and to sport more generally as 'an institution within which power [over race] is constantly at play'.

Sport and 'the resources of hope'

In conclusion we want to indicate that Williams's cultural pragmatism does not restrict his utopian vision. While Williams would encourage concentration within the cultural analysis of sport and other cultural arenas on detecting and explicating counter-hegemonic alternatives, he would, at the same time, keep an eye to the future possibilities of socialist/democratic cultural arrangements, the oppositional cultures within his formulation of hegemony. Although not referring to Williams, Gary Whannel looks to a socialist future for sport in his book *Blowing the Whistle* (1983). Whannel assembles an agenda for a socialist sport future under four guiding principles. First, the place of elite sport within a socialist democratic sporting future must be challenged. To be truly democratic, sporting culture must dispense with favour to supposedly elite athletes and with the allocation of public funds to elite sporting programmes. Rather, public spending on sport should be concentrated at the grassroots level with 'no special privilege [availing] to those who excel' (Whannel 1983: 103).

Whannel's second proposal is for the abolition of international sporting competition organised in the form of contestation between nations. This comes back to the point raised earlier in the chapter that national sport has served an important ideological function for capitalism by fostering an illusory consensus and glossing over the social divisions of class spawned by capitalism. In short, sport nullifies class dissent and arouses a delusional conflict steeped in imagined nation. In a socialist and, therefore, genuinely classless society this ideological need for sport disappears and sport with other nations could be conducted purely on a basis of goodwill. We could, as Whannel (1983: 106) suggests, return to the original Olympic spirit where sporting competition was conducted by individuals as cultural ambassadors of nations rather than the contemporary version of international sport in which representatives of countries are charged with the quest for national honour.

Whannel's (1983: 103) third proposal is for the diminishment of competition in sport. As Marxist sport sociologists have argued, sport has been used to socialise individuals into the competitive ethos of capitalist society. Within socialism the sporting ethos will emphasise co-operation, camaraderie and common purpose. Competition will remain but will be subsumed within a humane and socialistic value system; taking part in sport will be genuinely more important than winning (Whannel 1983: 108). Whannel's fourth proposal is that a sport policy agenda be entirely based on humane and democratic goals. Consideration must be given to widening sports participation and, accordingly, funding must be prioritised to the sporting activities of women and people from racial and ethnic minority groups. Funding priority should also be given to sports that are inexpensive and accessible and to those that are naturally democratic in structure, such as korfball, a form of unisex handball. While dangerous sports might not be banned, they would not qualify for public funding or support, and debate would be had about the outlawing of sports that are deemed inhumane (Whannel 1983: 108–10).

Whannel's agenda presents a utopian socialist vision and is in keeping with Williams's own hopes for culture under socialist arrangements. Although not discussing sport, Williams had imagined the possibilities for the arts within a socialist society and in *The Long Revolution* (1961) called for the placement of arts, particularly the theatre, into public hands. As we have noted, Williams was a pragmatist and he was aware of the obstacles to socialism in capitalist society, in culture as in industry and politics. However, he believed that within culture the 'resources of hope' spring eternal and that socialistically minded individuals are duty bound to point the way to the future. Williams's cultural materialism appropriates the Marxist cultural project; he keeps its materialist roots but returns it to humanistic principles, indeed to the socialist utopianism that Marx rejected in his turn to economism. Alternative cultures challenge hegemony in the present while oppositional cultures challenge hegemony in the future; both are important to Williams. Indeed, without hoping and planning for oppositional culture there can be little chance of achieving alternative cultures. For Williams, thinking about what can be achieved stems from thinking about what might be. The possibilities for the future reside within human creativity, which for Williams (1961: 115) is 'the root of ... personality ... and society'. It is thus, for Williams, the creative aspects of human nature, expressed through culture, that will sustain humans against oppressive relations of power and provide the inspirational means of overcoming them. Sport plays its part. Williams (1961: 336) regards soccer as 'a wonderful game' and by this expresses his own aesthetic enjoyment of that sport as well as his belief that this sport constitutes part of what he refers to as the 'good living culture'. Williams thus sees soccer as a sportive expression of human creativity and desires societal arrangements that will not encumber but nurture the intrinsic goodness of sporting cultures. As Willis (1982: 134) has argued, in keeping with the humanistic intent of Williams, sport can be about emphasising human similarity rather than dissimilarity, where sport is reduced to measurement, quantification and comparison, values of capitalism rather than those of socialism and democracy, those values instilled within the agenda for sport promulgated by Whannel. The utopian socialist vision derived from Williams's cultural humanistic account of hegemony glimpses the possibilities of a democratic future for sport, not only for overcoming the ideological and systemic barriers of class but also those of gender and race.

Note

1   An interesting contrary position is to be found in the sociology of the Scottish Enlightenment. Adam Ferguson (1995 [1767]: 28–9) believed that the sports of man 'are frequently an image of war', and that this symbolism is desirable because without the 'practice of war' and the 'rivalship of nations' civil society would collapse. Sport is particularly important because it allows for the mixing of 'friendship' with 'animosity' and a perpetuation of the 'national spirit' during times of peace.

CONNECTIONS

The chapter has argued the case for the importance of Raymond Williams in considerations of power and ideology within culture. The utility of his cultural materialist position was stressed and we noted continuity in this position with Williams's explicit humanism in earlier work. In this Connections section we identify other writers who have seen the relevance of Williams beyond the dimension of class and have used cultural materialism to examine gender and race. We also note an emergent recognition of humanism in the work of key writers on gender and race, and consider the implications for sport studies scholarship as it connects with relevant themes such as postcolonialism.

As noted in the chapter, cultural materialism emerges from Williams's debate with Marx's economic materialism and, accordingly, Williams's focus is on class. Indeed, the very notion of cultural materialism is formulated within a framework that specifically addresses class relations, and cultural materialism might reasonably be considered potentially tenuous as an explanatory means for relations of gender and race. Our examples from sport studies in the chapter were intended to show otherwise, whether or not they make explicit reference to Williams. Not surprisingly, the relevance of Williams has been debated within feminist and race focused Cultural Studies. Of concern to both has been that a framework for analysing class cannot be neatly applied to gender and race, and that, most importantly, it cannot account for the nature of pertinent power relations and politics. However, some feminists have recognised a 'convergence' between Williams and feminist writing of a more culturalist – as opposed to structuralist and poststructuralist – kind (Kaplan 1995). Shiach (1995: 51), although noting an absence of women within Williams's writing, maintains that cultural materialism does provide insight into the 'contemporary social formation' in a manner that renders it highly useful to feminist cultural analysis. Dollimore and Sinfield (1994) claim that cultural materialism is necessarily political in its commitment to revealing the material basis of all forms of socially exploitative power relations. Cultural materialism allows for the examination of the particularities of culture within respective domains of power relations. Much of the work of Dollimore and Sinfield focuses on sexuality (for a discussion of cultural materialism in relation to homosexuality, see Sinfield 1998) but they insist on the broad relevance of cultural materialism to race, ethnicity, gender, sexuality and class.

The prominent Cultural Studies theorist Paul Gilroy has been a key critic of Williams with regard to the latter's account of race. Gilroy (1992: 49–50) accuses Williams (referring to Williams's discussion of race in *Towards 2000* (Williams 1983)) of reproducing distinctions of 'authentic and inauthentic national belonging' similar to those found in the diatribes of advocates of 'new racism' (culturally rather than biologically concocted racism). Gilroy stops short of calling Williams a racist but he claims that Williams works with a notion of national community that is exclusionary and 'strategically silent' in discussing 'social identities'. Gilroy has, in turn, been criticised for misinterpreting Williams. Milner (2002: 120) points out that Gilroy is fundamentally incorrect to claim that Williams did not believe that 'blacks can share a significant "social identity" with their white neighbours'. Williams was actually sounding a cautionary note to the liberal tendency to reduce questions of social identity to legal definitions and to seek solutions to inequality purely in such terms. For Williams, this was a totally inadequate means of accounting for the culturally shaped nature of social identity and for dealing with the cultural underpinnings of racist hegemony. Furthermore, Williams did not work with an exclusionary notion of community in either idealist or material terms. Williams was a multiculturalist, believing that the mesh between cultural diversity and common interest in lived community contexts served as the basis for 'real grounds of hope' (Williams 1983: 196). Williams thus held to an organic notion of community relations, people working out a common culture together through experiences of shared interest and need. This is what he meant by 'long experience', and it is rather unfortunate that Gilroy (1992: 49) contorted this into the rhetorical question, 'how long is long enough to become a genuine Brit?'

It is clear enough that Williams's ongoing hope for a common culture, embracing cultural diversity, was inspired by a humanistic outlook, and it would seem that humanism can provide the grounds on which theorists on race and gender are able to be reconciled into a broadly cultural materialist position. In recent writing Gilroy (2000) explicitly advocates what he refers to as 'planetary humanism', a 'pragmatic' form of humanism aimed at overcoming the divisive aspects of 'race' categorising in cultural analysis and theorising on race. According to Gilroy (2000: 17), 'this radically non-racial humanism exhibits a primary concern with forms of human dignity that race-thinking strips away'. Gilroy is aware that this is a provocative position but he is insistent that we can have a form of humanism – focused on the primacy of human dignity – removed from more familiar notions of essentialist humanism within the traditions of Western discourse. There is reason to believe that Williams would have been sympathetic to this revised form of humanism, and that it is amenable to cultural materialism. With regard to gender, a humanistic position has been advocated by the feminist scholar Michele Barrett (1999). Barrett accepts familiar criticisms within Cultural Studies of 'liberal humanism', but warns against this leading into 'anti-humanism'. In a related point, Barrett (1999: 174) contends that feminist and cultural theory more generally need not claim 'anti-essentialist' bearings to maintain analytical import with regard to power relations. She notes that a revised form of essentialism – 'strategic essentialism' – has emerged within feminist debates about culture and power.

This notion of 'strategic essentialism' has emerged at the intersection of gender and race studies and specifically in the theoretical (cum political) domain known as postcolonialism. The term strategic essentialism, associated most readily with Gayatri Spivak (1987), works well at the political level, the very name suggesting that subaltern groups do well to strategically employ essentialist discourses where and when doing so suits their purposes. Beyond this pragmatic level some postcolonial intellectuals indicate a philosophical commitment to essentialist notions of humanity. Milner (2002: 161) observes that, in his classic *Culture and Imperialism* (1993), Edward Said evinces a 'radicalised humanism' that has much in common with Williams's humanistic orientation. Despite being critical of the Anglo-centrism of Williams's theorising on culture (Williams's Welsh nationalism notwithstanding), Said believes that humanity overrides the classification of peoples into cultural groups. A related position was espoused by Frantz Fanon, one of the founding figures of postcolonial intellectualising and activism. Fanon (1986 [1952]: 10–11) maintained that the oppression of the 'black man' is 'the result of a series of aberrations of affect'. There exists a natural state of affairs, a 'cosmic harmony', behind the inequalities of race that have been imposed and administered politically and embedded psychologically and culturally. Even Fanon's advocacy of violence against colonial rule is based on his unswerving commitment to humanistic values.

7

SPORT, CULTURE AND EMBODIED EXPERIENCE

In this chapter we turn to consider the embodied practices of sport, that is to say how sport is experienced through bodily movement. In doing so we provide a cultural study to an area within sport studies that has traditionally been dominated by physiologists concerned to measure and quantify human movement as a means towards the improvement of sporting performance.[1] Meier (1995: 93) argues that under the gaze of sports assessment methods based in physiology, the body is 'reduced to the status of an object to be altered and manipulated or an obstacle to be surmounted ... in preparation for athletic endeavours the body is drilled, trimmed, strengthened, quickened and otherwise trained to improve its fitness and functioning'. We hold no such interest, our concern being with how to understand the significance of movement made by people during sporting engagement. This largely involves the difficult task of trying to understand sporting bodily movement from the perspective of the participant. This involves more than just asking the participant about their bodily movement as such explanation usually escapes articulation, as our examples from professional sportspeople show. We turn to the philosophical area known as phenomenology to help us gain understanding of how sports participants make sense of their bodily practices within the sportive experience.

Phenomenology and sporting action

The word 'phenomenology' derives from the Greek terms *phenomenon*, which in English means 'thing', and *logos*, which means 'study or analysis' of something. Thus the literal meaning of 'phenomenology' is 'the study of things'. In a less literal way, phenomenology is the study of how a person or persons perceive(s) particular things. Phenomenology involves the study of the consciousness of the person or people under investigation – how they 'see' the world about them, how they understand it, and the feelings and emotions they feel when engaged in such perceptions. Phenomenology is concerned with how particular persons or groups of people see, perceive, understand, experience, make sense of, respond to, emotionally feel about and engage with particular objects or circumstances. As it has developed over the last century or so, phenomenology has become less concerned with the nature of human consciousness in general, and more concerned with particularities: how *this* person (or persons) experiences and feels about *this* particular event, object or circumstance (Luijpen, 1969; Lauer, 1965). In philosophy, the brand of phenomenology that looks at the details of a particular person's ways of looking at and making sense of the world is called *existential* phenomenology. This is because it is concerned with understanding what the world looks like from the viewpoint of the existence of a particular human being or group. This sort of phenomenology is associated with a number of famous philosophers, including Maurice Merleau-Ponty, whose ideas we look at in some detail in this chapter.

The sociologist Alfred Schutz (1899–1959) gave phenomenology a decidedly social and cultural edge in his book *The Phenomenology of the Social World* (1972). Schutz sees phenomenological sociology as getting at the details and particularities of how people live their lives. Schutz uses the term 'lifeworld' to define the mundane, everyday existences in which people operate. This is made up of the ways in which individuals view the world they are in, and ways in which they act within it. The lifeworld is formed by the culture of the particular society in question. The culture creates the common sense ways in which people experience the world. These are the ways through which people in a given cultural context make sense of and experience the world around them. People do not generally subject their common sense perceptions about life to rational reflection or criticism; such perceptions are generally just accepted without being thought about. As the actions of people are based on taken for granted assumptions, sociology needs to investigate the cultural contexts – the lifeworld – within which practical decision making occurs. Schutz provided the inspiration for a phenomenological approach to sociology that became known as 'ethnomethodology'. Ethnomethodology refers specifically to the study of the methods people use to make sense of the social world they are part of. Ethnomethodologists are intent on reconstructing what goes on in particular 'lifeworlds'. Like Schutz, ethnomethodologists are interested in describing in detail the actual ways in which people perceive and act upon the social world they live in. However, ethnomethodology adds to this focus a stress on how social actors (who are referred to as 'members' of particular social realities) are constantly in the process of actively achieving the sense of reality that they have. In other words, society is not something that exists 'outside' people's everyday thoughts and activities, and imposes itself on them, but rather, society is seen as constantly *being made* by people in their everyday actions (Garfinkel 1967). Ethnomethodologists therefore study routine practices in order to understand the nexus between mind and body in human actions.

For example, Sudnow (2002) looked at the processes involved in carrying out a particular skill, playing jazz piano. Sudnow sought to understand how

139

a jazz pianist skilled in improvisation actually plays the piano, by focusing on his own personal endeavours in this direction. By paying close attention to how he himself played jazz piano, he sought to express in words the physical activities his mind and body were simultaneously engaged in. The conclusion he comes to is that when he felt he was playing well, it was as if his hand had 'a mind of its own'. The best playing happened when he was no longer 'trying', but as if the playing was 'just happening' all by itself. He seemed no longer to be in fully conscious control of the hand: the 'hand chooses where to go as much as "I" do' (Sudnow 2002: 2). Here we have a demonstration of the central phenomenological idea that activities obey a logic of their own, and are not generally guided by the person engaged in them fully and explicitly reflecting on what s/he is doing while s/he is doing them. In trying to understand at a later date what was going on in his own playing, Sudnow believes that his playing was at its best when 'my hand was so engaged with the keyboard that through its own configurations and potentialities it laid out a setting of sounding places right up ahead of itself' (Sudnow 2002: 46). Thus the hand – rather than the 'mind' *per se* – was working in a way such that 'it' was always planning ahead as to what the next series of notes to strike would be. The most successful improvisations occurred when not only Sudnow's hand but his whole bodily posture felt as if it were 'at one with' the music: 'I sing with my fingers ... [it is] *my body* ... that sings' (Sudnow 2002: 130). Such an approach to piano playing may be applicable to sportive play too. It is possible to reconstruct how a particular sportsperson operates by thinking about how their actions are carried out in ways that are beyond explicit reflection. The sportsperson does not 'think' about what they are doing; rather they just are what they *are* doing.

For example, the psychologist Steve Blinkhorn notes of the playing of the England national team and Liverpool soccer star Michael Owen, that when he gets control of the ball 'there is a plan there. Players like him can see the possible range of consequences. They have a plan that goes beyond the mere next contact with the ball' (cited in Midgley 2003: 5). The capacity to plan ahead, but without explicitly thinking about what the next moves are, is perhaps a crucial feature of play in many sports. In the case of piano playing, the planning ahead of what the next notes would be was being achieved without Sudnow's brain consciously trying to make this happen. Prebish (1993: 227) gives the example of an amateur American footballer he knew, whose goal scoring capacities were particularly remarkable. Asked to explain how in practice sessions he had such a great capacity to make the ball glide effortlessly past the goalposts every time, the player replied: 'the ball, the grass, the crossbar, the leg ... are all one'. There was no sense of dislocation between 'mind' and 'body', or between 'body' and 'pitch'. All of these were experienced by the player as if they were of one entity. Prebish argues that the secret of the player's success was that:

he could temporarily transcend his sense of self while on the football field ... he had discovered how to remove the distinction between self and others ... [but only] as long as he didn't crave the result. ... When he tried to kick them through, they all went astray.

(1993: 227)

Thus as long as the player did not explicitly reflect on what he was trying to do, or what he was trying to achieve by doing it, the goals kept coming. But once rational reflection entered into it, the 'spell' was broken, and the perceived and experienced connection between body, ball and pitch was destroyed.

A similar unity of vision and purpose is no doubt held by the greatest of sportspeople, and perhaps the greater their talent the more difficulty they have in explaining it. For example, the mercurial French soccer player Zinedine Zidane when asked about one of his most dazzling goals, responded as follows:

I ask myself, how did I do that?! They [my fellow players] were just as surprised as I was. You can make that particular move a hundred times, but only once might it work. ... [After the match] I looked at it again [on video], although I generally don't tend to watch replays of my games. But that particular move, I watched it fifteen times, in order to dissect it. And it is beautiful! It is so beautiful![2]

Faced with a demand to explain precisely how he carried out such a manoeuvre, Zidane's on-pitch mastery deserts him. All he can do is point to the beauty of what he has achieved, rather than be able to explain in detail the resources that he could draw upon to that end. Here we have the paradox of how a master of his art cannot explain in words how that art works or where it comes from. This is not a unique problem on Zidane's part. Time and again, when top ranking sportspeople are asked to put into words how they do what they do, they stumble and grasp awkwardly for ways of expressing themselves. This kind of inexpressive failure is in stark contrast to their often highly elegant and expressive movements when engaged in their own partic-ular sport. This difference in capabilities in different contexts often leads to remarks by others along the lines of 'all her brains are in her feet'. The tacit suggestion here is that the person in question may possess physical intelli-gence, in that he or she can participate very effectively in certain sportive activities, but lacks the mental intelligence that goes along with verbal expres-sion and other more 'intellectual' skills.

However, such a view prejudges the issue. It might be better to see sportive and verbal skills as parts of two distinct, but equally valuable, forms of human intelligence. The aim of this chapter is to inquire into the nature of the former. What does it feel like to be engaged in a particular sportive practice?

141

How does one know, and what does it feel like, when one is playing it 'well' or 'badly'? In addition, how can another person go about attempting to understand what another person feels when engaged in a sport? What are the best ways of accessing and understanding the experiences of sportspeople, aspects they themselves often have difficulty putting into words? We take up this enquiry in the next part of the chapter.

Understanding bodily experience

We proceed by examining the phenomenology of the French philosopher Maurice Merleau-Ponty. Merleau-Ponty's phenomenology can be summarized into five main ideas.

First, Merleau-Ponty (1996) was concerned to get away from, and to transcend, the age old divide in Western philosophy between a conscious human mind and its passive, inert body (Schmidt 1985). For Merleau-Ponty, we can overcome this unhelpful way of thinking about human beings by seeing that the mind and the body are not two separate entities, but are in fact always thoroughly bound up with each other. Mind and body are not two separate things but are instead just two aspects of the same substance, the individual human being. Each person is not just a subject, but also a *body–subject*. This idea goes beyond merely saying that a subject has a body. Instead, the idea of body–subject is an attempt to express the idea that subjectivity and the body are not just interrelated, but completely indissociable. The body *is* the subject, and the subject *is* the body.

Second, Merleau-Ponty wished to think about how space was experienced by particular body–subjects. Like other phenomenologists, Merleau-Ponty is concerned with the 'practical', lived experience of particular people, rather than the world that natural scientific viewpoints can see. Merleau-Ponty's phenomenology distinguishes between an abstract space perceived by sciences such as geometry, and a practical, 'lived' space perceived by body–subjects (Merleau-Ponty 1996). Both spaces are products of ways of thinking, with different modes of thought generating different types of space. Generally speaking, 'lived' space involves the spatial things, and relations between them, which body–subjects encounter in their everyday lives (Priest 1998). This is the space encountered in the lifeworld of everyday activities and practices. By contrast, abstract space is space as presented to a subject engaged in reflection, not in practical activity. This is space that is thought rather than practically lived.

Third, Merleau-Ponty wanted to get away from a view that placed a fundamental divide between a conscious human mind on the one side, and an inert world of objects confronting it on the other. He wanted to see the ways in which the person and his or her environment are instead wrapped up in one another. Just as 'mind' and 'body' are seen to be interpenetrating entities rather than isolated and separate substances, so too for Merleau-Ponty are the human being and the lifeworld s/he inhabits thoroughly bound up with each other. Merleau-Ponty's terminology points to a situation whereby the body–subject is constituted by his or her lifeworld, and the lifeworld is simultaneously constituted by the body–subject. Consciousness is seen to penetrate the 'world', and the 'world' likewise is seen to penetrate consciousness.

Fourth, for Merleau-Ponty consciousness is always situated. Perceptions of the world are never from a privileged, transcendental position, a 'bird's eye view' as it were. Instead, because each person is a body–subject, perception is rooted in the body of each human subject. What each body–subject can see and experience is its own visual field. A visual field is perceived – and thus constituted – from the perspective of a subject who has a body (Merleau-Ponty 1996). The visual field constitutes the body–subject just as, simultaneously, the body–subject constitutes the visual field (Schmidt 1985). The way Merleau-Ponty (1965: 168–9) expresses this situation is through a description of the mutual constitution of body–subject and visual field as a 'dialectic of milieu and action'. The world should be seen as being made up of a diversity of embodied subjects perceiving, constituting, and in turn being constituted by, a plurality of visual fields relative to them. It is this fact that perception is embodied that allows Merleau-Ponty to assert that all views are from a certain position.

Fifth, human subjectivity is not a pure consciousness that passively reflects on external objects, but is rather an active consciousness that exists in a practical relation to its visual field. More than that, in fact, the body–subject is a form of practical consciousness. Each body–subject has practical knowledge of how to operate in its own visual field, and acts practically on the basis of that knowledge. According to Merleau-Ponty, then, the primordial condition of the body–subject is a state prior to reflective consciousness. The claim here is that the abstract modes of thought involved in reflective consciousness (those ways of thinking that are 'rational', 'logical' and 'scientific') are secondary products, generated on the basis of the pre-reflective modes of knowing and doing characteristic of the primitive existential condition of the body–subject practically engaged in manoeuvring through its own visual field. Quite simply, 'doing' is prior to 'thinking'.

Now that we have outlined in brief Merleau-Ponty's ideas, we can see why he can be said to have provided a general language that can be used to investigate particular types of embodied doing and being (Crossley 1995). Phenomenological analysis on this view seeks to reconstruct the contours of the 'lived' spaces, the visual fields, created and experienced by particular body–subjects in their practical orientations towards their environments. Merleau-Ponty himself briefly applied his ideas to the study of sportive activities. He described the movements of the soccer player in this way:

> For the player in action the soccer field is not an 'object', that is, the ideal term which can give rise to an indefinite multiplicity of perspectival *views* and remain equivalent under its apparent transformations. It

is pervaded with lines of force (the 'yard lines'; those which demarcate the 'penalty area') and is articulated into sectors (for example, the 'openings' between the adversaries) which call for a certain mode of action and which initiate and guide the action as if the player were unaware of it. The field itself is not given to him, but present as the immanent term of his practical intentions; the player becomes one with it and feels the direction of the 'goal' for example, just as immediately as the vertical and the horizontal planes of his [or her] own body. It would not be sufficient to say that consciousness inhabits this milieu. At this moment consciousness is nothing other than the dialectic of milieu and action. Each manoeuvre undertaken by the player modifies the character of the field and establishes new lines of force in which the action in turn unfolds and is accomplished, again altering the phenomenal field.

(1965: 168–9)

This quotation is Merleau-Ponty's analysis of what it might feel like to be a *player–body–subject*. The lifeworld of the player–body–subject is the soccer field as it is viewed and experienced by him or her. Since the field is constituted by the player–body–subject, it is his or her 'property'. But at the same time the field constitutes the player–body–subject. It follows that both the player –body–subject and the soccer field are mutually creative of each other. Viewed in this way, soccer play is not the result of the perceptions and reactions of a player logically reflecting on what they are doing. Instead, play is generated by more 'practical' forms of engagement with the sportive environment. From this perspective, the player 'feels' the direction of the different parts of the pitch, for example the movement towards the goal area, as much as s/he experiences the endowments of his or her own body. He or she 'knows' the pitch not at the level of reflection but at the level of pre-reflective, practical engagement. The player's actions are generated on the basis of that form of practical under-standing (Inglis and Hughson 2000).

Play can thus be seen as a *flow* of embodied practical activities rather than as a series of discrete actions presided over and decided by a reflecting conscious-ness. The player–body–subject does not carry out 'strategies', if these are defined as the results of reflective monitoring and decision. Instead, the player–body–subject practically produces 'moves', which are felt (rather than thought) to be compelled by the spatial contours of the soccer field. As these contours are also 'felt' by the player–body–subject, they are transformed into dynamics of space, in this case the space of the soccer field. Thus there pertains a fundamental relationship between the dynamics of the perceived pitch, and the movements that the player–body–subject enacts. Both player and field are in movement together, the one orienting and reorienting the other simultane-ously and constantly as long as the player is playing. The succession of 'moves', the very substance of play itself, constantly lead to reconfigurations both of the dynamics of the field, and of the subsequent moves 'demanded' of the player by those dynamics. Those dynamics are produced by the permanent interpenetration of the body and the field (Hughson and Inglis 2000).

The Merleau-Pontian notion of there being a *stream* of play is an attempt to encapsulate in words the rhythm of play on the pitch. Whilst the player sometimes has to perform relatively 'discrete' movements (e.g. to stop running with the ball in order to take aim at a target), such activities are seen as only relatively rather than absolutely distinct from the flow of play that preceded them and follows them. The terminology used to describe forms of play should, on a Merleau-Pontian view, draw upon metaphors of processual and ongoing movement, and not utilise language that conveys an impression of jerky, stop-start forms of motion.

However, the differences between words that suggest process and fluidity and words that emphasise jerkiness and a lack of flow could be said to be illustrative of the differences between what are taken as 'good' and 'bad' forms of play in particular sports. The philosopher David Best (1995: 382) describes 'good' play in a particular sport as involving 'actions which ... approach ... the ideal of totally concise direction towards the required end of the particular activity', such as scoring goals in soccer or hitting the ball in a particular way in tennis. Best (1995: 383) argues that play of this kind involves a 'unified structure which ... [is] the most economical and efficient method of achieving the required end'. From this viewpoint the difference between relatively highly skilled participants in a particular sport and those who have less refined skills is that the former can avoid expending extra energy when carrying out their sportive activities, as they possess the ability to be completely 'at one with' the activities they are carrying out.

It might therefore be the sheer powers of concentration on the task at hand that mark out the very good player from the merely competent one. To take an example again from soccer, the agent Paul Stretford has speculated in this manner on the capacities of the young virtuoso player Wayne Rooney:

> I imagine that if we had the technology to look into his head we'd see that he sees everything at a slowed-down pace. While everyone else sees the football being played at 100 miles an hour, it's all slow motion in his mind ... [and so] situations don't faze him, no matter how great the pressure.
>
> (cited in Midgley 2003: 5)

Rooney's capacity to enact forms of play that other players cannot is on this account a result of his ability to 'see' the pitch, and the potential moves it allows and he can enact within it, in ways very different from those other players have access to. The fluidity of Rooney's play comes from his being able to engage as a body–subject with the pitch in fashions not accessible to the other body–subjects on the field.

If words associated with fluidity and smoothness of movement can be used to describe 'successful' forms of sportive movement, it follows that words associated with the opposite kind of images, to do with jerky, ill coordinated actions, can be used to reproduce the experience of playing 'badly'. When the sport player has to reflect on what s/he is doing while s/he is doing it, there is no feeling of 'oneness' between mind and body, because the mind has turned the body into an object of reflection. Once that occurs, movement will lack fluidity and will not feel 'right'. Bayley's description of his failure to play good tennis is indicative of this process:

> I dug deep. Got in the ready position. Tossed the ball. Tried and tried and tried to remember to look at it while I brought the racket back in the mechanically difficult beginning of the service action. Struggled to remember to stretch up to wallop it at the apogee. All the time teeth gritting, concentrating on where I want the wretched thing to go. Managed none of those things very well. The toss I was never really, really looking at the ball, just faking it. What should have been a smooth continuous arabesque was more like a juddering ratchet and I (eventually) hit the ball at shoulder height in a crabbed action that was Quasimodo swatting flies. Instead of a lustrous and sexually pleasing pling into the service court, I delivered an emasculating thwarp as the ball spewed wildly into space.
>
> (Bayley 2003: 1)

While the service should have been describable as a 'smooth continuous arabesque', it in fact feels like a 'juddering ratchet'. Bayley's account is of particular interest because in seeking to put into words what he feels as an embodied subject, he draws upon sexual metaphors. The pleasure that good play gives is said to be akin to sexual satisfaction, but failure to carry out a smoothly delivered service feels 'emasculating'. His masculine power is undercut by his inability to serve effectively, just as it would if he had failed in an intimate encounter to perform well sexually. Instead of seeing himself as a handsome and virile figure equipped with potent sexual and sportive prowess, the failed service means he sees himself more as the disfigured and pitiful figure of Quasimodo, whose bodily actions are the opposite of elegant. In searching for metaphors to describe a lack of fluidity in play, Bayley has reached towards words and images that suggest the impotent grotesque.

The sportive body, space and power

Now that we have laid out how various forms of phenomenology can be applied to the understanding of sports, we can turn to look at some of the limitations of phenomenology in this area. If one were to take a strongly phenomenological stance against other forms of studying sport, one would be committed to saying that 'sport is only truly capable of being known as it is existentially lived' (Morgan 1993: 128). But if we only looked at sports as they are experienced by players 'from the inside', then we would be unable to connect how sports are played and experienced with social and cultural factors beyond the immediate context of sportive practice. In particular, by only looking at sports experiences isolated from wider social and cultural issues, we would be ignoring the various ways in which forms of power can influence how particular sports are played. The task, then, is to try to connect the micro-level issue of how particular sportspeople experience their sportive actions with more macro-level concerns about forms of social and cultural power. What we have to do is connect phenomenological accounts of experience with the more 'structural' aspects of culture and society examined within Cultural Studies and sociology. We will now look at various ways in which this can be done.

The first way of linking experience to wider factors concerns thinking about the nature of the spaces in which sports occur. We saw above that Merleau-Ponty conceives of the sportive arena, in this case the soccer pitch, as being seen from the point of view of the player–body–subject. The player and pitch are 'as one', with the player practically rather than reflectively 'feeling' the contours of the pitch. Thus Merleau-Ponty's phenomenology wants us to see the space where the sport occurs solely from the vantage point of the player. But this means downplaying or ignoring altogether some crucial questions about how the game of soccer is organised.

In Merleau-Ponty's analysis, there is a complete omission of questions such as who enforces the rules on the pitch, who polices the stadium, in whose interests the game is being staged, and so on, all questions about the nature of power (Bourdieu and Wacquant 1996). Merleau-Ponty's innovation is to talk about body–subjects, rather than just subjects. But in his work the body–subject is still a 'philosophical' idea, an abstraction, rather than a real flesh and blood person who lives in a particular culture and society (Lefebvre 1991: 183n). Thus the Merleau-Pontian player–body–subject is an 'ideal' player, rather than a 'real' person. However, if we move the focus away from Merleau-Ponty's ahistorical abstractions towards looking at particular individual sportspeople engaged in sports at particular historical periods, we can use the idea of body–subject in a more concrete fashion.

This involves us thinking in more detail about the ways in which the places designated as areas where sports are to occur have become ever more tightly organised over the last 100 years or so. The French Marxist thinker Henri Lefebvre argues that throughout the twentieth century, there was an increasing

> predominance of 'amenities', which are a mechanism for the localization and 'punctualization' of activities, including leisure pursuits, sports and games. These are thus concentrated in specially equipped

'spaces', which are as clearly demarcated as factories in the field of work.

(1991: 227)

Thus sports stadia and other such spaces are developed in part to concentrate sports in a particular locale, such that access to participating in them can be regulated (e.g. by having to be a member of an athletic club), and that the viewing of them by spectators can be controlled (e.g. by buying a ticket to watch an athletics event). Moreover, sports stadia allow certain sports like athletics or cycling to be ever more subject to precise rules and regulations, and the activities involved in them to be more rigorously timed and measured (Brohm 1978). From his Marxist perspective, Lefebvre (1991: 408) sees such stadia as 'a repressive and oppressive space', where the activities of athletes and others come more and more under regulation and control by an array of authorities.

The historian Henning Eichberg (1998: 153) discerns such a process characterising the development of the arenas for ball games such as soccer and baseball. He argues that we must understand how players of such games play, and how they experience their play, in the context of the changing demands made upon them by sporting authorities who are constantly recasting stadia spaces in the direction of more and more control over the nature of play. Eichberg traces out a movement away from the relatively unformed and 'open' spaces of the pre-modern soccer pitch towards a much more formalised and demarcated type of space, which is ever more strictly regulated in terms of the size of the pitch, the spaces between the goal posts, and so on. Simultaneous with this spatial development is a chronological process. The commercialised sports industries, seeking to turn the game into profitable mass entertainment, require the production of 'tense' and exciting moments which appeal to potentially huge audiences, and the abolition of the looser, more unpredictable actions of the pre-modern game.

The imposition of rule changes and devices to speed up play in a number of sports has altered the lived spaces occupied by players on the pitch and, thus, has implications for the application of a Merleau-Pontian phenomenological analysis of sport play. Taking soccer as an example: the player–body–subject, under pressure to keep the game moving quickly, has less time at his or her disposal, 'either to think before passing the ball, or to gain some respite during breaks in play' (Giulianotti 1999: 143). The body of the footballer and the spaces of soccer that s/he experiences are both thus compelled to change in order to provide novel means of rapid-fire 'entertainment' (Inglis and Hughson 2000). The experience of actually playing soccer is today being transformed by the imperatives of entertainment and profit, such that the way the pitch 'feels' to the contemporary player might fairly be said to have little resemblance to the way that this space was experienced in the past. Here we have a prime example of how macro-level forces, in this case economically driven, can have profound implications for the nature of sportive experience.

The sportive body and gender

The preceding example points to one way of linking the micro-level of sportive experience with more macro-level forces, by considering how the latter can transform the nature of the spaces in which the former is located. A further mechanism whereby we can link issues of experience and power is through thinking about how forms of power are embedded in the nature of the sporting body itself. We will first consider how this can be thought about in terms of gender, and then we will turn towards examining how the same can be done in terms of social class.

We noted above the fact that Merleau-Ponty's phenomenology describes the nature of the movements of a body–subject in general terms, not particular, individual body–subjects living within specific social and cultural conditions. His abstract notion of body–subject needs therefore to be fleshed out in particular ways. One of these ways concerns gender. The feminist theorist Judith Butler (1989: 95, 98) argues that 'although Merleau-Ponty intends to describe the universal structures of bodily existence', he nonetheless 'fails to acknowledge the historicity of sexuality and of bodies'. She and other feminist writers have argued that the specific bodily experiences of women, living in particular times and places, need to be accounted for so that Merleau-Ponty's phenomenology of bodily movement can be made more satisfactory. On this view, the differences in the experience of playing sports felt by men and women in particular societies can be accounted for in ways opened up by Merleau-Ponty, but these ways need to be augmented by a specific focus on the gendered dynamics of sportive activity.

A particularly striking example of gendered differences in sportive activity comes from baseball in the USA. At the beginning of the 1994 baseball year, President Bill Clinton was photographed throwing the ceremonial first pitch of the season. At around the same time, but at another venue, Hillary Clinton was also photographed carrying out the same act. A number of newspapers the next day carried the two photos together. An interesting difference was made apparent in each of the Clintons' throwing styles. Bill 'had turned his shoulders sideways to the plate in preparation for delivery [and brought] … the ball forward from behind his head in a clean-looking throwing action' (Fallows 1996). By contrast, Hillary was pictured throwing the ball with her 'body facing the target, rather than rotating [her] shoulders and hips ninety degrees away from the target and then swinging them around in order to accelerate the ball'. As a result, to even a relatively uneducated baseball observer, while the President looked as if he was throwing effectively, the First Lady looked wholly ineffective in her stance. She was, it seemed, 'throwing like a girl'.

It is precisely this phenomenon, of the female apparently lacking the confident bodily movement of the sports playing male, that is the subject of the most well known study of sportive and other corporeal actions from a feminist inspired Merleau–Pontian perspective. This is Iris Marion Young's (1990) paper entitled 'Throwing like a girl'. Young denies that observable differences in male and female bodily movement in modern Western societies are rooted in 'sex', biology or 'nature'. Instead, the matter is one explicable in terms of culturally constructed gender categories. The differences in bodily use rest in how people in each gender category use their bodily capacities. Young sees such differences in bodily use as functions of different forms of socialisation. In a patriarchal form of society, as modern Western societies are, women are brought up in ways that deny them the 'subjectivity, autonomy and creativity' that such a society accords to men (Young 1990: 144). Women are encouraged in childhood to act in 'ladylike' ways, such as keeping the legs close together, and not using 'masculine' gestures such as walking with a bold stride. Such bodily dispositions are learned and acquired, not inevitable or innate. Males, by contrast, are taught implicitly and explicitly to walk, talk, throw, run, and so on 'like a man'; the common characteristic of all these male forms of bodily activity is one of confidence and openness, psychological (and thus also, as mind and body are fused entities, corporeal) qualities that a patriarchal society accords to men but not to women.

In a Western patriarchal context, therefore, the female body–subject is one that tends to be less sportively efficacious than its male counterpart. The space around the female is one that she has, through a process of socialisation and enculturation, been discouraged from confidently reaching out towards. Women tend to be more corporeally reactive than active in comparison to men, because the space that they 'feel' through their bodies seems more restricted to them than the space around the body felt by their male counterparts. For example,

> in softball or volleyball women tend to remain in one place more often than men do, neither jumping to reach nor running to approach the ball. Men more often move out toward a ball in flight and confront it with their own countermotion. Women tend to wait for and then react to its approach, rather than going forth to meet it.
>
> (Young 1990: 146)

Not only on this view do women tend to be less 'open' to the space they perceive around them than men are, but it is also the case that, as a result of the socialisation processes described above, 'women tend not to put their whole bodies into engagement in a physical task with the same ease and naturalness as men' (Young 1990: 145). The jerky type of movement that lacks smoothness and fluidity, that we saw above may often be characteristic of poorer forms of sportive action, can now be seen in the light of gender factors. Women often seem less good at sports not because they are 'naturally' less talented, but because their sense of themselves as body–subjects has been created, at least in part, by a patriarchal cultural context in which feminine autonomy and confidence are looked on with suspicion.

Clearly many criticisms could be made of Young's account. Has she not overestimated the degree to which women lack corporeal confidence? How does this account deal with the changing nature of female self-understanding, partly brought about by feminist movements and their encouragement of female pride in oneself? Is it really the case that all women are as she alleges? In relation to the last point, Young is careful to note that she is describing the bodily subjective dispositions associated with the condition of femininity in a modern Western society. This means that women who for one reason or another are not as 'feminine' as others will not correspond to the model she sets out, either fully or at all. Some women do indeed 'escape or transcend the typical situation and definition of feminine bodily existence', in her view (Young 1990: 144). Clearly the training of female athletes might be oriented around very different forms of bodily conduct from the feminine 'norm'. However, Young argues that it remains the case that 'typically' women in a society such as ours do undergo forms of socialisation that turn them into body–subjects who have a rather different sense of their own corporeal, and thus sportive, capacities than do men. The main point here is that Young has suggested an important way of connecting large scale social and cultural conditions, in this case those associated with patriarchy, with the micro-level experience of engaging in particular sportive actions.

The sportive body and class

Just as wider gender factors can be combined with a Merleau-Pontian understanding of the experience of sporting activities, so too can issues associated with social class. The understanding of why in modern Western societies people in different classes tend to be involved or interested in different types of sport has been taken up by the French sociologist Pierre Bourdieu. Bourdieu – in similar fashion to Gans, as discussed in Chapter Four – seeks to explain what he sees as a social fact revealed time and again by the statistical results yielded by large scale surveys carried out in France and other Western nations, namely that working class people prefer certain types of sportive activity, whilst middle class people prefer other types of sport. Within the middle classes, there are also divisions in sporting preferences, with the lower middle classes (e.g. nurses, primary school teachers) preferring activities such as yoga and jogging, and upper middle class people (e.g. lawyers, academics, senior civil servants) preferring activities such as horse riding and polo.

Bourdieu (1993a) adduces some of the more obvious reasons why people in different classes have differing sporting tastes. Obviously money plays a role, with the equipment to play polo for example – not just the stick and the riding gear, but a horse, stabling for it, membership of a club, etc. – ruling out a large sector of the population, because they lack that kind of disposable income. There is also an explicitly 'social' element: membership of certain sporting groups, such as polo or yacht clubs, is often less centred around the sporting activity itself and more oriented around social functions and individuals wishing to be 'in' with the 'smart set'. In such cases, the sport is often just a pretext for the rituals associated with a particular social group, with elite groups imposing exclusive forms of membership on their sporting clubs in order to 'keep the riff-raff out', and maintain their own sense of prestige. In addition, some sports are socially defined as being more 'refined' than others, and thus those people wishing to be seen as distinctive and superior to others would wish to be associated with an activity such as grouse shooting, but would have no desire to participate in, for example, what is seen as the much less refined activity of dog racing.

Bourdieu believes that there is a profound reason why certain types of people prefer certain types of sports, and dislike the idea of participating in other types. Here Bourdieu follows the ideas of both Merleau-Ponty and Marcel Mauss. The latter is one of the classic authors in the history of French sociology. Mauss (1979) argued that the bodily posture of human beings is profoundly shaped by the culture in which they grow up. Thus people in different societies hold themselves, walk, gesticulate, eat and perform other bodily actions differently. Precisely how they do these things is a result of enculturation, for each society expects its members to operate according to certain bodily norms. Socialisation processes embed in the physical constitution of a person 'the most automatic gestures or the most apparently insignificant techniques of the body [such as] ways of walking or blowing one's nose, ways of eating or talking' (Bourdieu 1992: 466). Socialisation in childhood, which gets reinforced as the child grows up, means that both the mind and body of the individual are shaped in ways typical of the group's characteristic ways of thinking and acting. Even the minutest details of an individual's bodily behaviour will reflect the ways in which other people in the group do the same things. The mental and physical set of dispositions that the group inculcates into the individual Mauss calls the *habitus* of the group. It is not only the case that everyone in the group tends to think and act in similar ways. It is also the case that each individual person's various activities will tend to 'fit' with each other in terms of style (Bourdieu 1977: 143). If a person is a member of group X, then s/he will walk, talk, dance, run, and so on, in distinctively 'group X-style ways'. How s/he does each of these things will mark him or her out as a member of that group. In addition, what s/he likes and dislikes will be functions of the tastes of the group. In other words, his or her habitus dictates his or her tastes and preferences.

It was Bourdieu's innovation to assert that different groups within a particular society each have their own distinctive habitus. For Bourdieu the main groups in any modern Western society are social classes. Thus each class has its own habitus. In bodily terms, this means that each identifiable class has not only 'its own' distinctive set of ways of thinking, and likes and dislikes, but also its own particular forms of bodily activity. Thus there is a distinctively 'working class' way of playing sports, just as there is a distinctively working class way of holding the body, eating, and so on. This set of ways of operating bodily is different from those produced by the habitus of each of the other two main classes in modern societies, the lower middle class and the upper middle class. Each of these groups has its own particular ways of functioning, characteristics that each group passes on to its individual members.

The nature of each class's habitus is produced by that class's social and economic position in the wider society. Here the Merleau-Pontian aspect comes in and is yoked to a socio-economic analysis of how privileged or unprivileged particular classes are in terms of wealth and power. How particular body–subjects experience life, and how their bodily dispositions function, is the product of their class position. The most powerful class, the upper middle class, enjoys a privileged social and economic position, for it is both wealthy and esteemed (even if grudgingly) by people in the other classes. Its habitus expresses a lifestyle that Bourdieu characterises as a *life of ease*. As a result of being relatively highly wealthy, life for people in this class involves 'the suspension and removal of economic necessity' and thus a sense of 'distance from practical urgencies' (Bourdieu 1992: 54). Consequently body–subjects in this group generally feel very *at ease* with themselves and their surroundings, and feel an apparently effortless confidence in most situations.

By contrast Bourdieu (1992) characterises the habitus of the working class, the least powerful class in terms of both wealth and prestige, as involving the 'taste of the necessary'. The working class do not have a life of ease as do the upper middle class, because they are located nearer to the hard edge of life, and are faced more with constant struggles to 'make ends meet'. The habitus of the working class is characterised by a set of tastes which favour things that are seen to be unpretentious and 'not too fancy'. This is an 'instrumental' rather than an 'aesthetic' attitude that favours immediate results and instant gratifications. Anything deemed to be pretentious, like most modern art, is disliked and rejected. As for the lower middle class, they occupy a position between the other two classes. They have more wealth and prestige than the working class but less than the upper middle class. The habitus of the lower middle class is characterised by what Bourdieu (1992: 318ff) calls 'cultural goodwill'. On Bourdieu's view, the lower middle class is fundamentally aspirational: while looking down on working class people as being 'common', people in the lower middle class want to be seen to be as 'refined' and 'distinctive' as their upper middle class counterparts seem. But such is the cultural power of people in the upper middle class that they can always define their own tastes and activities as being more refined than those of the lower middle class. For example, once an 'exclusive' holiday resort starts being frequented by large numbers of lower middle class people (mere 'tourists'), upper middle

153

class trendsetters declare that the resort is no longer fashionable and the upper middle class bandwagon moves on to another locale now defined as the new 'in' place. For Bourdieu, then, there is a constant cultural class struggle going on, with upper middle class people despising the tastes and activities of the lower middle and working classes, and the lower middle class seeking to be like the upper middle class and unlike the working class. People in the working class react to all of this with feelings either of humiliation, indifference or mocking scepticism at the pretensions of their social 'superiors'.

It is in this light that Bourdieu locates what he sees as the most profound aspect of sportive experience. There is an 'affinity' between the habitus of each class and the nature (or what each habitus perceives as the nature) of each particular sport (Bourdieu 1993a: 352). The upper middle class habitus is based around ideals of 'ease' and 'elegance', hence sports such as fencing and polo are favoured over others, because they offer (or seem to offer) the capacity to move in elegant and refined ways. Thus it is not just the social opportunities afforded by membership of the polo club that attract upper middle class people; for some of them it is the very nature of the bodily movement that the sport itself affords. The lower middle classes like jogging and yoga because they are activities that ascetically train the body; people in this class like this kind of thing because their whole lifestyle is based around renouncing immediate enjoyments in favour of rewards that they feel will come later. By punishing themselves now they convince themselves they will be rewarded in the future, and that reward will be to become a more 'refined' and 'distinguished' (i.e. upper middle class) person. Finally, the working class taste in sports such as boxing or weightlifting derives from a habitus that likes immediate gratifications (e.g. knocking out the opponent, getting a muscular body) and embraces (or at least is not disgusted by) physical violence. Looking at the tastes different classes have for different sports in this way also reveals why a particular group does not tend to like a particular sport. For example, team sports such as soccer are not appealing to someone with an upper middle class habitus, as that habitus is based around notions of individualism and the sacrosanct nature of the self; bending to collective discipline in the team does not, at a sub- or semi-conscious level, appeal to the upper middle class person. Finally, it should be stressed that on Bourdieu's view (which follows Merleau-Ponty's ideas on practical consciousness), in all these cases the affinity between a habitus and particular sports is rarely a subject of conscious reflection by individuals; they just practically 'feel', rather than reflectively think, that a sport is 'right for me' or 'not for me at all'.

Many objections could be made about the particularities of Bourdieu's account of taste in sports in modern Western societies. In terms of his wider sociology of tastes in cultural goods, it could be said that he has over-privileged class as the determining factor and under-recognised factors such as age, ethnicity and gender (Brubaker 1985). Bourdieu may also have overemphasised the cultural subordination of lower classes by higher classes (Honneth

1986; Fowler 1997; Frow 1987). Moreover, his ideas may now be somewhat outdated. The system of cultural tastes in Western societies may have changed substantially since his research was carried out in the 1960s and 1970s, with class boundaries in taste now perhaps being less rigid (Warde *et al.* 1999). In specifically sporting terms, is it really the case that participation in sports can be as neatly packaged in class based ways as Bourdieu alleges? Are all soccer fans working or lower middle class, for example? If not, how significant is upper middle class soccer support, and what does this tell us about the changing dynamics of sport and other forms of culture in a particular society? Moreover, is the taste in a particular sport wholly a product of one's habitus? For example, rugby is played and enjoyed by people of quite diverse social backgrounds, so how does this fit into Bourdieu's (too?) neat schema of sports and class tastes?

Despite these objections, one might say that Bourdieu's reworking of Merleau-Ponty's ideas about bodies is an impressive one. Bourdieu said that what was lasting about his work was not what it said about particular societies at particular times, but the terminology and ideas it provided for analysing other social and cultural contexts. Bourdieu's notion of habitus provides us with a way of thinking about how sportive experience, the focus of phenomenological study, can be tied to analysis of wider structures of power and domination, in this case class power. The benefit of his work is to point out that *how* sports are played and *why* particular people are interested in them (or not) are issues always thoroughly bound up with questions of power and the organisation of wider society. The essential message of Bourdieu is that sportive practices are never innocent of power relations.

In this chapter we have examined various approaches to the study of sportive experience from a phenomenological perspective. We have looked in particular at the ways of understanding sporting activities provided by ethnomethodologists and by Maurice Merleau-Ponty. We have also looked at the ways in which the ideas of the latter have been developed by scholars whose concern is to combine a phenomenological perspective on what sportive practices feel like 'from within', with analysis of wider social and cultural forces, especially power relations in terms of gender and class. While a phenomenological perspective taken purely on its own is perhaps too narrow a focus for understanding many aspects of how sports are played, it nonetheless remains a crucial component of any study of sport that wishes to get to the often subtle details of what happens when sports are enacted. Quite simply, a phenomenological approach is an indispensable element in understanding the nature of sports, both today and at any time.

Notes

1   The most systematic account of expressive bodily movement, in a manner sympathetic to the humanities and social sciences, is provided in the work of the dance analyst Rudolf Laban (1879–1958). Laban (1980 [1950]) meticulously recorded

and explained every form of dance movement by notation method. The system known as Labanotation has become of particular interest to sports formally assessed on the basis of quality of movement, for example gymnastics (Hutchinson 1972: 411). Importantly, Laban provided a 'naturalistic account of dance', focused on the 'flow of movement', rather than a compartmentalised breakdown of a series of movements (Brennan 1999: 287).

2   Interview with Zinedine Zidane, online at http://www.indirekter-freistoss.de (in German).

CONNECTIONS

In this Connections section we consider the important concept of the 'field' within Bourdieu's sociology of culture and in specific relation to sport(s) as an arena of social practice. While the notion of habitus is central to understanding the embodied practices of sport, the field provides the conceptual means of explaining how these practices occur within socially and culturally constituted sites. For Bourdieu, the field is not a material institution as it is within functionalist sociology but a metaphor for a 'social arena within which struggles or manoeuvres take place' (Jenkins 1992: 84). Bourdieu sees fields as occupied by 'partially autonomous' actors who are engaged in positional power struggles (Mahar et al. 1990: 8). Positions are taken up in relation to the dominant interests that have been established within fields over time. Thus, according to Bourdieu (1990a: 88), 'every field, as a historical product, generates the interest which is the precondition of its functioning'. The main difference between Bourdieu and functionalist sociologists (and Marxist theorists for that matter) is that he wants to downplay the determining role that social structure has on the lives of individuals and social groups. Thus Bourdieu is interested in individuals as *agents* within the field and he advises the mapping of a 'social typology' of the positions occupied by individuals as social agents (Jenkins 1992: 88). Bourdieu emphasises the dynamic nature of human action and his sociology of culture recognises that it is individuals who give shape to social fields.

The 'field' is notoriously hard to define beyond the level of metaphor. Richard Jenkins (1992: 89) asks whether fields 'exist in the social consciousness of those actors who inhabit [their] social space' or 'simply [as] analytical constructs'. Bourdieu offers no precise delineation of fields but alludes to fields existing on a macro-societal plane. One of the fields to which Bourdieu (1993b: 119) refers is the 'sporting field', and he suggests that this field is governed by its own specific forms of logic which, in practice, have a determining effect on what transpires within the field. An overarching 'sporting field' does not initially appear to allow for an understanding of the vastly complex social world of sport comprised of a host of different sports and intersected by dichotomies such as amateurism and professionalism, and elite and community sport. Bourdieu did speak of 'subsectors' existing within fields (Bourdieu and Wacquant 1996: 100), and this would provide some means for considering how particular sports would operate as distinctive arenas of social practice while also operating in relation to a broadly conceived 'sporting field'. Defrance (1995: 126) contends that a Bourdieuian study of sport demands the reconstituting of the field into 'subfields' to account for particular sports. This subdivision of fields shows the distinctive nature of sport as a multilayered and fragmented social arena, even more so than other undoubtedly complex fields such as education. Sport as a decidedly cultural domain bears similarity to the arts, which also benefit from subfield categorisation.

The paper by Defrance referred to above appeared in a special edition of the *Sociology of Sport Journal*, published in 1995. This edition was dedicated to papers on sport based in French social theory, and included three papers on Bourdieu: Defrance's paper and papers by Suzanne Laberge and J.P. Clement. Laberge challenges Bourdieu's emphasis on class by looking at gender as the dominant social force within fields. According to Laberge (1995: 142), 'although the exercise and sports field has historically been male dominated', subfields of sport are differently gender divided so that some are perceived and experienced as feminine rather than masculine. Laberge then constructs a four dimensional typology to look at how gender orientations of social actors will impact upon those actors within gendered sports fields. Laberge (1995: 142) contends that we can draw insights from the studied experiences of women venturing into male dominated sports fields, as well as those of men venturing into female dominated sports fields, to guide wider consider-ation of the 'complex dynamics of the articulation of multiple gendered dispositions within our contemporary societies'. Clement's paper highlights the illustrative nature of the language of sport and suggests that through the study of the social practice of sport we can clearly see the reliance of the concept of habitus on that of the field. Clement (1995: 154) notes, via Bourdieu, that the social actor's 'inclination to act ... is produced by the rela-tionship between the field of a game and a system of positions adapted to the game'.

On a more critical note, in a recent paper Noble and Watkins (2003) contend that Bourdieu overstates the unconscious dimension of habitus to the extent that the conscious dimension in social action is left unaccounted for. Indeed, they claim that, 'in trying to emphasise the largely unconscious nature of embodied practice [Bourdieu] mistakes automaticity for absence of consciousness' (Noble and Watkins 2003: 535). Noble and Watkins accept that 'much of what we do remains unconscious' but believe that many of our social practices display a high level of conscious awareness that is removed from habitus as discussed by Bourdieu. The authors offer as an example the training processes in sport that rely on the individual's capacity for conscious reflection to seek improvement in technique and playing style. Via reference to sports training, they seek to invert Bourdieu's conceptual priority for unconsciousness over consciousness: 'Intervention reshapes bodily capacity to the dialectic of consciousness and habituation. Intervention reshapes bodily capacity through continuous acts of calibration; and, through repetition, this refined technique becomes habitus' (Noble and Watkins 2003: 536). In offering this reformulation Noble and Watkins seek to lift habitus – or their preferred term habituation – above the conceptual constraints of the field. This intellectual manoeuvre would be unacceptable to theorists such as Defrance and Clement, who maintain that habitus can only maintain validity in strict conceptual relation to the field as theorised by Bourdieu. It could also be maintained that Noble and Watkins have imposed a false dichotomy between consciousness and unconsciousness onto Bourdieu. Bourdieu (1990b: 62–3) referred to a 'doxic relationship' between habitus and field, through which a 'practical sense as the feel for the game' is produced. However, although this 'feel for the game' results more from 'second nature' than 'rational calculation', Bourdieu remained very much aware of the existence of individual social actors as conscious 'reflecting subjects'.

Debates stemming from the work of the late Pierre Bourdieu will continue and, whatever the outcome of such debates, Richard Jenkin's (1992: 176) simple declaration that Bourdieu is 'good to think with' remains paramount. From the brief discussion here we can see not only is Bourdieu's theorising useful to our studies in the sociology and cultural study of sport, but that the cultural example of sport can provide insight into Bourdieu's social and cultural thinking for academics and students within the broader fields of the sociology of culture and Cultural Studies.

8

SPORT, CULTURALISM AND ETHNOGRAPHY

We have referred at various points in this book to ethnographic work and its value in making sense of the creative aspects of culture as lived and experienced by specific social groups. In this chapter we elaborate on ethnography as a methodology as a way of identifying and gathering 'data' to empirically inform our understanding of lived cultural experience. We comment on the fruitfulness of ethnography in the study of sport, and on the value of a 'culturalist' inflection to ethnography as a mode of inquiry. Within this discussion we locate ethnography within Cultural Studies, while making relevant connections to the closely related sociological tradition of ethnography. Our considerations of empirical examples and possibilities from sport cover sport spectator and supporter and sport participant contexts. We believe that the discussion indicates not only that sport is an important area of cultural life that should be studied by ethnographic means, but also that debates that have occurred between ethnographers focusing on sporting contexts have significant implications for the controversies that rage on within ethnography about such issues as the biographical positioning of the researcher, the authorial status of the ethnographer and the ethics of fieldwork. The chapter commences with a consideration of ethnography within the culturalist tradition and provides evidence of a culturalist ethnographic influence within writing on sport. We then move on to discuss the knowledge status of ethnographic research with a view to assessing the ability of ethnography to inform us about what is going on in particular cultural domains and how people engage with sporting cultures in ways meaningful to them.

Signposts to a culturalist ethnography

The fascination with lived cultural experience is, as we have seen throughout this book, at the core of culturalist Cultural Studies. It is not surprising then that ethnography – defined by Barker (2000: 384) as 'an empirical and theoretical approach which seeks detailed holistic description and analysis of cultures based on intensive participative fieldwork' – emerged within Cultural Studies as a major research undertaking in the post-graduate programme at the CCCS in the 1970s. However, prior to the emergence of a named and dedicated interest in ethnography, an ethnographic temperament was evident in the work of early culturalist writers. Of the founding figures, Richard Hoggart is widely recognised as an unwitting ethnographer. His narration in *The Uses of Literacy* (1958 [1957]) of working class life in the north of England in the 1930s is based on keen observation, and although not ethnographic in an anthropological or sociological sense, Hoggart is entirely concerned with the meanings people invest into and take from their cultural activities. Hoggart's proto-ethnographic writing is highly impressionistic and, in this manner, comparable to an English journalistic-cum-ethnographic tradition exemplified in the social reportage of George Orwell, in his books *Down and Out in Paris and London*, *The Road to Wigan Pier* and *Homage to Catalonia*. Interestingly, Hoggart's observations of the decline of working class culture in *The Uses of Literacy* are reminiscent of similar observations, made in an earlier time, by the protagonist George Bowling in Orwell's novel *Coming Up for Air*.[1]

Raymond Williams is not usually associated with ethnography, although Aronowitz (1994) has argued that Williams's work prior to his Marxist theoretical turn offered a form of 'historical ethnography'. Crucial to this interpretation is Williams's notion of the 'structure of feeling'. Specifically, Williams (1961: 48) referred to 'the structure of feeling [as] the culture of a period'. Although a notoriously vague term, the structure of feeling suggests that particular social periods are characterised by a collective mood that informs values and attitudes about life. For Williams, the 'structure of feeling' provides the intellectual and emotional base for the 'lived culture'. Importantly, the structure of feeling does not reflect a dominant ideology, although not isolated from dominant ideas it will evince aspects of contrary collective opinion arising from class difference and in working class response to conditions of social dominance. The term 'structure of feeling' indicates a unique combination of sociology with culturalism; the recognition of a social structure that embraces a collective cultural mood at a particular point in time. Although *The Uses of Literacy* (1958 [1957]) is decidedly less 'sociological' than *The Long Revolution* (1961), Hoggart was no less interested than Williams in providing an overview of the 'whole way of life' of the English working class. The keen observations of both of these writers make up what we would refer to as a *panoramic ethnography* of working class culture. Although neither Hoggart nor Williams wrote much about sport, as we can see from Chapter Two, their observations led both to believe that sport existed as a key component of working class cultural life. However, for a culturalist ethnography focused on sport in working class life it is useful to turn to other writers.

Culturalist ethnography in sport: the 'football man' meets the 'sporting alien'

Published originally in 1968, *The Football Man: People and Passions in Soccer*, by Arthur Hopcraft, locates soccer within a Hoggartian style account of English working class culture. The descriptive language is completely in keeping with the culturalist temperament:

> [Soccer] is inherent in the people. It is built into the urban psyche, as much a common experience to our children as are uncles and schools. It is not a phenomenon; it is an everyday matter. There is more eccentricity in deliberately disregarding it than in devoting a life to it. It has more significance in the national character than theatre has. Its sudden withdrawal from the people would bring deeper disconsolation than to deprive them of television. The way we play the game, organise it and reward it reflects the kind of community we are.
>
> (Hopcraft 1988 [1968]: 9)

Hopcraft's method is autobiographical objectivism, in the manner of Hoggart, in that he draws on his own life experience of football following, but in an attempted objective way to give wider insight into the intrinsic cultural relevance of the sport. His writing is highly sensuous, the sights, sounds and smells of soccer pervade the book, which is unquestionably panoramic in its ethnographic scope. Hopcraft (1988 [1968]: 10) distances himself from conventional sport authorship, his book 'is not a gallery of heroes' it is 'more concerned with people than with technique', it is about 'explor[ing] the character of football', by which Hopcraft clearly means the cultural and social character. *The Football Man* is mainly organised into chapters focusing on the types of personnel associated with soccer: players, managers, club directors, referees and fans. It is in his chapter 'The fan' that Hopcraft's culturalist ethnographic insights come into full view. Hopcraft's account of the 'working-class communion' that thrives within the precarious domain of the football end is especially telling:

> For those of us who first learned our professional football jammed against the crush barriers down at the bottom of [the standing areas behind the goals] … they are more evocative of the wonder of childhood than even old comic-strips are. They are hideously uncomfortable. The steps are as greasy as a school playground lavatory in the rain. The air is rancid with beer and onions and belching and worse. The language is a gross purple of obscenity. When the crowd surges at a shot or a collision near the corner flag a man or a boy, and sometimes a girl, can be lifted off the ground in the crush as if by some massive, soft-sided crane grab and dangled about for minutes on end, perhaps never getting back to within four or five steps of the spot from which the monster made its bite. In this incomparable entanglement of bodies and emotions lies the heart of the fan's commitment to football. The senses of triumph and dejection experienced here are

never quite matched in any seated section of a football ground. It is physical interaction which makes the monster the figure of unavoidable dreams it becomes.

(Hopcraft 1988 [1968]: 188–9)

Hopcraft is aware of and notes the problematic nature of the football terrace as a point of public gathering. It has served as a refuge for the hooligan scoundrel and, obviously enough from his own description, presented an ongoing concern for public safety. On each of the few occasions when large losses of life have occurred in British football grounds blame can be attributed to the overcrowded terraced ends. However, with the implementation of the Taylor report in the 1990s, largely a response to tragedies at Bradford and Hillsborough in the 1980s, the football end was dismantled and replaced by the all-seated stadium. With this reform football lost what Hopcraft (1988 [1968]: 189) affectionately called a 'monstrous, odorous national pet', that place 'where the love of the game is fiercest'. Even in 1968, Hopcraft realised that the terraces were close to having their day, but he hoped that architects would redesign them with sensitivity to keep them as places of excitement and relatively unbridled human expression. As it has turned out in most cases, 'the merchants of blandness' (Hopcraft 1988 [1968]: 190) have stripped the football stadium of the crude but earthy sensuality that Hopcraft so evocatively sketched.

Hopcraft uses his ethnographic insights from football to provide a moral commentary on working class culture, again in the manner of Hoggart. He has stern words to say about the football hooliganism that had emerged on the terraces by the time he was writing *The Football Man*. With Hopcraft's (1988 [1968]: 184) socio-historical distinction between the 'committed fan with a bit of a temper' and the 'gang member' we can see the Hoggartian 'old order yielding to the new' and it is similarly a transformation into decline. Hopcraft (1988 [1968]: 182) suggests that violence at the soccer match was traditionally an isolated occurrence and a non-group affair, at worst the odd punch up but even then violence was more usually threatened than enacted. Considering the level of 'delirium' generated on the old terraces Hopcraft (1988 [1968]: 179) finds it surprising that people have not behaved more violently and done more physical harm to each other than has actually been the case. Hopcraft's (1988 [1968]: 184) moral gaze descends onto the 'older men in the football crowd' for not taking the 'young troublemakers' into hand. Hopcraft regards this failure to act as being attributable to either the fear or indifference of the older men towards the misbehaving youths. Either way, he sees it as indicative of a general malaise pervading 'contemporary social life'.

Writing in the mid-1990s, Mihir Bose (1996: 29) declares *The Football Man* a classic and, despite being focused on the 1960s, to be of 'tremendous contemporary relevance'. Bose believes that Hopcraft successfully conveys the 'complex emotions' embedded within football supporting culture. This comment highlights the importance of *The Football Man* as a culturalist ethnography of sport, a veritable record of 'lived experience'. It is a product of its time, but it stands the test of time by remaining of interest to future generations in the way that it captures the 'structure of feeling' of football during the period of the author's observation. An understanding of the autobiographical positioning of the author is key to a sympathetic reading of the Hoggart and Hopcraft style of culturalist ethnography. Both authors can appear as fuddy-duddies in their moralistic criticism of emergent youth, but how many of us can claim not to feel discomfiture with aspects of youth culture as we grow older? More importantly, their failure to personally reconcile the new with the old is an interesting part of the auto-ethnographic process, and provides a glimpse within the lived record into the slow change of the 'structure of feeling'. It is with such an understanding in mind that we can best appreciate the praise and criticism made of *The Football Man* by Bose in his own auto-ethnographic offering *The Sporting Alien: English Sport's Lost Camelot* (1996).

Bose came to live, work and study in England in the late 1960s. He was born in Calcutta and raised in Bombay; of privileged background, he was privately educated according to the ways of a lingering imperialist system. Englishness pervaded Bose's life. The English focus of his formal education extended into wider cultural interests, particularly sport. Bose's sporting interests traverse the English class system, and while cricket is prominent amongst these interests – he has written a number of books on cricket, including *A History of Indian Cricket* – his deepest passion seems to be for soccer, as a supporter of the famous Tottenham Hotspur Football Club. As a young man Bose's interest in Tottenham was aroused by that team's Cup and League double success of 1961. From the next season Bose would anxiously await the arrival of the Monday morning newspapers to check on Tottenham's weekend fortunes. By the time of his migration to Britain, which coincided with the publication of *The Football Man*, Bose had developed his own long distance love for English soccer and an imagination for the culture of the sport in keeping with Hopcraft's evocations. However, Bose was jolted into a new awareness once he reached the final pages of Hopcraft's penultimate chapter, 'Football and foreigners'.

In this chapter Hopcraft criticises the traditional insularity of English soccer culture but suggests this insularity was shaken by the success of the England national team on home soil at the 1966 World Cup. Hopcraft notes the warm reception that England supporters gave to the North Korean team during their matches in the competition at grounds in the Midlands and the north. It is Hopcraft's description of the North Koreans that understandably bothers Bose. While meaning to show respectful affection, Hopcraft is patronising and unintentionally racist in his use of language. At this point in the book Hopcraft fails Bose (1996: 30) as an empathetic writer. Bose had taken

Hopcraft's vision of football culture as his own, but from page 221 he became aware that Hopcraft was describing a different culture to the one that he was about to come into contact with. From this critical standpoint Bose interrupts with his own auto-ethnographic account of soccer culture, no less panoramic than Hopcraft's and from an important biographical position given the changes that were occurring in the racial and ethnic relations of football in Britain. Bose extrapolates fascinatingly and skilfully from personal experience of racism of varying degree – from subtle to the most blatant and deliberately abusive racism – to the wider scope of how forms of racism have become embedded within soccer, and English sport more generally. Nevertheless, Bose (1996: 73–4) retains his love of soccer and Tottenham Hotspur and wishes that the indigenous English could 'appreciate their [sporting] heritage' in the way that he appreciates it.

An appreciation of the sporting heritage requires facing up to the reality of the present, and to this end Bose warns against the indulgence of sports romanticism, particularly with regard to the historical link between premier level football clubs and local community. The increasing affluence and middle class aspirations of a good section of the working class has resulted in football no longer being integral to community life in the traditional image:

> with the ground often bang in the middle of the town, a few minutes walk from the railway station, next to the shops and buses and surrounded on all sides by terraced houses. … Going to the football chimed neatly with the very fixed contour of what was the Saturday ritual for most working-class men. … In the morning the usual factory grind, knock off at one o'clock, then a quick walk to the pub [and] a walk to the ground just in time for a three o'clock start.
>
> (Bose 1996: 138)

According to Bose, the football supporting working class (those who can afford match tickets) now tend to live in suburban hinterland areas of cities and towns and commute on match days. Whereas, 'the houses, shops, schools they have left behind are peopled by the so-called ethnics, mostly Asians and blacks, but also Greeks, Cypriots, Turks, etc., for whom the old English tradition of pub, football, then home for tea is about as familiar as jam butties'.

Bose (1996: 139) goes on to ask whether football can be reconnected with community once the traditional community relationship has been fractured. He does not forecast an answer but, as indicated above, contends that the cultural reality of this situation has to be faced if mention of football and community is to refer to anything other than a mythologised (white English) working class past. Bose thus gives us a very different picture of football and culture to that of Hopcraft, but there is striking similarity in the descriptive style – as apparent from our use of quotations from each – both writers offering keen glimpses into the minutiae of everyday life in the English neighbourhood: very sensuous writing assuming respective moral high grounds, working from the autobiographical lens to the wider cultural scope. Both map changes within the 'structure of feeling' of the period under their observation, and take their place within an undeclared lineage of culturalist ethnographic writing on sporting culture. As indicated above (and as claimed by Bose), Hopcraft's *The Football Man* holds great contemporary relevance, and this relevance is enhanced and renewed by subsequent works that allow books such as *The Football Man* to continue to be read as expressions of the lived cultural reality of football rather than as historical curiosities. Hopcraft benefits thus from his critical yet sympathetic treatment by Bose. It is hoped that Bose will benefit similarly from the critical engagements and offerings of future writers.

From Chicago to Birmingham: ethnography and the sociology/Cultural Studies connection

As mentioned above, Hoggart – and by implication the subsequently discussed sport writers – is not an ethnographer in the specifically anthropological or sociological sense. He has not purposefully gone into 'the field' and conducted participant observation study. The collection of 'data' via participative research is usually given as the key marker of ethnography in the aforementioned disciplines. Malinowski's fieldwork in the Trobriand Islands, published in the 1920s, is most often cited as the early classic in anthropological ethnography (Atkinson and Hammersley 1994: 249). Ethnographic work in sociology emerged not long after, chiefly in association with the 'Chicago School' and placing emphasis on researching the contemporary urban milieu. The main inspirational figure behind the ethnographic work in the Chicago School was the journalist turned academic Robert Park. Park (1952: 47), described Chicago's cultural heterogeneity as 'a mosaic of little worlds which touch but do not interpenetrate' mutually exclusive or overlapping geographical neighbourhoods distinguished by class and/or ethnicity, and as corresponding 'moral regions' with distinctive and possibly conflicting sets of beliefs and behaviours. These, he argued, must be studied 'as part of the natural … life of the city' (Park 1952: 51) to allow us to understand the meanings given to urban life from the perspectives of city inhabitants.

Park thus proposes a humanistic and experiential focused understanding of the life of city dwellers that is sympathetic to the culturalist emphasis on 'lived culture'. Park does not, however, propose a panoramic ethnography of a unitarily perceived urban working class culture in the manner of Hoggart. Rather, Park was interested in examining the contrasting urban diversity of social and cultural worlds. He coined the term 'marginal man' to designate the uncomfortably in-between positions of so many urban citizens; neither immigrant nor American, working nor middle class, they were people caught in movement between cultural worlds. Park thus encouraged ethnographic studies to illuminate the marginality and complexity of urban cultural relations and identities, always emphasising the symbolic meanings of these relations and identities from the perspective of the examined human subject. This approach was extremely influential upon the early Cultural Studies ethnographic work at the CCCS. Like Park the British youth subculture researchers were interested in the plurality of lived cultural formations rather than in a singular notion of lived cultural experience. The status of ethnography within early Cultural Studies reflects a working distinction between that emergent discipline's forbearing in literary studies and sociology. Hoggart's ethnography stems from the literary studies understanding of lived experience whereas the youth subculture ethnographies offer one of the clearest representations of sociology within Cultural Studies to date.

As noted in Chapter Four, little of the youth subculture work at the CCCS concentrated on sport. However, we believe the ethnographic methodological approach of some of this work to be relevant to the study of sport cultural formations. We examine this potentiality through discussion of the relevant work of Paul Willis. Willis, an inveterate ethnographer and currently chief editor of the international journal *Ethnography*, remains the leading contributor to the ethnographic reputation of the CCCS in the 1970s. Willis conducted two well known ethnographic studies during this period; the first, based on his doctoral research, presented a comparative study of biker and hippie subcultures in the West Midlands. This study was published in 1978 as the book *Profane Culture* (1978). His best-known book *Learning to Labour: How Working-class Kids get Working-class Jobs* (1977), was published in 1977 and based on ethnographic fieldwork conducted subsequent to his biker and hippie study. In *Learning to Labour* Willis studies a group of male working class youth – the 'lads' – in their later school and early work years, with a specific interest in how the young men construct a culture of resistance to social authority that results in the reproduction of subordinate class relations.

Both *Learning to Labour* and *Profane Culture* are pertinent to our considerations about the possibilities and potential limitations of ethnographic study into the lived cultural domains of sport. *Profane Culture* is of particular interest in its comparative focus on oppositional youth cultural groupings of the day. Willis (1978) highlights the 'homologous' relationship between the cultural items and uses of items and the social values of the respective groups. The hippies advocated peace and love and passive non-conformity, and listened to mellow forms of folk and progressive rock music. The bikers advocated rebellion and an aggressive non-conformity, and listened to early rock and roll music. It would be difficult to replicate the study into sport ethnography because sport subcultures are not subcultures in the sense of the hippies and bikers, drawn together by an all-consuming lifestyle and clearly defined alternative value systems. However, what sporting subcultures do have in common with these non-sporting subcultures is that particular cultural activities are integral to the existence of the subculture. Quite simply, a rugby college subculture would not exist without rugby. Rugby, within the parameters of sporting engagement, sanctions aggressive conduct. In an inversion of Willis's inquiry we might ask whether aggression in the sport is 'homologous' to the off-field cultural interests of the members of the rugby college subculture, in music, film and other activities. For a comparative ethnographic study, the rugby college subculture, which would likely be regarded as culturally conformist, could be contrasted with a non-conforming sporting subculture such as skateboarding. The members of this subculture could also be examined for the homological fit between the character of their sporting conduct and their non-sporting cultural interests. It also seems apparent – following our discussion in Chapter Four (Connections section) – that a comparative focus between such groups in the one piece of research would offer a fertile ground for a direct consideration of the difference between sport subworlds (the rugby group) and sport subcultures (the skateboarder group).

We now look at *Learning to Labour* with especial interest in Willis's personal positioning as an ethnographer with a closely established relationship with the 'lads'. The particular theme we concentrate on is *cultural identification*. This is a thorny issue within ethnographic debate. Although it is generally agreed that close rapport and identification with a group under study is an important part of the ethnographic process – getting to know the culture from the perspective of the researched – and that the most successful ethnographies are characterised by identification achievement, critics warn that there is a fine line between an appropriate level of identification and over-identification. Willis has been accused of developing 'over-rapport' with the 'lads' (Hammersley and Atkinson 1995: 110), symptomatic of this are his failure to maintain a researcher's 'distance' from the group and too uncritical acceptance of their socially rebellious behaviour as a form of quasi-political institutional resistance. More generally, Willis is accused of 'celebrating' the masculinity of the 'lads' (Hammersley and Atkinson 1995: 111) and this is a critical theme we want to consider further with regard to sport related ethnographies.

The line of criticism we take follows the 'feminist critique' of Angela McRobbie (1991) in her well known article 'Settling accounts with subculture'. In this article, originally published in 1981, McRobbie accuses the CCCS subculture researchers, particularly Willis, of over-concentrating on class as a site of social subordination to the neglect of gender. Largely as a result of the over-rapport Willis had established with the group, he was blinded to the overtly sexist and chauvinistic behaviour of the 'lads', and interpreted it as working class rebellion. By interpreting the lad's degrading behaviour towards female teachers and female pupils in this way, Willis fails to recognise the misogyny of their subculture and overlooks the gendered power relations of their lives (Skeggs 1992: 191). It is our current concern that these shortcomings be avoided in ethnographic studies of sport cultures and subcultures. In a recent article two of the authors (Free and Hughson 2003) contend that the gender blindness to which McRobbie referred has found its way into the so-called 'new ethnographies' of soccer supporter subcultures. We look specifically at the studies by Giulianotti (1991; 1993; 1995a; 1995b) and Armstrong (1993; 1998) of the fan subcultures in their respective native cities of Aberdeen and Sheffield, and argue that, in their honourable intention to give a fair account of much maligned and media stereotyped male youth groupings, these authors replicate the errors of Willis, as noted by McRobbie.

Among the thugs: insights from football supporter ethnographies

Our criticisms of Giulianotti and Armstrong need to be balanced with the respect we afford them as researchers (Hughson 1998a) and with the recommendation that their work be read by all would-be ethnographers of spectator and participant sport. Their careful consideration of the ethnographic process provides an example of the reflection in which sport ethnographers should engage with regard to issues such as field relations and ethics, and both of these issues are considered further below. Despite the ethnographic self-reflection that generally characterises their work, both Giulianotti and Armstrong say little about matters of gender and sexuality arising in the field, neither in regard to their relations with the supporter groups nor to the gender and sexual relations of the men being studied (Free and Hughson 2003: 138). We can assume from what is told that these are ostensibly ardent and exclusively heterosexist subcultures. However, apparent episodes of homophobic and misogynistic behaviour remain unanalysed and the authors do not reveal how they came to terms with such behaviour as researchers. It would have been insightful to know whether Giulianotti and Armstrong were expected to trade in sexist banter and, if so, how they negotiated such situations. Did the young men know of the researcher's sexual orientation? Indeed, given that Giulianotti and Armstrong highlight their biographical similarity to group members in terms of age, class background, birthplace and gender, it seems inadequate that they do not declare their own sexual orientation in ethnographic write-up. Readers are left to assume that Giulianotti and Armstrong share heterosexuality in common with the men under study. It is to be hoped that future studies into sport related subcultures avoid such silences, as explicit discussion of the sexual positioning of the researcher in relation to the studied group will help to reveal further insights into both homophobic and homoerotic dimensions of subcultural life, moving sport ethnography beyond the potential uncritical celebration of hyper-heterosexual social practices.

Such awareness will also help guard against conceptual excess as researchers look for novel theoretical means to explain their findings. With regard to football supporter ethnographies Giulianotti (1991; 1995b) and Hughson (1998b) have employed the concept of *carnivalesque* to explain the rowdy social conduct of young men. The term carnivalesque has entered Cultural Studies via the work of the Russian literary theorist Mikhail Bakhtin

(1895–1975). Bakhtin (1984) used the term in a social context to explain how occasions of uproarious collective behaviour not only provide relief from the drudgery of normal life but can effect a meaningful, if symbolic and ephemeral, challenge to dominant power relations. The carnival inverts the normal course of worldly affairs and from this upside down perspective people are given a glimpse of how life might otherwise be. Inevitably, vulgarity and uncouth demonstrations enter into the fun of the carnival, most importantly as a nose tweak to the conventions of social authority. Carnivalesque has been discussed by a number of writers within Cultural Studies – Kristeva (1980) being the first – as involving *transgression* (the breaking of moral if not official laws) rather than radical political protest. Stallybrass and White (1986: 201) note the important qualification that transgression occurs only in situations where groups in 'low or marginal positions' challenge hierarchical discourse and sites thereof.

Sporting events, obviously enough, involve carnival, but carnival understood more generally as festivity without any political purpose. The recent trend at test cricket matches in England for some male spectators to dress in 'drag' registers with an aspect of Bakhtin's carnival (gender reversal) and such displays have at times annoyed cricket officialdom. However, given that the young men in question are likely to be from privileged social backgrounds it is difficult to see their behaviour as transgression in a Bakhtinian sense. The association of rowdy, even hooligan, soccer supporters with carnivalesque seems more terminologically appropriate as these supporters do disrupt the official order and occupy a more marginal social position. However, even this latter point is made problematic by Giulianotti and Armstrong's insistence that contemporary soccer hooligan groupings in Britain are not exclusive to men of lower working class background (as the traditional stereotype would have it) (Free and Hughson 2003: 138). If this is so, young men *per se* appear as the marginalised in the carnivalesque equation. Such a positioning could be supported by Armstrong's (1998: 302) contention that contemporary football hooligans (so labelled) take on a derisory status of 'newly discredited male' within dominant media discourses, and in turn serve a 'folk devil' function to the benefit of the media as a capitalist and moralistic enterprise.

However pertinent this criticism of the media representation of 'football hooliganism' might be, care needs to be taken with subsequent conceptualisations within Cultural Studies. Specifically here – despite previous usage of the term by one of the current authors – we are cautious about associating the term carnivalesque with young male football supporting rowdies. The football supporting related social practices of these young men appear to regularly involve the degradation of women and therefore involve a symbolic reinforcement of sexism and patriarchal power relations. Identifying rowdy behaviour as carnivalesque can serve as an unintended masking of the sexism and chauvinism that perpetuates within male subcultural groupings. Importantly – to relate this to our discussion of ethnography – this cautionary observation is

169

made from a considered distance. When ethnographers such as Giulianotti have used the term carnivalesque it has coincided with or followed recent intensive and highly immersed field research with young men. Carnivalesque sounds a note of identification with the young men; a conceptual means of explaining the sport supporting experience from their perspective. However, our point is that such conceptualisation is at once indicative of ethnographic over-rapport and compounds the problem in male subculture studies recognised by McRobbie many years ago.

Sport presents a particularly problematic research field in terms of over-rapport. Ethnographic researchers in sport are likely to have fairly similar socio-demographic biographies to those they are researching, given that sport is a classed, gendered, age differentiated and regionally marked cultural activity. Related to these factors, ethnographers are likely to conduct studies on sports that they know well, and that are often dear to them, as participants or spectators, or both. Although we have taken issue with how Giulianotti and Armstrong deal with themes of gender and sexuality in the research context, we believe that both authors offer useful advice on how sport ethnographers can negotiate and reflect upon their dual existence as researcher and sport participant/fan. Both authors claim an 'insider' status in the sense that they shared significant biographical similarities to the groups being studied and, furthermore, that they knew some of the members of the respective groups prior to the research being undertaken (Hughson 1998a: 50). Added to this, both researchers are soccer enthusiasts and fans of the Aberdeen (Giulianotti) and Sheffield United (Armstrong) association football teams.

Giulianotti (1995a: 12) uses the term 'relative insider' to describe himself as an ethnographer 'manag[ing] an empathetic and preinformed entrée to the cultural values of the research subjects'. Armstrong (1993: 20) reflects similarly but places more emphasis on the irresolvable yet necessary tension in the insider/outsider status of the ethnographer. He describes himself as a 'marginal native', a midpoint location between 'stranger' and 'friend'. This description seems particularly apt for ethnographers studying sport. Many will be friends to the study participants in the common literal sense, while being friends in the research context in that they share and participate in the same cultural interest as the research subjects, often as teammates within sport. Sport ethnographers are 'strangers' in that, by adopting the role of researcher, they take on a set of instrumental goals that are pursued within the cultural domain of the studied group while having no personal or collective relevance to members of the group. This is a situation the researcher needs to handle carefully, particularly where the research goals have the potential to disrupt organisational goals and imperatives, for example team cohesion. In considering how such pitfalls are best avoided the sport ethnographer will need to make choices early on whether to conduct research in overt or covert mode, a choice faced by ethnographers in a host of cultural contexts (Bryman 2001: 293).

Armstrong's preferred description of the ethnographer as 'marginal native' reminds us of the well-worn concern about the ethnographer 'going native'. By giving the term native this definitional status, Armstrong makes the 'going native' concern redundant, as the ethnographer can be considered native from the outset. With regard to research on football hooliganism, Armstrong (1993: 30) claims that an ethnographer who engages in violent conduct in the field cannot be presumed to have 'gone native', because this assumes that the researcher would not have behaved violently at a football match outside of the research context in the company of football hooligans. The possibility of the researcher behaving violently in the field raises the issue of research ethics and, although the football hooliganism example is very particular and pertains to sport supporting, the implications of Armstrong's argument have interesting relevance to ethnographers undertaking participant observation of sports in which they are actively involved. This pertains especially to ethnographers partaking in competitive sport where the goal of sporting success is assumedly elevated over the goal of academic research, at least during episodes of sporting engagement. Whether or not the researcher behaves violently or in some other way constituting misconduct is not conditional to his/her 'going native'. By the very fact that, in the context of field research, the researcher has relegated the research agenda by fully taking on the cultural goals of the group under study (assumedly the sport team), he/she can be said to have gone native. However, like Armstrong's 'marginal native', sport ethnographers engaged in the study of sporting activities in which they normally partake are able to declare their 'native' status prior to undertaking the research, therefore avoiding concerns about 'going native'.

While in general agreement with Armstrong about the practice of ethno-graphic research, Giulianotti is more circumspect than his colleague on the issue of violence. Giulianotti (1995a: 11) explicitly connects his thoughts about violence with ethical considerations. He has imposed a working rule on his field research, to 'not get involved in fighting'. Giulianotti's decision is in keeping with what is widely recognised as one of the key ethical principles to which ethnographers should adhere, namely *non-maleficence* (researchers should avoid harming participants) (Murphy and Dingwall 2001: 339). The principle goes beyond the idea of harming participants physically to an avoidance of harming participants or other humans met during the research process in any way that might be anticipated. While there are always going to be some grey areas, an avoidance of violent conduct would seem a minimal expectation of the researcher. For sport ethnographers involved in less controversial case studies (than those of Armstrong and Giulianotti) of sport players or supporters, ethical problems associated with violence might not arise. However, for all ethnogra-phers employed as academics or enrolled as post-graduate students, the issue of ethics remains of paramount concern, as university researchers, academics and students accept the codified versions of ethical standards set by professional bodies (such as sociological and anthropological associations) and external

171

funding institutions upon which social research projects have become increasingly reliant.

While we assume that most social science researchers are instinctively driven to conduct their research ethically, procedural compliance with ethical guidelines can create practical difficulties for researchers, and this is especially the case for ethnographers. For example, social science researchers studying human subjects are commonly expected, if not required, to obtain informed consent from their participants prior to the commencement of a study. In some cases, most obviously those intending to use covert observational research, seeking informed consent from participants will debilitate the planned course of study. Sport ethnographers planning observational participant studies of team sporting activities are likely to be hindered by the need for informed consent. It might be assumed that as members of sports teams, ethnographic researchers – at least those engaging in overt research – will easily be able to gain informed consent from their participants. However, even presuming they are able to facilitate such consent, this can generate an initial status problem for the researcher as a participant observer, by highlighting the seriousness of his/her non-sporting ambitions to other members of the team. More so than in many other ethnographic situations, the sport ethnographer needs to be seen to be on an equal footing with participants and to completely share their organisational and subcultural goals. Obtaining informed consent for an academic study of these goals must necessarily reinforce awareness in other members of the team of the ethnographer's difference from them.

Another key ethical principle within social science research is *justice* (Murphy and Dingwall 2001: 339). In the research context this involves the fair and equal treatment of participants and all humans encountered within the ambit of study. Again, this can raise difficulties for the ethnographer, despite the best of intentions to behave in a just way as researcher. By the nature of their research, ethnographers are often placed in partisan and parochial situations. Willis would claim to be doing justice to the lads studied in *Learning to Labour* (1977) by giving a fair interpretation of their social behaviour from their own standpoint and by viewing the behaviour as a form of resistive practice in response to conditions of social alienation. His sympathetic interpretation of their social practices is in keeping with the leftist political project of the CCCS youth subculture studies. However, as we have seen, Willis has been accused of 'over-rapport' and, to relate this to the current point, it might be said that in his enthusiasm to act justly towards the lads he has inadvertently acted unjustly as a researcher to others, namely the women treated chauvinistically and abusively by the lads. Sport ethnographers potentially face related problems. Whether studying collective situations of sport participation or supporting, sport ethnographers find themselves in highly parochial contexts where it is very difficult to establish an empathetic distance between themselves and the group in immediate and constant focus.

For the football supporter subculture ethnographers, identifying with the team supported by the studied group promotes a very obvious parochialism. This is most apparent with Armstrong (1993: 30), who admits to sharing a particular dislike of the supporters of the local rival team Sheffield Wednesday. Giulianotti (1994b) deliberately sets out to provide a more even handed, and hence just, ethnographic account by incorporating first hand participant observation of Hibernian supporters (Scottish east coast rivals to his home team Aberdeen's fan group) into his study. This was a rather problematic undertaking by Giulianotti and risked the possibility of ostracism by the core participants should they view his research association with the rival fans as a betrayal of an expected subcultural allegiance. Again we find a tension between practical considerations and those concerned with ethics, indirectly in this case. For many sport ethnographers, the comparative participant focus adopted by Giulianotti will not be practicable, and other means of fair dealing in research will need to be found. Neither will it often be the case that sport ethnographers are studying 'oppressed' groups or subcultures, with some justi-fication to expression of 'underdog sympathy'. Accordingly, sport ethnographers must be especially alert to avoid celebrating sport groups and contexts that have no basis in wider political and social subordination.

Sport ethnography and the representation of 'inner experience'

The ethically committed ethnographer adheres to the principle of justice not only in regard to fieldwork relations but also in regard to the writing up and presentation of research. Fair minded ethnographers are at pains to justly and accurately represent research participants and other social actors encountered during research. However, this good intention hits upon another difficulty arising from debates within contemporary ethnography, about the very term 'representation'. Indeed, it is reasonable to speak of an unresolved 'crisis of representation' (Denzin 1997: 4) occurring within ethnography over the last twenty years or so. During this time a number of critics have challenged the taken for granted privilege of the ethnographer to write about the life experi-ences of groups and communities under study. For example, Richardson (1992: 119) argues that ethnographers need to give more consideration to 'who/what constitutes the author/subject', and in doing so calls for 'breaking genre[s]' in ethnographic writing. One aspect of this involves a shift to 'community authorship' where research participants are encouraged to write on their own behalf. For Richardson this is as much about destabilising the authority of the ethnographer as it is about giving democratic voice to those being researched.

Despite the challenge posed to the ethnographer by the proposal for 'collab-orative writing', Richardson (1992: 119) assures us that we need not yet give up on ethnography. Non-academic writing on sporting life offers significant substantiation of this latter claim. The first hand accounts of football hooligan subcultures provide a particular case in point. There is now a plethora of books by former 'hooligans' or those who claim to have had close contact with such groups, each giving vivid accounts of life within the subculture. While these authors are perfectly entitled to present their version of life in the hooligan midst, the ethnographic status of their writing remains doubtful. This is not only because these authors do not hold formal credentials as anthropologists or sociologists, but also because their claims to 'community authorship' are likely to be tenuous. In an early example of this genre, *Bloody Casuals: Diary of a Football Hooligan*, Jay Allan (1989) claims to have been an early leader of the Aberdeen Soccer Casuals (ASC), and describes a number of public incidents involving the group. Upon undertaking his ethnographic study of the same group as a doctoral student at Aberdeen University, Richard Giulianotti learnt that a number of ASC members disputed Allan's claim to group leadership and also his version of a number of events (Hughson 1998a: 53). Allan's account is shown to be idiosyncratic rather than that of a community author, and this is always likely to be the case with books written by sport supporters and participants, including the autobiographies of prominent sportspeople. Of course, most of these books do not make claim to the status of social research, our criticism is intended more towards academics who overstate the point that all writing is fiction and of equal truth value. We agree with Hammersley and Atkinson (1995: 257) that the 'craft-skilled' ethnographer still has a good deal to offer in the pursuit of knowledge about social and cultural life.

The 'crisis of representation' within ethnography stems from the related challenge to knowledge claims made by the ethnographer. The ethnographer's raison d'être is to learn about a particular social reality and to report on it. However, reportage or representation is necessarily destabilised if the preceding claim to knowledge of social reality is disputed. At question is whether there is a reality that actually exists beyond the ethnographer's own mindset. For example, Bruner (1986: 5) contends that 'reality only exists for [*us*] in the facts of consciousness given by inner experience'. From this view, the ethnographer's reality is always a matter of personal perspective and interpretation; he/she can never get into the realm of 'inner experience' of those being studied. However, the unavoidability of the researcher reporting from within his/her own experiential frame need not result in an ethnographic solipsism where other people's views of the world are entirely 'filtered out' of the interpretation process. For Bruner (1986: 9) 'vitality' can be retained within ethnography by the use of 'illustrative snatches of personal narrative, bits of biography, or vivid passages from … field-notes' (Bruner 1986: 9). In this sense a writing of the researcher's own experience of interactions with others in the field becomes not simply a statement of anthropological awareness but also a useful 'by-product' which enlivens the documentary account. Sport provides a very lively avenue for eclectic forms of report writing inspired by auto-ethnographic reflection, in which the author's story exudes an empathetic understanding of what sportspeople within the field of study are experiencing (emotionally, physically, intellectually and spiritually) in their sporting endeavours (cf. Richardson 2000: 11).

Nevertheless, as indicated above, the subjective questioning of experience entails the raising of significant doubts about ethnographic reality. From Bruner's perspective, while there might be a 'reality out there', the ethnographic project is about describing how the experience of reality is manifested into audible and observable expressions (Bruner 1986: 6). The ethnographer relies on field-notes and diaries as 'the accepted genres of expression'; they provide the narrative insight into the ethnographer's 'lived experience in the field' (Bruner 1986: 7). However, Bruner questions whether the written narrative is ultimately able to capture the 'richness', not only of the cultural field and the inhabitants under study, but also of the ethnographer's own engagement within the field. From a culturalist perspective we must sympathise with this reservation. Cultural life in all its dimensions and contexts, including sport, is sensuous, and ethnographic writing can only partially capture its sensuality. Again however, sport as an area of culture to be studied by the ethnographer provides hope against surrender to critical nihilism. That 'sport and movement experiences can be elusive, bodily, intense, and contradictory' (Denison and Markula 2003: 9) highlights the need to explore them introspectively as *subjective* experiences comprising holistic human significance and meaning, as suggested at the end of the previous paragraph.

In conclusion, we propose that sport ethnography is best approached with the epistemological understanding referred to by Hammersley (1992: 43) as 'subtle realism'. Subtle realism emerges from the tension, pervading the social sciences, between realism and relativism. The conventional 'doctrine of realism' – holding that there is a reality independent of the researcher whose nature can be known, and that the aim of the research is to produce accounts that correspond to that reality – Hammersley agrees, is now passé. However, he does not accept that an increasing focus on the constructed nature of cultural life should result in a relativist attitude towards social knowledge and in relativistic modes of discourse to describe social and cultural life (Hammersley 1992: 45). For Hammersley relativism is logically anti-ethnographic and, therefore, epistemological and methodological acceptance of it has dire implications for ethnography. Importantly, however, the answer does not rely on reversion to 'naive realism' but on an appreciation that ethnography does provide insight into the subjective experiences that mediate cultural life. For Hammersley (1992: 45), and in distinction from the tradition he departs from, ethnographic realism does not involve attempting to assess the validity of the cultural perspectives of those being studied. The 'commitment' to 'understand the perspectives of others' need not involve questioning the truth or falsehood of cultural representations. For Hammersley, and his associate Paul Atkinson, the goal of ethnography has always been the 'production of knowledge' (Atkinson and Hammersley 1994: 254), and this goal can remain, providing the qualifications of the subtle realist approach are accepted. Researchers planning ethnographic studies of sporting cultures thus need not be deterred by ongoing debates about representation and reality. Indeed, the ethnographic study of sport can help to cast an empirical ray of hope back onto these debates and to restate the research importance of ethnography to Cultural Studies.

Note

1   Orwell comments little about sport in his books but his awareness of the importance of sport to everyday life is glimpsed in passing encounters with a hotel manager and a communist newspaper editor in Paris in *Down and Out in Paris and London* (Orwell 2003 [1933]: 41, 49).

CONNECTIONS

In this Connections section we look at ethnographic research on sport as a mediated form of culture. In contemporary society, sport is increasingly 'consumed' indirectly through media forms, mainly television, and hence the cultural study of sport is inextricably linked to the study of the media. This has been apparent enough throughout the book and, not surprisingly, there are a number of books by other authors dedicated to studying the relationship between the media and sport (Rowe 1999; Whannel 1992; Boyle and Haynes 2000; Wenner 1998). Our specific interest in this brief section is to look at how ethnography provides a useful research methodology for examining sport within a mediated 'circuit of culture'. Ethnographic work on the media tends to concentrate on the audience, and relates to our discussion in Chapter Four on Cultural Studies academics that move beyond traditional conceptions of the audience as passive consumers – the media 'effects' approach – to look at audiences as active users of media technologies, and the cultural messages disseminated via these technologies.

An importance of studying mediated culture ethnographically is that it provides an appreciation of how media texts become meaningful through their location in cultures of production and consumption; it gives an experiential view of the lived culture process that runs through the media in an ongoing circuitous way, from production to consumption and back again. A pioneering figure of media ethnography within Cultural Studies, and another CCCS luminary, is Dorothy Hobson. Hobson was involved in some of the collective feminist projects at Birmingham (Van Loon 2001: 277), but is best known for her groundbreaking ethnographic study of a beleaguered English soap opera based in the West Midlands. The study takes the name of the soap opera and was published in 1982 as *Crossroads:*

The Drama of Soap Opera. Hobson's approach to the study was refreshingly humanistic; discarding the social science preoccupations of previous media attitudinal research, she joined women in their homes to watch *Crossroads* to gain a sensuous familiarity with the meanings the women derived from this programme and invested in it within their own domestic domains. In her own way, Hobson extended the Hoggartian tradition and activated a feminist strand of culturalism. Hobson favours a panoramic approach to ethnography, unlike other CCCS ethnographers she is interested more broadly in working class women and does not focus on a subcultural group. Hobson (1982: 11) also looks across the media process, stating at the outset a concern 'with the production of popular television programmes and the understanding or appeal of those programmes for their audience'.

In appraisal of *Crossroads* Turner (1996: 128) refers to Hobson's 'exemplary account of how culture industries work, through [the] examination of the articulation among broadcasting institutions, the production company, the programme makers and the audience'. Sport is a particularly complex 'culture industry', with each of the elements identified by Turner having overlapping and conflicting concerns and interests that give effect to and continually reconstitute the 'MediaSport' (to borrow Wenner's term) process. To understand this process as lived cultural experience it makes good sense to study it ethnographically and, to comprehend it in totality, to employ Hobson's holistic ethnographic approach. Thus far, media ethnographies dealing with sport have tended to look at production and consumption as polarities on a continuum rather than as shifting points within a circuit of culture. Nevertheless, these studies have been fruitful, and sport has provided a particularly interesting area of ethnographic investigation into the behind the scenes goings on of media production. These studies have focused mainly on television production of sports events (Kinkema and Harris 1998: 30). Recent research of this kind has been undertaken by Silk (1999) into the broadcasting of a Canadian soccer tournament in New Zealand. Via intense ethnographic study of the Canadian television crew, Silk was able to gain insight into a production regime formulated according to a global logic that assumed the existence of a global sport audience, irrespective of national peculiarities and local cultural nuances. In connection with other similar studies in different locations we might be able to view an international trend in sport production strategies, as Silk appears to predict.

Hobson's study is best known for its focus on the audience, and it is this aspect of her work that has been most prone to criticism. McGuigan (1992: 144) – from his anti-'cultural populist' standpoint – believes Hobson offers an 'extreme version' of the active audience position, whereby audiences always make their own judgements about the television programmes they watch. He likens this to John Fiske's position on audiences, 'a Panglossian view of popular culture: all is well in the best of all possible worlds'. This seems a somewhat caricatured representation of Hobson, but it is to be hoped that sport audience ethnographies do not go down the path of uncritical celebration. As Wenner (1998: 11) suggests, recognising 'empowered' and 'subversive' sport audiences is sometimes more a fulfilment of the researcher's desire than a reflection of the media consumption reality occurring beyond the research realm.

However, sport audience ethnographies will, on occasion, offer up case studies indicating subversive readings. Duncan and Brummett (1993) studied women watching American football in their homes and noted how the women lampooned commentary styles and ridiculed the hyper-masculinity of the players. They maintained that these 'resistant' readings were made possible by the fact that the football match was relocated from its 'actual' masculine and public context into the women's own domestic setting, in which the women were able to engage freely with the mediated (rather than the 'real') sport text as they pleased. This study compares inter-estingly with that of Strathmann (2001), which found that 'sports talk', based on mediated sport consumption, is a distinct 'male genre' used in workplaces as a 'community-creating activity' for men, largely to the exclusion of women. In light of this study, the lampooning of the football broadcast and the deliberate misinterpretation of the serious sport message by the women in Duncan and Brummett's study appears all the more to be a form of resistance, and these women might even be deemed to have engaged in carnivalesque dialogue.

The potential benefit of sport audience ethnography is that it provides a most telling way of understanding the meanings that people give to their mediated sport viewing experiences. In some cases these experiences will involve acts of transgression, and in others sheer pleasure and a release from the drudgery of nine-to-five work duties. The responsibility of the sport media ethnographer is to carefully identify the cultural significances of respective case studies of audiences. Media sport ethnography also holds much promise for the circuit of culture approach in the manner of Hobson, drawing relevant connections between the production and consumption of sport media texts. Dorothy Hobson may be more person-ally interested in viewing soap operas than sport, but her 'exemplary account' has great pertinence to those of us interested in the ethnographic study of mediated sport.

CONCLUSION

Sport and the 'City of Culture'

'Culture is everywhere' (Inglis and Hughson 2003: 4): we are faced with items of culture at every turn, in public and private life. Indeed, as the items of the high street – books, magazines, compact and digital discs – invade our homes along with other situated communication devices – the radio, television and the personal computer – culture blurs the distinction between public and private lives. Sport too is everywhere, and more than ever is connected symbolically and materially to other forms of culture. While we [the authors] might not recognise sport existing within a postmodern culture, we accept that debates about the breakdown of barriers between high culture and popular culture have implications for sport. These debates and sport's location within them have bearing on how sport must be reconsidered within the policy context.

The familiar and established policy relationship is between sport policy and social policy (Collins 2003). While this relationship remains relevant, we propose an explicit connection between sport policy and cultural policy. Contemporary governmental policy arrangements demand such an association. In Britain sport is formally incorporated into the bureaucratic realm of culture via its placement within the Department of Culture, Media and Sport. This, despite suggestions by some Cultural Studies academics that sport is qualitatively different from other forms of culture because of its inherent competitiveness, and, as such, should not be included among the 'culture industries' (Hesmondhalgh 2002: 13). A somewhat different understanding can be gleaned from the view of culture proffered by the former Secretary of Culture within the Blair Government, Chris Smith. Smith wanted all forms of culture to be organised into 'creative industries' that would maintain and nurture aesthetic integrity while embracing the marketplace possibilities of strategically commercialised culture. Smith set out a number of guiding principles for the creative industries, including 'access' and 'excellence', and in doing so reconciled two notions that had underpinned much of the acrimony within the cultural and arts policy arena between the respective advocates of grassroots and elite orientations (Hughson and Inglis 2001). Similar divisions have characterised debates over sport funding, but current government initiatives propose that sport policy can be reconciled in the same way as arts

179

policy, with access and excellence co-existing in a mutual inclusivity, one feeding off the other, both intrinsic parts of a 'democratic' vision of culture.

So sport policy, like cultural policy for the arts, seeks to strike not just a balance between funding for elite performance and grassroots participation but to foster a sporting culture in which these aims are entirely synchronised. The arts and sport funding bureaucracies have become increasingly similar. In recent years both have moved away from a devolved corporatist structure with considerable decision making responsibility divested to regional bodies to a more centralised system – and some would argue more autocratic – with decision making power returned to a central body and the regional and local agencies assuming more of a distributional role. This is not the place to debate such developments; the point here is to show that policy directions on sport mirror its increasing entanglement with culture in the public realm. This direction need not be regressive, but we are cautious about the ways in which sport is drawn into a bureaucratically envisioned cultural democracy with accompanying expectations of good cultural citizenship.

A recent example to illustrate our concern is the way in which sport featured within bids by English cities for the title of the European City of Culture. The title, to be invested in 2008, was keenly sought by the finalists Birmingham, Bristol, Cardiff, Liverpool, Newcastle/Gateshead and Oxford. The desire to win international recognition as a City of Culture was as much driven by pecuniary incentives as it was by 'cultural' incentives. The last British city to hold the title, Glasgow in 1990, has enjoyed a considerable economic upturn since its tenure as the European City of Culture. Each of the cities involved in the recent bid, but particularly those that have felt the brunt of post-industrial downturn, explicitly stated that winning the bid would lead to economic regeneration and the associated benefits to be enjoyed by all citizens. As Glancey (2003) has noted, the idea of culture driving the economy is a direct inversion of the nineteenth century notion that a healthy civic economy would result in a cultured city. Industrialists took it as their civic duty to invest in public culture and the arts. However, following the decline of traditional industries, culture has itself emerged as an industry in relation to leisure, tourism, heritage and the arts. Accordingly, it is through culture that cities now hope to seek economic revival: a City of Culture equates to a city of prosperity.

Sport found prominent place within the 'City of Culture' advertising campaigns, chiefly through the profile assumed by key sporting sites. For example, the Millennium Stadium was highly visible within the promotion for Cardiff's bid. Such promotion places sport on equal footing alongside other sites of cultural reverence. This is useful to the image of an inclusive City of Culture because sport has a certain democratising affect. The more traditional sites of culture benefit from association with the football stadium because sport helps to disseminate the catch-all understanding of culture to which the City of Culture appeals. The loyal citizenry of the City of Culture cannot be achieved by the arts alone, it must draw upon the truly popular elements of culture, and sport is perhaps the most popular form of culture of all in terms of cross-demographic appeal. Sport thus warrants its place amongst the material and symbolic iconography of the City of Culture: the football stadium is celebrated as a key site in the architectural landscape of the city, along with buildings, monuments and bridges.

A lift-out appearing in the Newcastle *Evening Chronicle*, in the days leading up to the announcement of the winning bid, featured a photographic montage of a number of familiar cultural sites around Newcastle/Gateshead. The Tyne bridge and the award winning Millennium Bridge, the Baltic Art Gallery (a splendidly refurbished flour mill), St. Nicholas's Cathedral, the Theatre Royal, the Life Centre (for popular science) and Earl Grey's Monument were joined in background with an interior shot of St. James Football Stadium on match day. The foreground of the montage shows the talismanic figure of Newcastle United soccer player Alan Shearer running in front of the striking image of Antony Gormley's mammoth sculpture 'The Angel of the North', which sits protectively on the hills outside Gateshead. The incorporation of sport into this iconography presumes that local sport will be supported and patronised along with other items and locations of culture. In a city such as Newcastle, with only one football team, it is assumed that support will be given to that team, an interesting twist on cultural democracy and contrary to the notion of sports citizenship developed by Rowe and Lawrence. The assumption of loyal cultural citizenship for the City of Culture hinges on the understanding that, as there is something there for all of us, we should accept the full cultural smorgasbord on offer within the city: our Baltic Gallery, our Tyne Bridge, our Newcastle United.

The blueprint for the City of Culture draws unwitting inspiration from the English tradition of cultural commentary discussed in this book, and particularly from the theme 'common culture' identified across the culturalist spectrum from Eliot to Williams to Willis. As different as the notion of common culture is within their respective writings, each of the aforementioned writers would be suspicious of the contrived cultural democracy to which the City of Culture appeals. Our interest, as indicated above, is to reveal how sport fits into the democratic vision of the City of Culture. Eliot, Williams and Willis recognised the place of sport within the common culture in rather idealised terms, but the mandarins of the City of Culture take a much more pragmatic view of its role. For them the importance of sport is in its ability to generate the consolidation of a necessary cultural consensus. Sport for all (the former policy catchphrase of the British Sports Council) can be equated to culture for all, and the related aim is to make the art gallery, the theatre and the opera house as popular as the football stadium; or at least, so it would seem. Sport appears to be a great cultural leveller, a bastion of cultural inclusion and a harbinger of the culturally classless society. Sport is of particular importance to the City of Culture because, more than other forms of culture and related sites, it offers an emotive, highly discernable and almost tangible means of civic and/or regional identity. Could Oxford really have been a serious contender for the City of Culture without a football team of the status of those from Liverpool, Birmingham and Newcastle?

The football stadium, as a cultural site, arouses an intense 'sense of place', an allure desired by other key sites within the City of Culture. John Bale (1991) adapts the term 'topophilia' (love of place) from cultural geography to describe the strength of emotions nurtured within sporting stadiums such as football grounds. The characteristics noted by Bale could each be attributed to the football stadium within the City of Culture: the stadium as a sacred place, a scenic place, as home, and as a tourist place. In the latter regard, some of the best known football stadiums within Britain draw tourists from home and abroad for guided tours. Liverpool's Anfield Stadium is listed by the Merseyside Tourist Authority as a 'category 1' tourist attraction (Bale 1991). However, Bale's model involves a binary opposition, and while the football stadium arouses topophilia it also, problematically, arouses the converse feeling, topophobia (fear of place). Bale discusses football topophobia in relation to nuisance factors external to the ground: residents' annoyance about traffic and parking problems; the noise of amplified music and announcements; vandalism caused by 'hooligans' on the rampage through the town after leaving the match. He also notes fears within the stadium to do with violence and overcrowding. Bale's research appears to have been conducted in 1989 at the peak of public concern about safety within English football stadiums, the year of the tragedy with Liverpool fans at Hillsborough Stadium in Sheffield. The level of these fears might have reduced since the late 1980s with the subsequent changes in safety provision in grounds, but the football stadium still occupies a precarious cultural position between love and fear.

The moral panic of the hooligan menace still stalks the football stadium if in a different guise to the traditional braced and booted skinhead stereotype. The modern (postmodern for some) hooligan has dispensed with obvious symbolic paraphernalia, and his anonymity can make him all the more dangerous: we are never sure who he is; it could be our next-door neighbour. What we can be sure of, however, is that the football hooligan has no place within the City of Culture, he is a social and cultural pariah and it is the duty of the good cultural citizen to help eliminate his presence whenever possible. Accordingly, the Newcastle *Evening Chronicle* (10 June 2003), under a front page headline 'Shop a Yob', displayed photographs of eighteen men suspected of engaging in football support related violence outside a recent England international match against Turkey at Sunderland's 'Stadium of Light'. Readers of the newspaper were invited to notify the police if they were able to identify one of the photographed suspects, thus establishing their own good cultural citizenship against the reviled cultural deviant. The deviant supporters are customarily distinguished from the 'vast majority of England supporters', isolating them from the good citizens and providing reassurance that the cultural credentials of sport are essentially intact.

Nevertheless the football stadium (or its surrounds) remains a potential site of deviance, unlike most other key cultural sites within the City of Culture. Fist fights are unlikely to break out in, or in association with the cultural life of, the art gallery or the theatre. However, this does not mean that these sites produce unidirectional emotional responses of the topophilic kind. The art gallery, theatre and concert hall are very likely to be loved places of heightened aesthetic experience but, conversely, these places are likely to be a source of topophobia for some. The thought of going to a symphony concert or to see Shakespeare at the Theatre Royal is not just off-putting to some people for fear of boredom, but induces a tacit fear of not knowing the cultural customs and protocols of perceived high art cultural sites. We come here to the realisation that visiting cultural sites, be it the football stadium or the concert hall, is always a classed experience, and the respective responses and anticipations expressed in terms of topophilia and topophobia are reflections of the classed perceptions that people have of cultural sites. The City of Culture attempts to gloss these discrepancies of class in the uses of culture in its assumption that we live in a cultural democracy. Left culturalists, Williams being the outstanding example, argue for a cultural democracy, but for a cultural democracy that genuinely addresses issues of class rather than trying to conceal them behind an illusory and unstable consensus.

To some considerable surprise it was announced in June 2003 that Liverpool would be the European City of Culture for 2008. Newcastle/Gateshead was well established as the bookmakers' favourite for the honour, and shortly before the formal announcement was made that same city was polled as the 'people's choice'. There has been some speculation that Newcastle/Gateshead and the other leading contender Birmingham became victims of the success of the regeneration of cultural life that had already been achieved in those cities. This is to suggest that the award went to Liverpool based on the perception that it needed the title of the City of Culture to invigorate the progress already achieved in the regional capitals of the West Midlands and the North East. However, if this speculation is in any way correct, it also highlights a worrying tendency to allow the cultural regeneration of city centres to mask the continuing social deprivation of many of the suburban residents of those cities. Newcastle and Birmingham may exhibit something more of a cultural swagger on their inner city streets than Liverpool, but both have very depressed suburban areas within a few stones' throws from a number of their key cultural sites, and very close indeed to their football stadiums. Should the City of Culture title result in significant social improvements for the people of Liverpool then it would seem churlish to begrudge their city the honour. However, residents of Newcastle/Gateshead and Birmingham, who do not feel that they benefit from the revival of culture within their cities, are likely to be aggrieved that the award went to Liverpool under a pretence that may well have been attributable to their circumstances as well.

If culture is to be used politically as a driving force of economic and social regeneration, then the processes through which this is done need to be transparent and, even more importantly, culture should not be used as the last bastion of egalitarian hope. The most disturbing aspect of the City of Culture discourse is the implicit reintroduction of a separation between culture and society and the accompanying acceptance that equality is moribund in the social realm. The rhetoric suggests not only that culture will revive the economy but also that it can reverse the social decline of the underprivileged. In itself this is not an unreasonable aim, and attempts to overcome social exclusion through programmes in culture, sport and the arts are often undoubtedly well intentioned and partially successful. However, when culture is separated from society and invested with a presumed potential to foster a happy consensus, the democratic vision is but an illusion. The City of Culture projects such a chimera. Of the various forms of culture, sport is most likely to shatter the City of Culture's illusory cultural democracy, and for this, as much as other reasons discussed in the book, should be of importance to cultural analysts. From the foregoing discussion it can be seen that sport is an unwieldy cultural beast, hard to tame within the City of Culture, because unlike other forms of culture (but not all) it harbours elements of incivility that can only be dismissed to an extent as aberration. The social roots of sport break through the carefully concreted pavements of the City of Culture. The job of Cultural Studies is to see what the cracks reveal and to be vigilant of attempts by cultural architects and engineers to have them smoothed over. The *uses of sport* do occur within a common culture, but only to the extent that the people make their own culture will it be democratic.

QUESTIONS FOR FURTHER DISCUSSION

Chapter 1: Sport, culture, and civilisation

1   How does sport fit into T.S. Eliot's understanding of 'the whole way of life'?
2   How, from the Kulturkritik perspective, can sport be returned to culture?
3   How convincing is Scruton's attempt to defend foxhunting as a natural activity?

Chapter 2: Sport, community and the common culture

1   How does sport reflect Hoggart's characterisation of 'Us' and 'Them'?
2   How might sport be located within Williams's understanding of the 'common culture'?
3   Discuss the merits of supporters' trusts in relation to the communal ownership of sport.

Chapter 3: Sport, public culture and community: letters from America

1   On what basis does Lasch argue that contemporary sport has become degraded?
2   Why would Sennett be dubious about appeals to community sport?
3   How might Putnam's respective notions of social capital be developed through sport?

Chapter 4: Sport and popular culture

1   What reasons can be given for the marginal treatment of sport within Cultural Studies?
2   How might the uses of sport be explained in terms of Willis's notion of 'grounded aesthetics'?
3   What factors would be raised in a political economy critique of sporting culture?

Chapter 5: Sport, postmodernism and culture

1   What are the implications of Baudrillard's 'crisis of representation' for the culture of sport?
2   How can we speak of 'authenticity' within sporting culture from a post-modernist perspective?
3   How does postmodernism account for the construction of cultural identities, cultural identities associated with sport in particular?

Chapter 6: Sport, power and the material relations of culture

1   How are the inequalities of sport explained from a structural Marxist perspective? Why is this perspective considered inadequate within Cultural Studies?
2   How does Williams's notion of 'cultural materialism' help to explain power relations within sporting culture?
3   How might sporting culture look under genuine conditions of democratic socialism?

Chapter 7: Sport, culture and embodied experience

1   Consider a particular example of someone playing a sport and outline a phenomenological analysis of their bodily experience.
2   How does a phenomenological analysis benefit the cultural study of sport?
3   Assess the merits of Iris Marion Young's analysis of the gendered aspects of sporting play and Bourdieu's account of the connections between class and sport.

Chapter 8: Sport, culturalism and ethnography

1 What are the distinctive features of culturalist ethnography? Identify and discuss books that might be regarded as culturalist ethnographies of sport.
2 What strategies can sport ethnographers adopt to avoid 'gender blindness' in their research?
3 How can sport ethnographers ensure that they conduct fieldwork in an ethical way?

BIBLIOGRAPHY

Ackroyd, P. (1976) *Notes for a New Culture: An Essay on Modernism*, London: Vision Press.

Adorno, T.W. (1996) *The Culture Industry: Selected Essays on Mass Culture*, London: Routledge.

Allan, J. (1989) *Bloody Casuals: Diary of a Football Hooligan*, Glasgow: Famedram.

Andrews, D.L. and Jackson, S.J. (2001) 'Introduction: sport celebrities, public culture, and private experience', in D.L. Andrews and S.J. Jackson (eds), *Sport Stars: The Cultural Politics of Sporting Celebrity*, London: Routledge, pp. 1–19.

Andrews, D.L., and Loy, J. (1993) 'British Cultural Studies and sport: past encounters and future possibilities', *Quest*, 45 (2), pp. 255–76.

Andrews, D.L., Carrington, B., Mazur, Z. and Jackson, S. (1996) 'Jordanscapes: a preliminary analysis of the global popular', *Sociology of Sport Journal*, 13, pp. 428–57.

Armstrong, G. (1993) 'Like that Desmond Morris?', in D. Hobbs and T. May (eds), *Interpreting the Field: Accounts of Ethnography*, Oxford: Clarendon, pp. 3–39.

—— (1998) *Football Hooligans: Knowing the Score*, Oxford: Berg.

Arnold, M. (1932 [1869]) *Culture and Anarchy*, ed. J. Dover Wilson, Cambridge: Cambridge University Press.

Aronowitz, S. (1994) 'Between criticism and ethnography: Raymond Williams and the intervention of Cultural Studies', in *Dead Artists, Live Theories, and Other Cultural Problems* (essays by Stanley Aronowitz), New York: Routledge, pp. 169–87.

Atkinson, P. and Hammersley, M. (1994) 'Ethnography and participant observation', in N. Denzin and Y. Lincoln (eds), *Handbook of Qualitative Research*, London: Sage, pp. 248–61.

Bakhtin, M. (1984) *Rabelais and His World*, Bloomington, IN: Indiana University Press.

Bale, J. (1991) 'Playing at home: British football and a sense of place', in J. Williams and S. Wagg (eds), *British Football and Social Change*, Leicester: Leicester University Press, pp. 130–44.

—— (1994) *Landscapes of Modern Sport*, Leicester: Leicester University Press.

Barker, C. (2000) *Cultural Studies: Theory and Practice*, London: Sage.

Barrett, M. (1980) *Women's Oppression Today: Problems in Marxist Feminist Analysis*, London: Verso.

—— (1999) *Imagination in Theory: Essays on Writing and Culture*, London: Polity.

Baudrillard, J. (1975) *The Mirror of Production*, St. Louis, MO: Telos Press.

—— (1983) *In the Shadow of Silent Majorities*, New York: Semiotext(e).

—— (1990) *Fatal Strategies*, New York: Semiotext(e).

—— (1993) *Symbolic Exchange and Death*, London: Sage.

188

Bauman, Z. (1992) *Intimations of Postmodernity*, London: Routledge.

Bayley, S. (2003) 'Zen and the art of the grooved forehand down the line', Life Etc. supplement, *The Independent on Sunday* (London), 8 June, pp. 1–2.

Beamish, R. (1988) 'The political economy of professional sport', in J. Harvey and H. Cantelon (eds), *Not Just a Game*, Ottawa: University of Ottawa Press.

Benjamin, W. (1973) *Charles Baudelaire: A Lyric Poet in the Era of High Capitalism*, London: New Left Books.

Bennett, A. (1907) *The Grim Smile of the Five Towns*, London: Collins.

Bennett, T., Emmison, M. and Frow, J. (1999) *Accounting for Tastes: Australian Everyday Cultures*, Cambridge: Cambridge University Press.

Best, D. (1995) 'The aesthetic in sport', in W.J. Morgan and K.V. Meier (eds), *Philosophic Inquiry in Sport*, Champaign, IL: Human Kinetics, pp. 377–89.

Blake, A. (1996) *The Body Language: The Meaning of Sport*, London: Lawrence and Wishart.

Boorstin, D.J. (1961) *The Image: Or What Happened to the American Dream?*, London: Weidenfeld and Nicolson.

Booth, D. and Tatz, C. (2000) *One Eyed: A View of Australian Sport*, Sydney: Allen and Unwin.

Bose, M. (1996) *The Sporting Alien: English Sport's Lost Camelot*, Edinburgh: Mainstream Publishing.

—— (2002) *A History of Indian Cricket*, London: Andre Deutsch.

Bourdieu, P. (1977) *Outline of a Theory of Practice*, Cambridge: Cambridge University Press.

—— (1990a) *In Other Words: Essays Towards a Reflexive Sociology*, Stanford, CA: Stanford University Press.

—— (1990b) *The Logic of Practice*, Cambridge: Polity.

—— (1992) *Distinction: A Social Critique of the Judgement of Taste*, London: Routledge.

—— (1993a) 'How can one be a sports fan?', in Simon During (ed.), *The Cultural Studies Reader*, London: Routledge.

—— (1993b) *Sociology in Question*, London: Sage.

Bourdieu, P. and Wacquant, L. (1996) *An Invitation to a Reflexive Sociology*, Cambridge: Polity.

Boyle, R. and Haynes, R. (2000) *Power Play: Sport, the Media and Popular Culture*, Harlow: Longman.

Brailsford, D. (1992) *British Sport: A Social History*, Cambridge: Lutterworth.

Brennan, M.A. (1999) 'Every little movement has a meaning all its own', in S.H. Fraleigh and P. Hanstein (eds), *Researching Dance: Evolving Modes of Enquiry*, London: Dance Books, pp. 283–308.

Briggs, A. (1965 [1954]) *Victorian People*, Harmondsworth: Penguin.

Brohm, J.M. (1978) *Sport: A Prison of Measured Time*, London: Pluto Press.

Brubaker, R. (1985) 'Re-thinking classical theory: the sociological vision of Pierre Bourdieu', *Theory and Society*, 14, pp. 745–75.

Bruce, T. and Hallinan, C. (2001) 'Cathy Freeman: the quest for Australian identity', in D.L. Andrews and S.J. Jackson (eds), *Sport Stars: The Cultural Politics of Sporting Celebrity*, London: Routledge, pp. 257–70.

Bruner, E.M. (1986) 'Experience and its expressions', in V.W. Turner and E.M. Bruner (eds), *The Anthropology of Experience*, Urbana, IL: University of Illinois Press, pp. 3–30.

Bryman, A. (2001) *Social Research Methods*, Oxford: Oxford University Press.

Bryson, L. (1983) 'Sport and the oppression of women', *Australian and New Zealand Journal of Sociology*, 19 (3), pp. 413–26.

—— (1990) 'Challenges in male hegemony to sport', in M.A. Messner and D.F. Sabo (eds), *Sport, Men, and the Gender Order: Critical Feminist Perspectives*, Champaign, IL: Human Kinetics, pp. 173–84.

Butler, J. (1989) 'Sexual ideology and phenomenological description: a feminist critique of Merleau-Ponty's *Phenomenology of Perception*', in J. Allen and I.M. Young (eds), *The Thinking Muse: Feminism and Modern French Philosophy*, Bloomington, IN: Indiana University Press, pp. 85–100.

Cannadine, D. (2002) *In Churchill's Shadows: Confronting the Past in Modern Britain*, London: Penguin.

Carrington, B. (2002) 'Sport, masculinity and black cultural resistance', in S. Scraton and A. Flintoff (eds), *Gender and Sport: a Reader*, London: Routledge, pp. 141–55.

Cashman, R. (1995a) 'Packer cricket', in D. Headon, J. Hooton and D. Horne (eds), *The Abundant Culture: Meaning and Significance in Everyday Australia*, Sydney: Allen and Unwin.

—— (1995b) *Paradise of Sport: The Rise of Organised Sport in Australia*, Melbourne: Oxford University Press.

CCCS (Centre for Contemporary Cultural Studies) (1978) *On Ideology*, London: Hutchinson.

—— (1982) *The Empire Strikes Back: Race and Racism in 70s Britain*, London: Hutchinson.

CCCS Women's Studies Group (1978) *Women Take Issue*, London: Hutchinson.

Chambers, I. (1986) *Popular Culture: The Metropolitan Experience*, London: Routledge.

Clarke, J. (1973) 'Football hooliganism and the skinheads', *Stencilled Occasional Paper* no. 42, Birmingham: Centre for Contemporary Cultural Studies, University of Birmingham.

—— (1976) 'The skinheads and the magical recovery of community', in S. Hall and T. Jefferson (eds), *Resistance through Rituals: Youth Subcultures in Postwar Britain*, London: Hutchinson.

—— (1978) 'Football and working class fans: tradition and change', in R. Ingham (ed.), *Football Hooliganism: The Wider Context*, London: Inter-Action Inprint.

Clement, J.P. (1995) 'Contributions of the sociology of Pierre Bourdieu to the sociology of sport', *Sociology of Sport Journal*, 12 (2), pp. 147–57.

Coakley, J. (2001) *Sport in Society: Issues and Controversies*, 7th edn, Boston, MA: McGraw-Hill.

Coleridge, S.T. (1972 [1830]) *On the Constitution of the Church and State*, London: Dent.

Collings, M. (1998) *It Hurts: New York Art from Warhol to Now*, London: 21 Publishing.

Collingwood, R.G. (1958 [1938]) *The Principles of Art*, London: Oxford University Press.

Collins, J. (1991) *Migrant Hands in a Distant Land: Australia's Post-war Immigration*, 2nd edn, Leichhardt (Sydney): Pluto Press.

Collins, M.F. (2003) *Sport and Social Exclusion*, London: Routledge.

Collins, T. and Vamplew, W. (2002) *Mud, Sweat and Beers: A Cultural History of Sport and Alcohol*, Oxford: Berg.

Cox, O.C. (1970 [1948]) *Caste, Class and Race*, New York: Monthly Review Press.

Crick, B. (2001) 'Shareholders united against Murdoch', in S. Hamil, J. Michie, C. Oughton and S. Warby (eds), *The Changing Face of the Football Business: Supporters Direct*, London: Frank Cass, pp. 64–9.

Critcher, C. (1971) 'Football and cultural values', *Working Paper in Cultural Studies* no. 1, Birmingham: Centre for Contemporary Cultural Studies, University of Birmingham, pp. 103–19.

—— (1974) 'Women in sport', *Working Paper in Cultural Studies* no. 5, Birmingham: Centre for Contemporary Cultural Studies, University of Birmingham, pp. 3–20.

—— (1979) 'Football since the war', in J. Clarke, C. Critcher and R. Johnson (eds), *Working Class Culture: Studies in History and Theory*, London: Hutchinson.

Critcher, C. *et al.* (1977) 'Fads and fashions', *Stencilled Occasional Paper* no. 63, Birmingham: Centre for Contemporary Cultural Studies, University of Birmingham.

Crosset, T. and Beal, B. (1997) 'The use of "subculture" and "subworld" in ethnographic works on sport: a discussion of definitional distinctions', *Sociology of Sport Journal*, 14 (1), pp. 73–85.

Crossley, N. (1995) 'Merleau-Ponty, the elusive body, and carnal sociology', *Body and Society*, 1 (1), pp. 43–63.

Curtis, J., and Loy, J. (1978) 'Positional segregation in professional baseball: replications, trend data and critical observation', *International Review of Sport Sociology*, 4 (13), pp. 5–21.

Defrance, J. (1995) 'The anthropology of sociology of Pierre Bourdieu: genesis, concepts, relevance', *Sociology of Sport Journal*, 12 (2), pp. 121–31.

Dempsey, K. (1992) *A Man's Town: Inequalities Between Men and Women in Rural Australia*, Melbourne: Oxford University Press.

Denison, J. and Markula, P. (2003) 'Introduction: moving writing', in J. Denison and P. Markula (eds), *Moving Writing: Crafting Movement in Sport Research*, New York: Peter Lang, pp. 1–24.

Denzin, N. (1997) *Interpretive Ethnography: Ethnographic Practices for the 21st Century*, Thousand Oaks, CA: Sage

Docker, J. (1994) *Postmodernism and Popular Culture: A Cultural History*, Cambridge: Cambridge University Press.

Dollimore, J. and Sinfield, A. (1994) 'Foreword', in J. Dollimore and A. Sinfield (eds), *Political Shakespeare: Essays in Cultural Materialism*, Manchester: Manchester University Press.

Donnelly, P. (1981) 'Toward a definition of sport subcultures', in M. Hart and S. Birrell (eds), *Sport in the Sociocultural Process*, 3rd edn, Dubuque, IA: Wm.C. Brown, pp. 565–87.

—— (1988) 'Sport as a site for "popular" resistance', in R. Gruneau (ed.), *Popular Cultures and Political Practices*, Toronto: Garamond Press, pp. 69–82.

—— (1993) 'Subcultures in sport: resilience and transformation', in A.G. Ingham and J.W. Loy (eds), *Sport in Social Development: Traditions, Transitions, and Transformation*, Champaign, IL: Human Kinetics, pp. 119–45.

—— (2003) 'The great divide: sport climbing vs. adventure climbing', in R.E. Rinehart and S. Sydnor (eds), *To the Extreme: Alternative Sports, Inside Out*, Albany, NY: State University of New York Press, pp. 291–304.

Duncan, M.C. and Brummett, B. (1993) 'Liberal and radical sources of empowerment in sport media', *Sociology of Sport Journal*, 10 (1), pp. 57–72.

Dunning, E. (1999) *Sport Matters: Sociological Studies of Sport, Violence and Civilisation*, London: Routledge.

Dworkin, D. (1997) *Cultural Marxism in Postwar Britain: History, the New Left, and the Origins of Cultural Studies*, Durham, NC: Duke University Press.

Dwyer, C. (1998) 'Contested identities: challenging dominant representations of young British Muslim women', in T. Skelton and G. Valentine (eds), *Cool Places: Geographies of Youth Cultures*, London: Routledge, pp. 50–65.

Eagleton, T. (2000) *The Idea of Culture*, Oxford: Blackwell.

Edwards, H. (1969) *The Revolt of the Black Athlete*, New York: Free Press.

Eichberg, H. (1998) *Body Cultures: Essays on Sport, Space and Identity*, ed. J. Bale and C. Philo, London: Routledge.

Eisenstein, H. (1984) *Contemporary Feminist Thought*, London: George Allen and Unwin.

Elias, N. (1994 [1939]) *The Civilising Process: The History of Manners and State Formation and Civilisation*, Oxford: Blackwell.

—— (1996) *The Germans: Power Struggles and the Development of Habitus in the Nineteenth and Twentieth Centuries*, Cambridge: Polity.

Elias, N. and Dunning, E. (1986) *Quest for Excitement: Sport and Leisure in the Civilising Process*, London: Blackwell.

Eliot, T.S. (1964 [1948]) *Notes Towards a Definition of Culture*, London: Faber and Faber.

Fallows, J. (1996) 'Throwing like a girl', *The Atlantic Monthly*, August. Online at http://www.theatlantic.com/issues/96aug/throw/throw.htm

Fanon, F. (1986 [1952]) *Black Skin, White Masks*, London: Pluto Press.

Ferguson, A. (1995 [1767]) *An Essay on the History of Civil Society*, ed. F. Oz-Salzberger, Cambridge: Cambridge University Press.

Firestone, S. (1971) *The Dialectic of Sex: The Case for Feminist Revolution*, New York: Bantam Books.

Fischer, E. (1963) *The Necessity of Art*, London: Penguin.

Fiske, J. (1987) *Television Culture*, London: Methuen.

—— (1989) *Understanding Popular Culture*, London: Routledge.

—— (1992) 'The cultural economy of fandom', in L. Lewis (ed.), *The Adoring Audience: Fan Culture and Popular Media*, London: Routledge, pp. 30–49.

—— (1993) *Power Plays, Power Works*, London: Verso.

Fowler, B. (1997) *Pierre Bourdieu and Cultural Theory*, London: Sage.

Free, M. and Hughson, J. (2003) 'Settling accounts with hooligans: gender blindness in football supporter subculture research', *Men and Masculinities*, 6 (2), pp. 136–55.

Frow, J. (1987) 'Accounting for tastes: some problems in Bourdieu's sociology of culture', *Cultural Studies*, 1 (1), pp. 59–73.

Galtung, J. (1994) 'Sport and international understanding; sport as a carrier of deep culture and structure', in M. Ilmarinen (ed.), *Sport and International Understanding*, Berlin: Springer-Verlag.

Game, A. (1991) *Undoing the Social: Towards a Deconstructive Sociology*, Toronto: University of Toronto Press.

Gans, Herbert (1974) *Popular Culture and High Culture: An Analysis and Elevation of Taste*, New York: Basic Books.

Gardiner, G. (2003) ' "Black" bodies – "white" codes: indigenous footballers, racism and the Australian Football League's racial and religious vilification code', in J. Bale and M. Cronin (eds), *Sport and Postcolonialism*, Oxford: Berg, pp. 29–43.

Garfinkel, H. (1967) *Studies in Ethnomethodology*, New York: Prentice Hall.

Giddens, A. (1990) *The Consequences of Modernity*, Cambridge: Polity.

Gilroy, P. (1992) *There Ain't No Black in the Union Jack: The Cultural Politics of Race of Nation*, London: Routledge.

—— (1996) 'British Cultural Studies and the pitfalls of identity', in J. Curran, D. Morley, and V. Walkerdine (eds), *Cultural Studies and Communications*, London: Arnold, pp. 35–49.

—— (2000) *Between Camps: Race, Identity and Nationalism at the End of the Colour Line*, London: Allen Lane.

Giulianotti, R. (1991) 'Scotland's tartan army in Italy: the case for the carnivalesque', *Sociological Review*, 39 (3), pp. 503–27.

—— (1993) 'Soccer casuals as cultural intermediaries: the politics of Scottish style', in S. Redhead (ed.), *The Passion and the Fashion*, Aldershot: Avebury, pp. 153–205.

—— (1994a) 'Social identity and public order: political and academic discourses on football violence', in R. Giulianotti, N. Bonney and M. Hepworth (eds), *Football, Violence and Social Identity*, London: Routledge.

—— (1994b) 'Keep it in the family: an outline of the social ontology of Hibs casuals', in R. Giulianotti and J. Williams (eds), *Football, Identity and Modernity: Fans and Players in the World Game*, Manchester: Manchester University Press.

—— (1995a) 'Football and the politics of carnival: an ethnographic study of Scottish fans in Sweden', *International Review for the Sociology of Sport*, 30 (2), pp. 191–217.

—— (1995b) 'Participant observation and research into football hooliganism: reflections on the problems of entrée and everyday risks', *Sociology of Sport Journal*, 12 (1), pp. 1–20.

—— (1996) 'A sociology of Scottish football fan culture', PhD thesis, University of Aberdeen, Scotland.

—— (1997) 'Enlightening the North: Aberdeen fanzines and local football identity', in G. Armstrong and R. Giulianotti (eds), *Entering the Field: New Perspectives on World Football*, Oxford: Berg.

—— (1999) *Football: A Sociology of the Global Game*, Oxford: Polity.

Giulianotti, R. and Gerrard, M. (2001) 'Evil genie or pure genius? The (im)moral football and public career of Paul "Gazza" Gascoigne', in D.L. Andrews and S.J. Jackson (eds), *Sport Stars: The Cultural Politics of Sporting Celebrity*, London: Routledge, pp. 124–37.

Glancey, J. (2003) 'Bright lights, big city', *The Guardian Review*, 29 March 2003, pp. 18–19.

Golding, P. and Murdock, G. (1991) 'Culture, communications, and political economy', in J. Curran and M. Gurevitch (eds), *Mass Media and Society*, London: Edward Arnold, pp. 15–32.

Gramsci, A. (1971) *Selections from the Prison Notebooks*, London: Lawrence and Wishart.

Greenberg, C. (1986 [1939]) 'Avant-garde and kitsch', in J. O'Brian (ed.), *Clement Greenberg: The Collected Essays and Criticism, vol. I: Perceptions and Judgements 1939–1944*, Chicago, IL: University of Chicago Press.

Grossberg, L. (1988) 'Patrolling frontiers: the articulation of the popular', in L. Grossberg, *It's a Sin: Essays on Postmodernism, Politics and Culture*, Sydney: Power Publications, pp. 35–71.

Gruneau, R. and Whitsun, D. (1993) *Hockey Night in Canada: Sport, Identities and Cultural Politics*, Toronto: Grammond Press.

Guttmann, A. (1989) *From Ritual to Record: The Nature of Modern Sports*, New York: Columbia University Press.

—— (1996) *The Erotic in Sports*, New York: Columbia University Press.

Hall, S. (1977) 'Culture, the media and the "ideological effect" ', in J. Curran, M. Gurevitch and J. Woollacott (eds), *Mass Communications and Society*, London: Arnold, pp. 56–90.

—— (1978) 'The treatment of football hooliganism in the press', in R. Ingham (ed.), *Football Hooliganism: The Wider Context*, London: Inter-Action Inprint, pp. 15–36.

—— (1981) 'Cultural Studies: two paradigms', in T. Bennett, G. Martin, C.Mercer and J. Woollacott (eds), *Culture, Ideology and Social Process: A Reader*, London: Open University Press, pp. 19–37.

—— (1992) 'The question of cultural identity', in S. Hall, D. Held and T. McGrew (eds), *Modernity and its Futures*, Cambridge: Polity, pp. 273–325.

Hall, S. and Jefferson, T. (eds) (1976) *Resistance through Rituals: Youth Subcultures in Postwar Britain*, London: Hutchinson.

Hall, S. and Whannel, P. (1964) *The Popular Arts*, London: Hutchinson.

Hallinan, C. (1991) 'Aboriginal and positional segregation in Australian rugby league', *International Review for the Sociology of Sport*, 26 (2), pp. 69–78.

Hammersley, M. (1992) *What's Wrong with Ethnography? Methodological Explorations*, London: Routledge.

Hammersley, M. and Atkinson, P. (1995) *Ethnography: Principles in Practice*, London: Tavistock.

Hargreaves, John (1982) 'Theorising sport: an introduction', in J. Hargreaves (ed.), *Sport, Culture and Ideology*, London: Routledge, pp. 1–29.

—— (1992) 'The hegemony thesis revisited', in C. Knox and J. Sugden (eds), *Rolling Back the Welfare State: Leisure in the 1990s*, Eastbourne: Leisure Studies Association, pp. 263–80.

Hargreaves, Jennifer (1993) 'Gender on the sports agenda', in A.G. Ingham and J.W. Loy (eds), *Sport in Social Development: Traditions, Transitions, and Transformation*, Champaign, IL: Human Kinetics, pp. 167–85.

—— (1994) *Sporting Females: Critical Issues in the History and Sociology of Women's Sport*, London: Routledge.

Harriss, I. (1990) 'Packer, cricket and postmodernism', in D. Rowe and G. Lawrence (eds), *Sport and Leisure: Trends in Australian Popular Culture*, Sydney: Harcourt Brace Jovanovich.

Hay, R. (1994) ' "British football, wogball or the world game?" Towards a social history of Victorian soccer', *ASSH Studies in Sports History* (Australian Society for Sports History), 10, pp. 44–79.

Haynes, R. (1998) *The Football Imagination: The Rise of Football Fanzine Culture*, Aldershot: Arena.

Hebdige, D. (1979) *Subculture: The Meaning of Style*, London: Methuen.

—— (1988) *Hiding in the Light: On Images and Things*, London: Routledge.

Herford, C.H. (1899) *The Age of Wordsworth*, London: George Bell and Sons.

Hesmondhalgh, D. (2002) *The Cultural Industries*, London: Sage.

Hetherington, K. (1998) *Expressions of Identity: Space, Performance, Politics*, London: Sage.

Hill, J. (2002) *Sport, Leisure and Culture in Twentieth Century Britain*, Basingstoke: Palgrave.

Hilton, T. (2002) *John Ruskin*, New Haven, CT: Yale University Press.

Hobsbawm, E. J. (1992) *Nations and Nationalism Since 1780: Programme, Myth, Reality*, 2nd edn, Cambridge: Cambridge University Press.

Hobson, D. (1982) *Crossroads: The Drama of Soap Opera*, London: Methuen.

Hoch, P. (1972) *Rip Off the Big Game: The Exploitation of Sports by the Power Elite*, Garden City, NY: Doubleday.

Hoggart, R. (1958 [1957]) *The Uses of Literacy: Aspects of Working-class Life with Special Reference to Publications and Entertainments*, Harmondsworth: Penguin.

—— (1992) *An Imagined Life (Life and Times, vol. III: 1959–91)*, London: Chatto and Windus.

—— (1995) *The Way We Live Now*, London: Pimlico.

—— (2001) *Between Two Worlds: Essays*, London: Aurum.

—— (2004) *Mass Media in a Mass Society: Myth and Reality*, London: Continuum.

Holmes, R. (1998) *Coleridge: Darker Reflections*, London: Flamingo.

Holt, R. (1989) *Sport and the British: A Modern History*, Oxford: Clarendon Press.

Honneth, A. (1986) 'The fragmented world of symbolic forms: reflections on Pierre Bourdieu's sociology of culture', *Theory, Culture and Society*, 3 (3), 55–67.

Hopcraft, A. (1988 [1968]) *The Football Man: People and Passions in Soccer*, London: Sports Pages/Simon and Schuster.

Horne, D. (1964) *The Lucky Country*, Sydney: Angus and Robertson.

Hughson, J. (1997) 'The Bad Blue Boys and the "magical recovery" of John Clarke', in G. Armstrong and R. Giulianotti (eds), *Entering the Field: New Perspectives on World Football*, Oxford: Berg, pp. 239–59.

—— (1998a) 'Among the thugs: the "new ethnographies" of football supporting subcultures', *International Review for the Sociology of Sport*, 33 (1), pp. 43–57.

—— (1998b) 'Is the carnival over? Soccer support and hooliganism in Australia', in D. Rowe and G. Lawrence (eds), *Tourism, Leisure, Sport: Critical Perspectives*, Melbourne: Cambridge University Press.

—— (1999) 'A tale of two tribes: expressive fandom in Australian soccer's A-league', *Culture, Sport, Society*, 2 (3), pp. 10–30.

—— (2000) 'The boys are back in town: football support and the social reproduction of masculinity', *Journal of Sport and Social Issues*, 24 (1), pp. 8–23.

—— (2002) 'Australian soccer's ethnic tribes: a new case for the carnivalesque', in E. Dunning, P. Murphy and A. Astrinakis (eds), *Football's Fighting Fans: Soccer Hooliganism as a World Problem*, Dublin: University College Dublin Press.

Hughson, J. and Inglis, D. (2000) 'Merleau-Ponty in the field: towards a phenomenology of soccer spaces', *Space and Culture*, 6.

—— (2001) ' "Creative industries" and the arts: towards a "third way" in cultural policy', *Cultural Policy*, 7 (3).

Huizinga, J. (1955 [1950]) *Homo Ludens: A Study of the Play Element in Culture*, Boston, MA: Beacon Press.

Hutchinson, A. (1972) *Labanotation: The System of Analysing and Recording Movement*, 2nd edn, London: Oxford University Press.

Ingham, A.G. and McDonald, M.G. (2003) 'Sport and community/*communitas*', in R.C. Wilcox, D.L. Andrews, R. Pitter and R.L. Irwin (eds), *Sporting Dystopias: The Making and Meaning of Urban Sport Cultures*, Albany, NY: State University of New York Press.

Inglis, D. (2004) 'Meditations on sport: on the trail of Ortega y Gasset's philosophy of sportive existence', *Journal of the Philosophy of Sport* (forthcoming).

Inglis, D. and Hughson, J. (2000) 'The beautiful game and the proto-aesthetics of the everyday', *Cultural Values*, 4 (3).

—— (2003) *Confronting Culture: Sociological Vistas*, Oxford: Polity.

Inglis, S. (1996) *Football Grounds of Britain*, 3rd edn, London: HarperCollins.

Jackson, B. (1968) *Working Class Community: Some General Notions Raised by a Series of Studies*, London: Routledge.

James, C.L.R. (1983 [1963]) *Beyond a Boundary*, London: Serpent's Tail.

James, D.G. (1961) *Matthew Arnold and the Defence of English Romanticism*, Oxford: Oxford University Press.

Jameson, F. (1992) *Postmodernism: Or, the Cultural Logic of Late Capitalism*, London: Verso.

Jary, D. and Jary, J. (1999) *Dictionary of Sociology*, 2nd edn, Glasgow: HarperCollins.

Jenkins, R. (1992) *Pierre Bourdieu*, London: Routledge.

Jenks, C. (1993) *Culture*, London: Routledge.

Johnson, L. (1979) *The Cultural Critics: From Matthew Arnold to Raymond Williams*, London: Routledge and Kegan Paul.

Johnson, R. (1986) 'What is Cultural Studies anyway?', *Social Text*, 6, pp. 38–80.

Jones, P. (1994) 'The myth of "Raymond Hoggart": on "founding fathers" and cultural policy', *Cultural Studies*, 8 (3).

Jones, S.G. (1988) *Sports, Politics and the Working Class: A Study of Organised Labour and Sport*, Manchester: Manchester University Press.

Kaplan, C. (1995) ' "What we have again to say": Williams, feminism and the 1840s', in C. Prendergast (ed.), *Cultural Materialism: On Raymond Williams*, Minneapolis, MN: University of Minnesota Press.

Kinkema, K.M. and Harris, J.C. (1998) 'MediaSport studies: key research and emerging issues', in L. Wenner (ed.), *MediaSport*, London: Routledge, pp. 27–54.

Kristeva, J. (1980) *Desire in Language: A Semiotic Approach to Literature and Art*, Oxford: Blackwell.

Laban, R. (1980 [1950]) *The Mastery of Movement*, 4th edn, revised by L. Ullmann, Plymouth: Northcote House.

Laberge, S. (1995) 'Toward an integration of gender into Bourdieu's concept of cultural capital', *Sociology of Sport Journal*, 12 (2), pp. 132–46.

Lasch, C. (1977) *The Culture of Narcissism: American Life in an Age of Diminishing Expectations*, New York: Warner Books.

Lauer, Q. (1965) *Phenomenology: Its Genesis and Prospect*, New York: Harper.

Leavis, F.R. (1930) *Mass Civilisation and Minority Culture*, Cambridge: The Minority Press.

—— (1993 [1948]) *The Great Tradition*, Harmondsworth: Penguin

Leavis, F.R. and Thompson, D. (1933) *Culture and Environment: The Training of Critical Awareness*, London: Chatto and Windus.

Leavis, Q.D. (1965 [1932]) *Fiction and the Reading Public*, London: Chatto and Windus.

Lechte, John (1994) *Fifty Contemporary Thinkers: From Structuralism to Postmodernity*, London: Routledge.

Lefebvre, H. (1991) *The Production of Space*, Oxford: Blackwell.

Lomax, B. (2001) 'How democracy saved Northampton Town FC', in S. Hamil, J. Michie, C. Oughton and S. Warby (eds), *The Changing Face of Football Business: Supporters Direct*, London: Frank Cass, pp. 102–10.

Luijpen, W. A. (1969) *Existential Phenomenology*, Pittsburgh, PA: Duquesne University Press.

Lynd, R.S. and Lynd, H.M. (1929) *Middletown: A Study in Contemporary American Culture*, London: Constable and Company.

Lyotard, J.F. (1984) *The Postmodern Condition: A Report on Knowledge*, Minneapolis, MN: University of Minnesota Press.

MacCannell, D. (1976) *The Tourist*, New York: Schocken.

MacDonald, D. (1957) 'A theory of mass culture', in B. Rosenberg and D. Manning White (eds), *Mass Culture and the Popular Arts in America*, New York: Free Press, pp. 59–73.

Maffesoli, M. (1996) *The Time of the Tribes*, London: Sage.

Maguire, J. (1988) 'Race and position assignment in English soccer: a preliminary analysis of ethnicity and sport in Britain', *Sociology of Sport Journal*, 5 (3), pp. 257–69.

Maguire, J., Jarvie, G., Mansfield, L. and Bradley, J. (2002) *SportWorlds: A Sociological Perspective*, Champaign, IL: Human Kinetics.

Mahar, C., Harker, R. and Wilkes, C. (1990) 'The basic theoretical position', in R. Harker, C. Mahar and C. Wilkes (eds), *An Introduction to Pierre Bourdieu: The Practice of Theory*, London: Macmillan.

Markula, P. (1995) 'Firm but shapely, fit but sexy, strong but thin: the postmodern aerobicizing female bodies', *Sociology of Sport Journal*, 12 (4), pp. 424–53.

Marx, K. (1977 [1859]) *A Contribution to the Critique of Political Economy*, Moscow: Progress Publishers.

—— (1981 [1844]) *Economic and Philosophic Manuscripts of 1844*, London: Lawrence and Wishart.

Mauss, M. (1979) 'Body techniques', in *Sociology and Psychology: Essays*, London: Routledge and Kegan Paul.

Mazer, S. (1998) *Professional Wrestling: Sport and Spectacle*, Jackson, MS: University Press of Mississippi.

McGuigan, J. (1992) *Cultural Populism*, London: Routledge.

McKay, J. (1991) *No Pain, No Gain? Sport and Australian Culture*, Sydney: Prentice Hall.

McKay, J., Miller, T. and Rowe, D. (1996) 'Americanisation, globalisation and rugby league', in D. Headon and L. Marinos (eds), *League of a Nation*, Sydney: ABC Books.

McKibbin, R. (1998) *Classes and Cultures: England 1918–1951*, Oxford: Oxford University Press.

McLuhan, M. and Fiore, Q. (2001 [1968]) *War and Peace in the Global Village*, Corta Madera, CA: Gingko Press.

McRobbie, A. (1991) 'Settling accounts with subculture: a feminist critique', in *Feminism and Youth Culture: From "Jackie" to "Just Seventeen"* (essays by A. McRobbie), London: Macmillan, pp. 16–34.

Meier, K.V. (1995) 'Embodiment, sport and meaning', in W.J. Morgan and K.V. Meier (eds), *Philosophic Inquiry in Sport*, Champaign, IL: Human Kinetics, pp. 89–95.

Merleau-Ponty, M. (1965) *The Structure of Behaviour*, London: Methuen.

—— (1996) *The Phenomenology of Perception*, London: Routledge.

Messner, M. (1992) *Power at Play: Sports and the Problem of Masculinity*, Boston, MA: Beacon Press.

Michie, J. (1999) *New Mutualism: A Golden Goal? Uniting Supporters and Their Clubs*, London: The Co-Operative Party.

Midgley, C. (2003) 'It takes all sports to make a genius', T2 supplement, *The Times* (London), 23rd April, pp. 4–5.

Milner, A. (1994) *Contemporary Cultural Theory: An Introduction*, London: UCL Press.

—— (2002) *Re-imagining Cultural Studies: The Promise of Cultural Materialism*, London: Sage.

Morgan, W.J. (1993) 'An existential phenomenological analysis of sport as a religious experience', in C.S. Prebish (ed.), *Religion and Sport: The Meeting of Sacred and Profane*, Westport, CT: Greenwood Press.

Mosely, P. (1994) 'Balkan politics in Australian soccer', *ASSH Studies in Sports History* (Australian Society for Sports History), 10, pp. 33–43.

Mulhern, F. (2000) *Culture/Metaculture*, London: Routledge.

Murphy, E. and Dingwall, R. (2001) 'The ethics of ethnography', in P. Atkinson, A. Coffey, S. Delamont, J. Lofland and L. Lofland (eds), *The Handbook of Ethnography*, London: Sage, pp. 339–51.

Myrdal, G. (1962) *An American Dilemma: The Negro Problem and Modern Democracy*, New York: Harper and Row.

Nash, R. (2001) 'English football fan groups in the 1990s: class, representation and fan power', *Soccer and Society*, 2 (1), pp. 39–58.

Noble, G. and Watkins, M. (2003) 'So how did Bourdieu learn to play tennis? Habitus, consciousness and habituation', *Cultural Studies* 17 (3/4), pp. 520–38.

Ortega y Gasset, J. (1961 [1932]) *Revolt of the Masses*, London: Allen and Unwin.

—— (1995 [1942]) *Meditations on Hunting*, Belgrade, MT: Wilderness Press.

Orwell, G. (1968 [1945]) 'The sporting spirit', in *The Collected Essays, Journalism and Letters of George Orwell, vol. IV: In Front of Your Nose (1945–50)*, ed. S. Orwell and I. Angus, London: Secker and Warburg, pp. 40–4.

—— (2003 [1933]) *Down and Out in Paris and London*, London: Penguin.

Owen, D. (1997) 'The postmodern challenge to sociology', in D. Owen (ed.), *Sociology after Postmodernism*, London: Sage, pp. 1–22.

Park, R. (1952) *Human Communities*, Glencoe, IL: Free Press.

Peterson, R. (1997) *Creating Country Music: Fabricating Authenticity*, Chicago, IL: University of Chicago Press.

Polley, M. (1998) *Moving the Goalposts: A History of Sport and Society Since 1945*, London: Routledge.

Pope, S.W. (1997) *Patriotic Games: Sporting Traditions in the American Imagination, 1876–1926*, New York: Oxford University Press.

Poulton, E. (2004) 'English media representation of football-related disorder: "brutal, shorthand and simplifying" ', *Sport in Society* (in press).

Prebish, C.S. (1993) 'Training into transcendence', in Charles S. Prebish (ed.), *Religion and Sport: The Meeting of Sacred and Profane*, Westport, CT: Greenwood Press.

Priest, S. (1998) *Merleau-Ponty*, London: Routledge.

Priestley, J.B. (1980 [1929]) *The Good Companions*, London: Heinemann.

Pronger, B. (1990) 'Gay jocks: a phenomenology of gay men in athletics', in M.A. Messner and D.F. Sabo (eds), *Sport, Men, and the Gender Order: Critical Feminist Perspectives*, Champaign, IL: Human Kinetics, pp. 141–52.

Putnam, R. (2000) *Bowling Alone: The Collapse and Revival of American Community*, New York: Simon and Schuster.

Rail, G. (1998) 'Seismography of the postmodern condition: three theses on the implosion of sport', in G. Rail (ed.), *Sport and Postmodern Times*, Albany, NY: State University of New York Press, pp. 143–61.

Read, H. (1974 [1968]) *A Concise History of Modern Painting*, revised edn, London: Thames and Hudson.

Redhead, S. (1997) *Post-fandom and the Millennial Blues*, London: Routledge.

Richards, I.A. (1976 [1927]) 'The lure of high mountaineering', in I.A. Richards, *Complimentarities: Uncollected Essays*, ed. J.P. Russo, Manchester: Carcanet New Press, pp. 235–45.

Richardson, L. (1992) 'Trash on the corner: ethics and technography', *Journal of Contemporary Ethnography*, 21 (1), pp. 103–19.

—— (2000) 'New writing practices in qualitative research', *Sociology of Sport Journal*, 17 (1), pp. 5–20.

Rigauer, B. (1981 [1969]) *Sport and Work*, New York: Columbia University Press.

Rinehart, R. (2000) 'Emerging/arriving sport: alternatives to formal sports', in J. Coakley and E. Dunning (eds), *Handbook of Sport Studies*, London: Sage, pp. 504–19.

Rinehart, R.E. and Sydnor, S. (2003) 'Proem' in R.E. Rinehart and S. Sydnor (eds), *To the Extreme: Alternative Sports, Inside Out*, Albany, NY: State University of New York Press, pp. 1–17.

Ross, A. (1989) *No Respect: Intellectuals and Popular Culture*, London: Routledge.

Roszak, T. (1970) *The Making of a Counter Culture: Reflections on the Technocratic Society and its Youthful Opposition*, London: Faber and Faber.

Rowe, D. (1995) *Popular Cultures: Rock Music, Sport and the Politics of Pleasure*, London: Sage.

—— (1999) *Sport, Culture and the Media: The Unruly Trinity*, Buckingham: Open University.

—— (2003) 'Sport and the repudiation of the global', *International Review for the Sociology of Sport*, 38 (3), pp. 281–94.

Rowe, D. and Lawrence, G. (1998) 'Framing a critical sports sociology in the age of globalisation', in D. Rowe and G. Lawrence (eds), *Tourism, Leisure, Sport: Critical Perspectives*, Sydney: Hodder Education, pp. 159–69.

Russell, D. (1997) *Football and the English: A Social History of Association Football in England, 1863–1995*, Preston: Carnegie Publishing.

Sage, G.H. (1990) *Power and Ideology in American Sport: A Critical Perspective*, Champaign, IL: Human Kinetics.

Said, E. (1993) *Culture and Imperialism*, London: Chatto and Windus.

Schmidt, J. (1985) *Maurice Merleau-Ponty: Between Phenomenology and Structuralism*, Basingstoke: Macmillan.

Schutz, A. (1972) *The Phenomenology of the Social World*, London: Heinemann.

Scruton, R. (1998a) *On Hunting*, London: Yellow Jersey Press.

—— (1998b) *An Intelligent Person's Guide to Modern Culture*, London: Duckworth.

Sennett, R. (1969) 'An introduction', in R. Sennett (ed.), *Classic Essays on the Culture of Cities*, New York: Appleton-Century-Crofts, pp. 3–19.

—— (1970) *The Uses of Disorder: Personal Identity and City Life*, London: Allen Lane.

—— (1991) *The Conscience of the Eye: The Design and Social Life of Cities*, New York: Alfred A. Knopf.

—— (2002 [1977]) *The Fall of Public Man*, London: Penguin.

Shiach, M. (1995) 'A gendered history of cultural categories', in C. Prendergast (ed.), *Cultural Materialism: On Raymond Williams*, Minneapolis, MN: University of Minnesota Press.

Shils, E. (1961) *Mass Society and Its Culture*, Indianapolis, IN: Bobbs-Merrill.

Silk, M. (1999) 'Local/global flows and altered production practices', *International Review for the Sociology of Sport*, 34 (2), pp. 113–23.

Sillitoe, A. (1975 [1972]) 'Sport and nationalism', in *Mountains and Caverns* (collected essays by Alan Sillitoe), London: W.H. Allen.

Simmel, G. (1950 [1903]) 'The metropolis and mental life', in K.H. Wolff (ed.), *The Sociology of Georg Simmel*, Glencoe, IL: Free Press.

Sinfield, A. (1998) *Gay and After*, London: Serpent's Tail.

Skeggs, B. (1992) 'Paul Willis: learning to labour', in M. Barker and A. Beezer (eds), *Reading Into Cultural Studies*, London: Routledge, pp. 181–96.

Spivak, G.C. (1987) *In Other Words: Essays in Cultural Politics*, London: Methuen.

Stallybrass, P. and White, A. (1986) *The Politics and Poetics of Transgression*, London: Methuen.

Steedman, C. (1986) *Landscapes for a Good Woman*, London: Virago.

Strathmann, C. (2001) 'Audience ethnography, sport in the mass media, and men's talk', in C. Hallinan and J. Hughson (eds), *Sporting Tales: Ethnographic Fieldwork Experiences*, Sydney: Australian Society for Sports History, pp. 59–69.

Sudnow, D. (2002) *Ways of the Hand: A Rewritten Account*, Cambridge, MA: MIT Press.

Swingewood, A. (1998) *Cultural Theory and the Problem of Modernity*, London: Macmillan.

Taylor, I. (1971) 'Soccer consciousness and soccer hooliganism', in S. Cohen (ed.), *Images of Deviance*, Harmondsworth: Penguin.

Theberge, N. (2002) 'Challenging the gendered space of sport: women's ice hockey and the struggle for legitimacy', in S. Scraton and A. Flintoff (eds), *Gender and Sport: a Reader*, London: Routledge, pp. 292–302.

Thompson, E.P. (1963) *The Making of the English Working Class*, London: Victor Gollancz.

Thornton, S. (1995) *Club Cultures: Music, Media and Subcultural Capital*, London: Polity.

Tocqueville, A. de (1952 [1835; 1840]) *Democracy in America*, ed. H. Steele Commager, London: Oxford University Press.

Tonnies, F. (1955 [1895]) *Community and Society*, London: Routledge.

Trollope, A. (1865) *Hunting Sketches*, London: Chapman and Hall.

Trondman, M. (1994) *Bilden av en klassresa. Sexton abetarklassbarn på väg till och i högskolan*, Stockholm: Carlssons Förlag.

Turner, G. (1996) *British Cultural Studies: An Introduction*, 2nd edn, London: Routledge.

—— (2003) *British Cultural Studies: An Introduction*, 3rd edn, London: Routledge.

Turner, V. (1969) *The Ritual Process: Structure and Anti-Structure*, London: Routledge and Kegan Paul.

Twitchell, J.B. (1992) *Carnival Culture: The Trashing of Taste in America*, New York: Columbia University Press.

Urry, J. (1990) *The Tourist Gaze: Leisure and Travel in Contemporary Societies*, London: Sage.

Vamplew, W. (1976) *The Turf: A Social and Economic History of Horse Racing*, London: Allen Lane.

—— (1988) *Pay Up and Play the Game: Professional Sport in Britain 1875–1914*, Cambridge: Cambridge University Press.

Van Loon, J. (2001) 'Ethnography: a critical turn in cultural studies', in P. Atkinson, A. Coffey, S. Delamont, J. Lofland and L. Lofland (eds), *The Handbook of Ethnography*, London: Sage, pp. 273–84.

Walsh, W. (1964) *A Human Idiom: Literature and Humanity*, London: Chatto and Windus.

—— (1967) *Coleridge: The Work and the Relevance*, London: Chatto and Windus.

Warde, A. *et al.* (1999) 'Consumption and the problem of variety: cultural omnivorousness, social distinction and dining out', *Sociology*, 33 (1), pp. 105–27.

Warner, W. Lloyd (1936) 'American class and caste', *American Journal of Sociology*, XLII (September), pp. 234–7.

Wenner, L. (ed.) (1998) *MediaSport*, London: Routledge.

Whannel, G. (1979) 'Football crowd behaviour and the press', *Media, Culture and Society*, 1 (2), pp. 327–42.

—— (1983) *Blowing the Whistle: The Politics of Sport*, London: Pluto Press.

—— (1992) *Fields in Vision: Television Sport and Cultural Transformation*, London: Routledge.

Wheale, N. (1995) 'Postmodernism: from elite to mass culture?', in N. Wheale (ed.), *The Postmodern Arts: An Introductory Reader*, London: Routledge, pp. 33–56.

Wheaton, B. (2003) 'Windsurfing: a subculture of commitment', in R.E. Rinehart and S. Sydnor (eds), *To the Extreme: Alternative Sports, Inside Out*, Albany: State University of New York, pp. 75–101.

White, R. (1980) 'Combating cultural aggression: Australian opposition to Americanisation', *Meanjin*, 39, pp. 275–89.

—— (1983) 'A backwater awash: the Australian experience of Americanisation', *Theory, Culture and Society*, 1 (3), pp. 108–22.

Williams, R. (1958) *Culture and Society 1780–1950*, London: Chatto and Windus.

—— (1961) *The Long Revolution*, London: Chatto and Windus.

—— (1974) *Television: Technology and Cultural Form*, Glasgow: Collins.

—— (1977) *Marxism and Literature*, Oxford: Oxford University Press.

—— (1980) *Problems in Materialism and Culture*, London: Verso.

—— (1983) *Towards 2000*, London: Chatto and Windus.

—— (1989a [1958]) 'Culture is ordinary', in R. Williams, *Resources of Hope: Culture, Democracy, Socialism*, ed. R. Gable, London: Verso, pp. 3–18.

—— (1989b [1977]) 'The importance of community', in R. Williams, *Resources of Hope: Culture, Democracy, Socialism*, ed. R. Gable, London: Verso, pp. 111–19.

Willis, P. (1977) *Learning to Labour: How Working-class Kids Get Working-class Jobs*, Farnborough, Hants: Saxon House.

—— (1978) *Profane Culture*, London: Routledge and Kegan Paul.

—— (1979) 'Shop floor culture, masculinity and the wage form', in J. Clarke, C. Critcher and R. Johnson (eds), *Working Class Culture: Studies in History and Theory*, London: Hutchinson, pp. 185–98.

—— (1982) 'Women in sport and ideology', in Jennifer Hargreaves (ed.), *Sport, Culture and Ideology*, London: Routledge and Kegan Paul, pp. 117–35.

—— (1990) *Common Culture: Symbolic Work at Play in the Everyday Cultures of the Young*, Milton Keynes: Open University Press.

—— (2000) *The Ethnographic Imagination*, Cambridge: Polity.

Wirth, L. (1938) 'Urbanism as a way of life', in R. Sennett (ed.), *Classic Essays on the Culture of Cities*, New York: Appleton-Century-Crofts, pp. 150–63.

Woodward, K. (1997) 'Concepts of identity and difference', in K. Woodward (ed.), *Identity and Difference*, London: Sage, pp. 7–50.

Young, I.M. (1990) 'Throwing like a girl: a phenomenology of feminine body comportment, motility and spatiality', in I.M. Young, *Throwing Like A Girl and Other Essays in Feminist Philosophy and Social Theory*, Bloomington, IN: Indiana University Press.

INDEX